Bugle Echoes

Also from Westphalia Press

westphaliapress.org

Bugle Echoes

A Collection of the Poetry of the Civil War

Edited by Francis F. Browne

WESTPHALIA PRESS
An imprint of Policy Studies Organization

Westphalia Press
An imprint of Policy Studies Organization
1527 New Hampshire Ave., NW
Washington, D.C. 20036
info@ipsonet.org

ISBN-13: 978-1-63391-073-7
ISBN-10: 1633910733

Cover design by Taillefer Long at Illuminated Stories:
www.illuminatedstories.com

Daniel Gutierrez-Sandoval, Executive Director
PSO and Westphalia Press

Rahima Schwenkbeck, Director of Marketing and Media
PSO and Westphalia Press

Updated material and comments on this edition
can be found at the Westphalia Press website:
www.westphaliapress.org

BUGLE-ECHOES

A COLLECTION OF THE

POETRY OF THE CIVIL WAR

Northern and Southern

EDITED BY

FRANCIS F. BROWNE

New and Revised Edition with Illustrations. Sold by Subscription Only

NEW YORK
WHITE, STOKES, & ALLEN
1886

MILITARY HEROES OF THE CIVIL WAR.

CONTENTS.

CONTENTS.

v

PREFATORY.

THIS collection of Poetry of the Civil War, be-gun several years ago for the compiler's personal satisfaction, has grown in extent and interest, until its publication is thought to be justified by the demand for books relating to the war, and by the literary and historical value of the material. Dur-ing the war, and soon after, various volumes ap-peared, containing indiscriminate collections of Northern or Southern war-songs. Viewed at this distance, most of them seem sad stuff. In that stormy period, patriotic fervor was stronger than poetic impulse, and rude doggerel was often lifted into favor by a buoyant tune. War-*songs*, whose popularity was due to their music rather than their words, have, with very few exceptions, been ex-cluded from this volume. Its aim has been to pre-sent a body of the really notable poetry which the war evoked : a record of the feelings and experi-ences of that heroic epoch, as they were wrought into lyrical expression. Time enough has elapsed to enable the war-poems of either side to be read without resentment ; and hence no piece is excluded for its political sentiments, if it has sufficient poetic merit. Some pieces containing strong passages,

which have enjoyed popular favor, are spoiled by
their coarseness ; while others, which were thought
" thrilling" in their time, now seem little more than
wild cries of rage and hate.

The two classes of poems, Northern and South-
ern, at first intended to be placed separately in the
volume, were finally brought together, for the suf-
ficient reasons that their interest is thus increased,
and in some cases it could not be determined to
which side a piece belonged ; and, further, that as
there is no political division between North and
South, there should be no division in their liter-
ature.   It is hoped that nothing in this volume will
shock the political sensibilities of anyone, least of
all the soldiers of the war.   The compiler is able
to speak authoritatively for only one soldier ; but,
judging by his own feelings, and by the cordial
approval and ready aid the project has received
from others, North and South, he believes there is
little to be feared in this direction.   Far from re-
viving sectional animosities, these echoes of a war
whose memory is brightened by so many heroic
deeds, in which the national mettle was so amply
proved and mutual respect came to succeed bitter-
ness and hate, should serve to unite more firmly
the bonds of a common patriotism.

It is too much to expect that, with the large mass
of material to select from, and the limited space of
this volume, every reader will find here the poem
which he seeks ; or to hope that no doubtful piece
has been admitted.   The compiler will feel satis-

fied if it shall be found that he has made, on the whole, a reasonably good use of the space at his command, and given a fairly representative collection of the war-poetry of both sections. The arrangement of pieces is in the main chronological according to subjects ; yet this rule is not invariable —pieces founded upon a particular event or period usually being grouped, thus affording an interesting study of the treatment from different standpoints. Wherever possible, poems have been given entire ; and extracts are so indicated by asterisks. The side whence a poem came may in most instances be inferred readily from its title, character, or author's name ; and in a few obscure cases the information is given in parentheses after the signatures. The Notes, which it is hoped will add to the interest of the volume, have aimed to present briefly such facts as may help to a better understanding of the poems, simple dates being often effective for this purpose.

The compiler wishes to make cordial acknowledgment of his obligation to various persons who have aided him by suggestions or material : especially to Mr. Rossiter Johnson of New York City, Captain Gordon MacCabe of Virginia, Colonel Paul H. Hayne of Georgia, and Mrs. Sidney Lanier of Baltimore. He is also indebted to the courtesy of many American authors and publishers for permission to use copyrighted matter—consent for which, he is gratified to state, has in no instance been refused. Especially to Messrs. Houghton, Mifflin &

Co. of Boston are his thanks due for their liberal concession of matter from their copyrighted publications, which include the works of twelve or fifteen of the leading American poets ; and also to Messrs. Harper & Brothers, Messrs. D. Appleton & Co., and Messrs. Charles Scribner's Sons, of New York City, and the J. B. Lippincott Co. of Philadelphia, for like favors.

F. F. B.

CHICAGO, March, 1886.

LIST OF ILLUSTRATIONS.

Across the years full rounded to a score
  Since Peace advancing with her olive wand
  Restored the sunshine to our desolate land,
Come thronging back the memories of War :
Again the drums beat and the cannons roar,
  And patriot fires by every breeze are fanned,
  And pulses quicken with a purpose grand
As manhood's forces swell to larger store.
Again the camp, the field, the march, the strife,
  The joy of victory, the bitter pain
Of wounds or sore defeat ; the anguish rife
  In tears that fall for the unnumbered slain,
And homes where darkened is the light of life,—
  All these the echoing bugle brings again.

MARCH, 1886.

BUGLE-ECHOES.

BEAT! BEAT! DRUMS!

BEAT! beat! drums!—blow! bugles! blow!
Through the windows—through doors—burst like
    a ruthless force,
Into the solemn church, and scatter the congrega-
    tion,
Into the school where the scholar is studying;
Leave not the bridegroom quiet — no happiness
    must he have now with his bride,
Nor the peaceful farmer any peace, ploughing his
    field or gathering his grain,
So fierce you whir and pound, you drums—so
    shrill you bugles blow.

Beat! beat! drums!—blow! bugles! blow!
Over the traffic of cities—over the rumble of wheels
    in the streets;
Are beds prepared for sleepers at night in the
    houses? no sleepers must sleep in those beds,
No bargainers' bargains by day—no brokers or
    speculators—would they continue?
Would the talkers be talking?—would the singer
    attempt to sing?
Would the lawyer rise in the court to state his case
    before the judge?
Then rattle quicker, heavier drums—you bugles
    wilder blow.

Beat ! beat ! drums !—blow ! bugles ! blow !
Make no parley—stop for no expostulation,
Mind not the timid—mind not the weeper or
    prayer,
Mind not the old man beseeching the young man,
Let not the child's voice be heard, nor the mother's
    entreaties,
Make even the trestles to shake the dead where they
    lie awaiting the hearses,
So strong you thump, O terrible drums—so loud
    you bugles blow.

WALT WHITMAN.

OUR COUNTRY'S CALL.

LAY down the axe, fling by the spade ;
    Leave in its track the toiling plough ;
The rifle and the bayonet-blade
    For arms like yours were fitter now ;
And let the hands that ply the pen
    Quit the light task, and learn to wield
The horseman's crooked brand, and rein
    The charger on the battle-field.

Our country calls ; away ! away !
    To where the blood-stream blots the green ;
Strike to defend the gentlest sway
    That Time in all his course has seen.
See, from a thousand coverts—see
    Spring the armed foes that haunt her track ;
They rush to smite her down, and we
    Must beat the banded traitors back.

Ho ! sturdy as the oaks ye cleave,
    And moved as soon to fear and flight,
Men of the glade and forest ! leave
    Your woodcraft for the field of fight.

The arms that wield the axe must.pour
  An iron tempest on the foe ;
His serried ranks shall reel before
  The arm that lays the panther low.
And ye who breast the mountain storm
  By grassy steep or highland lake,
Come, for the land ye love, to form
  A bulwark that no foe can break.
Stand, like your own gray cliffs that mock
  The whirlwind ; stand in her defence :
The blast as soon shall move the rock,
  As rushing squadrons bear ye thence.

And ye whose homes are by her grand
  Swift rivers, rising far away,
Come from the depth of her green land
  As mighty in your march as they ;
As terrible as when the rains
  Have swelled them over bank and bourne,
With sudden floods to drown the plains
  And sweep along the woods uptorn.

And ye who throng beside the deep,
  Her ports and hamlets of the strand,
In number like the waves that leap
  On his long-murmuring marge of sand,
Come, like that deep, when, o'er his brim,
  He rises, all his floods to pour,
And flings the proudest barks that swim,
  A helpless wreck against his shore.

Few, few were they whose swords of old
  Won the fair land in which we dwell ;
But we are many, we who hold
  The grim resolve to guard it well.
Strike for that broad and goodly land,
  Blow after blow, till men shall see
That Might and Right move hand in hand,
  And glorious must their triumph be.

                    WILLIAM CULLEN BRYANT.

A CRY TO ARMS.

HO, woodsmen of the mountain-side!
    Ho, dwellers in the vales!
Ho, ye who by the chafing tide
    Have roughened in the gales!
Leave barn and byre, leave kin and cot,
    Lay by the bloodless spade;
Let desk and case and counter rot,
    And burn your books of trade!

The despot roves your fairest lands;
    And till he flies or fears,
Your fields must grow but armèd bands,
    Your sheaves be sheaves of spears!
Give up to mildew and to rust
    The useless tools of gain,
And feed your country's sacred dust
    With floods of crimson rain!

Come with the weapons at your call—
    With musket, pike, or knife;
He wields the deadliest blade of all
    Who lightest holds his life.
The arm that drives its unbought blows
    With all a patriot's scorn,
Might brain a tyrant with a rose
    Or stab him with a thorn.

Does any falter? let him turn
    To some brave maiden's eyes,
And catch the holy fires that burn
    In those sublunar skies.
Oh, could you like your women feel,
    And in their spirit march,
A day might see your lines of steel
    Beneath the victor's arch!

What hope, O God! would not grow warm
    When thoughts like these give cheer?

The lily calmly braves the storm,
  And shall the palm-tree fear ?
No ! rather let its branches court
  The rack that sweeps the plain ;
And from the lily's regal port
  Learn how to breast the strain.

Ho, woodsmen of the mountain-side !
  Ho, dwellers in the vales !
Ho, ye who by the roaring tide
  Have roughened in the gales !
Come, flocking gayly to the fight,
  From forest, hill, and lake ;
We battle for our country's right
  And for the lily's sake !

HENRY TIMROD.

NO MORE WORDS !

[*Boston, April*, 1861.]

No more words ;
  Try it with your swords !
Try it with the arms of your bravest and your best !
You are proud of your manhood, now put it to the
    test ;
  Not another word ;
  Try it by the sword !

No more notes ;
  Try it by the throats
Of the cannon that will roar till the earth and air be
    shaken ;
For they speak what they mean, and they cannot be
    mistaken ;
  No more doubt ;
  Come—fight it out !

No child's play !
Waste not a day ;
Serve out the deadliest weapons that you know ;
Let them pitilessly hail on the faces of the foe ;
No blind strife ;
Waste not one life.

You that in the front
Bear the battle's brunt—
When the sun gleams at dawn on the bayonets
abreast,
Remember 'tis for government and country you
contest ;
For love of all you guard,
Stand, and strike hard !

You at home that stay
From danger far away,
Leave not a jot to chance, while you rest in quiet
ease ;
Quick ! forge the bolts of death ; quick ! ship them
o'er the seas ;
If War's feet are lame,
Yours will be the blame.

You, my lads, abroad,
" Steady !" be your word ;
You, at home, be the anchor of your soldiers young
and brave ;
Spare no cost, none is lost, that may strengthen or
may save ;
Sloth were sin and shame ;
Now play out the game !

FRANKLIN LUSHINGTON.

SUMTER.

[*On the 12th of April*, 1861, *Fort Sumter, in Charleston Harbor, South Carolina, garrisoned by United States troops, was bombarded by the Confederate forces, and, after resisting for thirty-four hours, capitulated. This was the first battle of the war.*]

CAME the morning of that day
When the God to whom we pray
Gave the soul of Henry Clay
    To the land ;
How we loved him, living, dying !
But his birthday banners flying
Saw us asking and replying
    Hand to hand.

For we knew that far away,
Round the fort in Charleston Bay,
Hung the dark impending fray,
    Soon to fall ;
And that Sumter's brave defender
Had the summons to surrender
Seventy loyal hearts and tender—
    (Those were all !)

And we knew the April sun
Lit the length of many a gun—
Hosts of batteries to the one
    Island crag ;
Guns and mortars grimly frowning,
Johnson, Moultrie, Pinckney, crowning,
And ten thousand men disowning
    The old flag.

Oh, the fury of the fight
Even then was at its height !
Yet no breath, from noon till night,
    Reached us here ;

We had almost ceased to wonder,
And the day had faded under,
When the echo of the thunder
    Filled each ear!

Then our hearts more fiercely beat,
As we crowded on the street,
Hot to gather and repeat
    All the tale;
All the doubtful chances turning,
Till our souls with shame were burning,
As if twice our bitter yearning
    Could avail!

Who had fired the earliest gun?
Was the fort by traitors won?
Was there succor?   What was done
    Who could know?
And once more our thoughts would wander
To the gallant lone commander,
On his battered ramparts grander
    Than the foe.

Not too long the brave shall wait;
On their own heads be their fate,
Who against the hallowed State
    Dare begin;
Flag defied and compact riven!
In the record of high Heaven
How shall Southern men be shriven
    For the sin!
              EDMUND CLARENCE STEDMAN.

BROTHER JONATHAN'S LAMENT FOR SISTER CAROLINE.

SHE has gone—she has left us in passion and
    pride—
Our stormy-browed sister, so long at our side!
She has torn her own star from our firmament's
    glow,
And turned on her brother the face of a foe!

O Caroline, Caroline, child of the sun,
We can never forget that our hearts have been
    one,—
Our foreheads both sprinkled in Liberty's name,
From the fountain of blood with the finger of flame!

You were always too ready to fire at a touch;
But we said, " She is hasty—she does not mean
    much."
We have scowled, when you uttered some turbulent
    threat;
But Friendship still whispered, " Forgive and for-
    get!"

Has our love all died out? Have its altars grown
    cold?
Has the curse come at last which the fathers fore-
    told?
Then Nature must teach us the strength of the
    chain
That her petulant children would sever in vain.

They may fight till the buzzards are gorged with
    their spoil,
Till the harvest grows black as it rots in the soil,
Till the wolves and the catamounts troop from
    their caves,
And the shark tracks the pirate, the lord of the
    waves:

In vain is the strife!   When its fury is past,
Their fortunes must flow in one channel at last,
As the torrents that rush from the mountains of
    snow
Roll mingled in peace through the valleys below.

Our Union is river, lake, ocean, and sky :
Man breaks not the medal, when God cuts the
    die !
Though darkened with sulphur, though cloven with
    steel,
The blue arch will brighten, the waters will heal !

O Caroline, Caroline, child of the sun,
There are battles with Fate that can never be won !
The star-flowering banner must never be furled,
For its blossoms of light are the hope of the world !

Go, then, our rash sister ! afar and aloof,
Run wild in the sunshine away from our roof ;
But when your heart aches and your feet have
    grown sore,
Remember the pathway that leads to our door !

OLIVER WENDELL HOLMES.

MEN OF THE NORTH AND WEST.

MEN of the North and West,
    Wake in your might,
Prepare, as the rebels have done,
    For the fight !
You cannot shrink from the test ;
Rise ! Men of the North and West !

They have torn down your banner of stars ;
    They have trampled the laws ;

They have stifled the freedom they hate,
　　For no cause !
Do you love it or slavery best?
Speak ! Men of the North and West !

They strike at the life of the State :
　　Shall the murder be done?
They cry, " We are two !"　And you?
　　" *We are one !*"
You must meet them, then, breast to breast ;
On ! Men of the North and West !

Not with words ; they laugh them to scorn,
　　And tears they despise ;
But with swords in your hands, and death
　　In your eyes !
Strike home ! leave to God all the rest ;
Strike ! Men of the North and West !

　　　　　　RICHARD HENRY STODDARD.

MY MARYLAND.

[This poem is probably the most famous, as it is the most stirring in its martial tone, of all that the war evoked. Its form is doubtless suggested by Mangan's " Karamanian Exile":

　　" *I see thee ever in my dreams,*
　　　　Karaman !
　　Thy hundred hills, thy thousand streams,
　　　　Karaman, O Karaman !
　　As when thy gold-bright morning gleams,
　　As when the deepening sunset seams
　　With lines of light thy hills and streams,
　　　　Karaman !
　　So now thou loomest on my dreams,
　　　　Karaman, O Karaman !"

But the previous use of this form, which is remarkably effective for a battle-lyric, in no wise detracts from the merits of Mr. Randall's fine poem. From his editorial desk in Augusta, Georgia, he has sent a corrected version of " My Maryland," with these interesting particulars of its history : " In 1860–61 he who pens these lines was, though very young, a professor at Poydras College, upon the Fausse Riviere of Louisiana. There, a stripling, just from college in Maryland, full of poetry and romance, he dreamed dreams, and was only awakened by the guns of Sumter. At an old wooden desk, in a second-story room of Poydras College, one sleepless April night in 1861, the poem of ' My Maryland' was written. . . . And now the desk is ashes, and the building too !" The poem first appeared in the New Orleans Delta.]

THE despot's heel is on thy shore,
          Maryland !
His torch is at thy temple door,
          Maryland !
Avenge the patriotic gore
That flecked the streets of Baltimore,
And be the battle queen of yore,
          Maryland, my Maryland !

Hark to an exiled son's appeal,
          Maryland !
My Mother State, to thee I kneel,
          Maryland !
For life or death, for woe or weal,
Thy peerless chivalry reveal,
And gird thy beauteous limbs with steel,
          Maryland, my Maryland !

Thou wilt not cower in the dust,
          Maryland !
Thy beaming sword shall never rust,
          Maryland !
Remember Carroll's sacred trust,
Remember Howard's warlike thrust,
And all thy slumberers with the just,
          Maryland, my Maryland !

Come! 'tis the red dawn of the day,
  Maryland!
Come with thy panoplied array,
  Maryland!
With Ringgold's spirit for the fray,
With Watson's blood at Monterey,
With fearless Lowe and dashing May,
  Maryland, my Maryland!

Dear Mother, burst the tyrant's chain,
  Maryland!
Virginia should not call in vain,
  Maryland!
She meets her sisters on the plain,
" *Sic semper!* " 'tis the proud refrain
That baffles minions back amain,
  Maryland!
Arise in majesty again,
  Maryland, my Maryland!

Come! for thy shield is bright and strong.
  Maryland!
Come! for thy dalliance does thee wrong,
  Maryland!
Come to thine own heroic throng
Stalking with Liberty along,
And chant thy dauntless slogan-song,
  Maryland, my Maryland!

I see the blush upon thy cheek,
  Maryland!
But thou wast ever bravely meek,
  Maryland!
But lo! there surges forth a shriek,
From hill to hill, from creek to creek,
Potomac calls to Chesapeake,
  Maryland, my Maryland!

Thou wilt not yield the Vandal toll,
  Maryland!

Thou wilt not crook to his control,
    Maryland !
Better the fire upon thee roll,
Better the shot, the blade, the bowl,
Than crucifixion of the soul,
    Maryland, my Maryland !

I hear the distant thunder-hum,
    Maryland !
The " Old Line's " bugle, fife, and drum,
    Maryland !
She is not dead, nor deaf, nor dumb ;
Huzza ! she spurns the Northern scum—
She breathes ! She burns ! She'll come ! She'll come !
    Maryland, my Maryland !

                JAMES R. RANDALL.

THE PROPHECY OF THE DEAD.

[*April,* 1861.]

Is the groaning earth stabbed to its core?
    Are the seas oozing blood in their bed ?
Have all troubles of ages before
    Grown quick in those homes of the dead ?
      The red plagues of yore—
    Must they to our season be wed ?

We thought the volcano of War
    Would belch out its flames in the East;
We knew where the winds were ajar
    With the quarrel of soldier and priest ;
      We shuddered—though far—
    To think how the vultures might feast.

We said, "We have Liberty's smile :
    Go to ! we are safe in the West !"

But the plague-spot was on us the while,
  And the serpent was warm in our breast :
    We can no more revile—
  The ox is for sacrifice dressed.

Do ye hear, O ye Dead, in your tombs—
  Ye Dead, whose bold blows made us free—
Do ye hear the *réveille* of drums ?
  Can ye say what the issue shall be ?
    Past the midnight that comes,
  Is the noon rising up from the sea ?

Who whispered ?   Is life underneath
  Astir in the dust of the brave ?
For there steals to my ear such a breath
  As can only steal out of the grave :
    " Ye must go down to death :
  Ye have drunk of the blood of the slave."

We have sinned, we have sinned, O ye Dead !
  Our fields with the out-crying blood
Of Abel, our brother, are fed :
  Must we therefore be drowned in the flood ?
    Waits no Ararat's head ?
  Is no ark guided there by our God ?

" Ye must go down to death : have ye heard
  The tale of the writings of yore—
How One in the sepulchre stirred,
  And cast off the grave-clothes he wore ?
    In the flesh dwelt the Word—
  Inheriting life evermore.

" When the foes of the nation have pressed
  To its lips the sponge reeking in gall ;
When the spear has gone into its breast,
  And the skies have been rent by its call ;
    It shall rise from its rest :
  It shall rise and shall rule over all."

                    AMANDA T. JONES.

THE OATH OF FREEDOM.

BORN free, thus we resolve to live :
  By Heaven, we will be free !
By all the stars which burn on high—
By the green earth—the mighty sea—
By God's unshaken majesty,
    We will be free or die !
      Then let the drums all roll !
        Let all the trumpets blow !
          Mind, heart, and soul,
          We spurn control
        Attempted by a foe !

Born free, thus we resolve to live :
  By Heaven, we will be free !
And, vainly now the Northmen try
To beat us down—in arms we stand
To strike for this our native land !
    We will be free or die !
      Then let the drums all roll !

Born free, we thus resolve to live :
  By Heaven, we will be free !
Our wives and children look on high,
Pray God to smile upon the right !
And bid us in the deadly fight
    As freemen live or die !
      Then let the drums all roll !

Born free, thus we resolve to live :
  By Heaven, we will be free !
And ere we cease this battle-cry,
Be all our blood, our kindred's spilt,
On bayonet or sabre hilt !
    We will be free or die !
      Then let the drums all roll !

Born free, thus we resolve to live :
  By Heaven, we will be free !
Defiant let the banners fly,
Shake out their glories to the air,
And, kneeling, brothers, let us swear
    We will be free or die!
    Then let the drums all roll !

Born free, thus we resolve to live :
  By Heaven, we will be free !
And to this oath the dead reply—
Our valiant fathers' sacred ghosts—
These with us, and the God of hosts,
    We will be free or die !
    Then let the drums all roll !

JAMES BARRON HOPE.

THE RÉVEILLE.

HARK ! I hear the tramp of thousands,
  And of armèd men the hum ;
Lo ! a nation's hosts have gathered
  Round the quick alarming drum—
      Saying, " Come,
      Freemen, come !
Ere your heritage be wasted," said the quick alarm-
    ing drum.

" Let me of my heart take counsel:
  War is not of life the sum ;
Who shall stay and reap the harvest
  When the autumn days shall come ?"
      But the drum
      Echoed, " Come !
Death shall reap the braver harvest," said the
    solemn-sounding drum,

" But when won the coming battle,
    What of profit springs therefrom?
What if conquest, subjugation,
    Even greater ills become?"
            But the drum
            Answered, "Come!
You must do the sum to prove it," said the Yankee-
    answering drum.

" What if, 'mid the cannon's thunder,
    Whistling shot and bursting bomb,
When my brothers fall around me,
    Should my heart grow cold and numb?"
            But the drum
            Answered, "Come!
Better there in death united than in life a recreant
    —come!"

    Thus they answered—hoping, fearing,
        Some in faith, and doubting some,
    Till a trumpet-voice proclaiming,
        Said, "My chosen people, come!"
            Then the drum,
            Lo! was dumb;
For the great heart of the nation, throbbing,
    answered, "Lord, we come!"

                        BRET HARTE.

————

"UNDER THE CLOUD AND THROUGH THE SEA."

So moved they when false Pharaoh's legion prest,
    Chariots and horsemen following furiously,—
Sons of old Israel, at their God's behest,
    Under the cloud and through the swelling sea.

So passed they, fearless, where the parted wave,
    With cloven crest uprearing from the sand,—

A solemn aisle before—behind, a grave,—
  Rolled to the beckoning of Jehovah's hand.

And Jordan raged along his rocky bed,
  And Amorite spears flashed keen and fearfully :
Still the same pathway must their footsteps tread,
  Under the cloud and through the threatening sea.

God works no otherwise. No mighty birth
  But comes by throes of mortal agony ;
No man-child among nations of the earth
  But findeth baptism in a stormy sea.

Sons of the Saints who faced their Jordan-flood
  In fierce Atlantic's unretreating wave,—
Who by the Red Sea of their glorious blood
  Reached to the Freedom that your blood shall
    save,—

O countrymen ! God's day is not yet done ;
  He leaveth not His people utterly ;—
Count it a covenant that He leads us on,
  Beneath the Cloud and through the crimson Sea !

Adeline D. T. Whitney.

APOCALYPSE.

[*Written in memory of Private Luther C. Ladd, killed by a mob which attacked his regiment, the Sixth Massachusetts, while passing through Baltimore on the way to Washington, April* 19, 1861 : *the first life lost in the war.*]

Straight to his heart the bullet crushed ;
Down from his breast the red blood gushed,
And o'er his face a glory rushed.

A sudden spasm shook his frame,
And in his ears there went and came
A sound as of devouring flame,

Which in a moment ceased, and then
The great light clasped his brows again,
So that they shone like Stephen's when

Saul stood apart a little space
And shook with shuddering awe to trace
God's splendors settling o'er his face.

Thus, like a king, erect in pride,
Raising clean hands toward heaven, he cried,
" All hail the Stars and Stripes !" and died—

Died grandly.   But before he fell,
(O blessedness ineffable !)
Vision apocalyptical

Was granted to him, and his eyes
All radiant with glad surprise
Looked forward through the centuries,

And saw the seeds which sages cast
In the world's soil in cycles past
Spring up and blossom at the last.

Saw how the souls of men had grown,
And where the scythes of Truth had mown
Clear space for Liberty's white throne.

Saw how, by sorrow tried and proved,
The blackening stains had been removed
Forever from the land he loved.

Saw Treason crushed and Freedom crowned,
And clamorous Faction, gagged and bound,
Gasping its life out on the ground.

Saw how, across his country's slopes,
Walked swarming troops of cheerful hopes,
Which evermore to broader scopes

Increased, with power that comprehends
The world's weal in its own, and bends
Self-needs to large, unselfish ends.

Saw how, throughout the vast extents
Of Earth's most populous continents,
She dropped such rare heart affluence

That from beyond the utmost seas,
The wondering peoples thronged to seize
Her proffered pure benignities.

Saw how, of all her trebled host
Of widening empires, none might boast
Whose love were best or strength were most,

Because they grew so equal there
Beneath the flag which, debonaire,
Waved joyous in the cleansed air.

With far-off vision gazing clear
Beyond this gloomy atmosphere
Which shuts us in with doubt and fear,

He—marking how her high increase
Ran greatening in perpetual lease
Through balmy years of odorous peace—

Greeted, in one transcendent cry
Of intense passionate ecstasy,
The sight which thrilled him utterly.

Saluting with most proud disdain
Of murder and of mortal pain,
The vision which shall be again !

So, lifted with prophetic pride,
Raised conquering hands toward heaven and cried,
" All hail the Stars and Stripes !" and died.

RICHARD REALF.

DIXIE.

[The original of this popular Southern song, of which there were many variations during the war, is believed to be a Northern melody—an old negro refrain, dating back to the time when slavery existed in New York ; a certain Mr. Dixy, or Dixie, owning large tracts of land on Manhattan Island, and many slaves, among whom the estate was known as " Dixie's Land."]

SOUTHRONS, hear your country call you !
Up, lest worse than death befall you !
   To arms !   To arms !   To arms, in Dixie !
Lo ! all the beacon-fires are lighted—
Let all hearts be now united !
   To arms !   To arms !   To arms, in Dixie !
    Advance the flag of Dixie !
    Hurrah ! hurrah !
For Dixie's land we take our stand,
  And live or die for Dixie !
    To arms !   To arms !
And conquer peace for Dixie !
    To arms !   To arms !
And conquer peace for Dixie !

Hear the Northern thunders mutter !
Northern flags in South winds flutter !
    To arms !
Send them back your fierce defiance !
Stamp upon the accursed alliance !
    To arms !
   Advance the flag of Dixie !

Fear no danger !   Shun no labor !
Lift up rifle, pike, and sabre !
    To arms !
Shoulder pressing close to shoulder,
Let the odds make each heart bolder !
    To arms !
   Advance the flag of Dixie !

How the South's great heart rejoices
At your cannons' ringing voices !
   To arms !
For faith betrayed, and pledges broken,
Wrongs inflicted, insults spoken,
   To arms !
  Advance the flag of Dixie !

Strong as lions, swift as eagles,
Back to their kennels hunt these beagles !
   To arms !
Cut the unequal bonds asunder !
Let them hence each other plunder !
   To arms !
  Advance the flag of Dixie !

Swear upon your country's altar
Never to submit or falter !
   To arms !
Till the spoilers are defeated,
Till the Lord's work is completed.
   To arms !
  Advance the flag of Dixie !

Halt not till our Federation
Secures among earth's powers its station !
   To arms !
Then at peace, and crowned with glory,
Hear your children tell the story !
   To arms !
  Advance the flag of Dixie !

If the loved ones weep in sadness,
Victory soon shall bring them gladness.
   To arms !
Exultant pride soon vanish sorrow ;
Smiles chase tears away to-morrow.
 To arms !   To arms !   To arms, in Dixie !
  Advance the flag of Dixie !
   Hurrah ! hurrah !

For Dixie's land we take our stand,
And live or die for Dixie!
To arms! To arms!
And conquer peace for Dixie!
To arms! To arms!
And conquer peace for Dixie!

ALBERT PIKE.

THE NINETEENTH OF APRIL.

[*Boston*, 1861.]

THIS year, till late in April, the snow fell thick and
    light;
Thy truce-flag, friendly Nature, in clinging drifts of
    white
Hung over field and city; now everywhere is seen,
In place of that white quietness, a sudden glow of
    green.

The verdure climbs the Common, beneath the leaf-
    less trees,
To where the glorious Stars and Stripes are floating
    on the breeze.
There, suddenly as Spring awoke from Winter's
    snow-draped gloom,
The passion-flower of Seventy-six is bursting into
    bloom.

Dear is the time of roses, when earth to joy is wed,
And garden-plat and meadow wear one generous
    flush of red;
But now in dearer beauty, to her ancient colors
    true,
Blooms the old town of Boston in red and white and
    blue.

Along the whole awakening North are those bright
    emblems spread ;
A summer noon of patriotism is burning overhead ;
No party badges flaunting now, no word of clique
    or clan ;
But " Up for God and Union !" is the shout of every
    man.

Oh, peace is dear to Northern hearts ; our hard-
    earned homes more dear ;
But freedom is beyond the price of any earthly
    cheer ;
And freedom's flag is sacred : he who would work
    it harm,
Let him, although a brother, beware our strong
    right arm !

A brother ! ah, the sorrow, the anguish of that
    word !
The fratricidal strife begun, when will its end be
    heard ?
Not this the boon that patriots' hearts have prayed
    and waited for ;
We loved them, and we longed for peace : but they
    would have it war.

Yes, war ! on this memorial day, the day of Lex-
    ington,
A lightning-thrill along the wires from heart to
    heart has run.
Brave men we gazed on yesterday, to-day for us
    have bled :
Again is Massachusetts blood the first for freedom
    shed.

To war, and with our brethren, then, if only this
    can be !
Life hangs as nothing in the scale against dear
    Liberty !

Though hearts be torn asunder, for freedom we
    will fight :
Our blood may seal the victory, but God will shield
    the right !

LUCY LARCOM.

THE STRIPES AND THE STARS.

O STAR-SPANGLED BANNER ! the flag of our pride !
Though trampled by traitors and basely defied,
Fling out to the glad winds your red, white, and
    blue,
For the heart of the Northland is beating for you !
And her strong arm is nerving to strike with a will,
Till the foe and his boastings are humbled and still !
Here's welcome to wounding and combat and scars
And the glory of death—for the Stripes and the
    Stars !

From prairie, O ploughman ! speed boldly away—
There's seed to be sown in God's furrows to-day !
Row landward, lone fisher ! stout woodman, come
    home !
Let smith leave his anvil and weaver his loom,
And hamlet and city ring loud with the cry :
" For God and our country we'll fight till we die !
Here's welcome to wounding and combat and scars
And the glory of death—for the Stripes and the
    Stars !"

Invincible banner ! the flag of the free,
Oh, where treads the foot that would falter for thee ?
Or the hands to be folded, till triumph is won
And the eagle looks proud, as of old, to the sun ?
Give tears for the parting—a murmur of prayer—
Then forward ! the fame of our standard to
    share !

With welcome to wounding and combat and scars
And the glory of death—for the Stripes and the
Stars !

O God of our fathers ! this banner must shine
Where battle is hottest, in warfare divine !
The cannon has thundered, the bugle has blown—
We fear not the summons—we fight not alone !
O lead us, till wide from the gulf to the sea
The land shall be sacred to freedom and Thee !
With love, for oppression ; with blessing, for scars—
One country — one banner — the Stripes and the
Stars !

EDNA DEAN PROCTOR.

THE BONNIE BLUE FLAG.

COME, brothers ! rally for the right !
    The bravest of the brave
Sends forth her ringing battle-cry
    Beside the Atlantic wave !
She leads the way in honor's path ;
    Come, brothers, near and far,
Come rally 'round the Bonnie Blue Flag
    That bears a single star !

We've borne the Yankee trickery,
    The Yankee gibe and sneer,
Till Yankee insolence and pride
    Know neither shame nor fear ;
But ready now with shot and steel
    Their brazen front to mar,
We hoist aloft the Bonnie Blue Flag
    That bears a single star !

Now Georgia marches to the front,
    And close beside her come

Her sisters by the Mexique Sea,
   With pealing trump and drum ;
Till, answering back from hill and glen
   The rallying cry afar,
A Nation hoists the Bonnie Blue Flag
   That bears a single star!

By every stone in Charleston Bay,
   By each beleaguered town,
We swear to rest not, night nor day,
   But hunt the tyrants down !
Till, bathed in valor's holy blood
   The gazing world afar
Shall greet with shouts the Bonnie Blue Flag
   That bears the cross and star !

ANNIE CHAMBERS KETCHUM.

TO THE AMERICAN PEOPLE.

THAT late, in half-despair, I said :
"The Nation's ancient life is dead ;
Her arm is weak; her blood is cold ;
She hugs the peace that gives her gold—
The shameful peace, that sees expire
Each beacon-light of patriot fire,
And makes her court a traitor's den,"—
Forgive me this, my Countrymen !

Oh, in your long forbearance grand,
Slow to suspect the treason planned,
Enduring wrong, yet hoping good
For sake of olden brotherhood,
How grander, how sublimer far,
At the roused Eagle's call ye are,
Leaping from slumber to the fight
For Freedom and for Chartered Right !

NAVAL HEROES OF THE CIVIL WAR.

Throughout the land there goes a cry:
A sudden splendor fills the sky;
From every hill the banners burst,
Like buds by April breezes nurst;
In every hamlet, home, and mart,
The fire-beat of a single heart
Keeps time to strains whose pulses mix
Our blood with that of Seventy-Six!

Draw forth your million blades as one!
Complete the battle then begun!
God fights with ye, and overhead
Floats the dear banner of your dead.
They, and the glories of the Past,
The Future, dawning dim and vast,
And all the holiest hopes of man,
Are beaming triumph in your van!

Slow to resolve, be swift to do!
Teach ye the False how fight the True!
How bucklered Perfidy shall feel
In her black heart the Patriot's steel;
How sure the bolt that Justice wings;
How weak the arm a traitor brings;
How mighty they, who steadfast stand
For Freedom's Flag and Freedom's Land!

BAYARD TAYLOR.

THE TWO FURROWS.

THE spring-time came, but not with mirth;
  The banner of our trust,
And with it the best hopes of earth
  Were trailing in the dust.

The farmer saw the shame from far,
  And stopped his plough afield;
"Not the blade of peace, but the brand of war,
  This arm of mine must wield.

" When traitor hands that flag would stain,
    Their homes let women keep ;
Until its stars burn bright again,
    Let others sow and reap."

The farmer sighed.   " A life-time long
    The plough has been my trust ;
In truth, it were an arrant wrong
    To leave it now to rust."

With ready strength the farmer tore
    The iron from the wood ;
And to the village smith he bore
    That ploughshare, stout and good.

The blacksmith's arms were bare and brown,
    And loud the bellows roared ;
The farmer flung his ploughshare down :
    " Now forge me out a sword !"

And then a merry, merry chime
    The sounding anvil rung ;
Good sooth, it was a nobler rhyme
    Than ever poet sung.

The blacksmith wrought with skill that day ;
    The blade was keen and bright ;
And now where thickest is the fray
    The farmer leads the fight.

Not as of old that blade he sways
    To break the meadow's sleep ;
But through the rebel ranks he lays
    A furrow broad and deep.

The farmer's face is burned and brown,
    But light is on his brow ;
Right well he wots what blessings crown
    The furrow of the Plough.

"But better is to-day's success"—
Thus ran the farmer's word—
"For nations yet unborn shall bless
This furrow of the Sword."

C. H. WEBB.

SCOTT AND THE VETERAN.

[*May,* 1861.]

AN old and crippled veteran to the War Department came;
He sought the Chief who led him on many a field of fame—
The Chief who shouted "Forward!" where'er his banner rose,
And bore its stars in triumph behind the flying foes.

"Have you forgotten, General," the battered soldier cried,
"The days of Eighteen Hundred Twelve, when I was at your side?
Have you forgotten Johnson, that fought at Lundy's Lane?
'Tis true I'm old and pensioned, but I want to fight again."

"Have I forgotten?" said the Chief; "my brave old soldier, no!
And here's the hand I gave you then, and let it tell you so:
But you have done your share, my friend; you're crippled, old, and gray,
And we have need of younger arms and fresher blood to-day."

" But, General," cried the veteran, a flush upon his
    brow,
" The very men who fought with us, they say, are
    traitors now ;
They've torn the flag of Lundy's Lane—our old red,
    while, and blue ;
And while a drop of blood is left, I'll show that drop
    is true.

" I'm not so weak but I can strike, and I've a good
    old gun
To get the range of traitors' hearts, and pick them,
    one by one.
Your Minié rifles, and such arms, it a'n't worth
    while to try ;
I couldn't get the hang o' them, but I'll keep my
    powder dry !"

"God bless you, comrade !" said the Chief ; " God
    bless your loyal heart !
But younger men are in the field, and claim to have
    their part ;
They'll plant our sacred banner in each rebellious
    town,
And woe, henceforth, to any hand that dares to pull
    it down !"

" But, General"—still persisting, the weeping veter-
    an cried,
" I'm young enough to follow, so long as you're my
    guide ;
And some, you know, must bite the dust, and that,
    at least, can I,—
So give the young ones place to fight, but me a
    place to die !

" If they should fire on Pickens, let the colonel in
    command
Put me upon the rampart, with the flag-staff in my
    hand :

No odds how hot the cannon-smoke, or how the
    shells may fly;
I'll hold the Stars and Stripes aloft, and hold them
    till I die!

" I'm ready, General, so you let a post to me be
    given,
Where Washington can see me, as he looks from
    highest heaven,
And say to Putnam at his side, or, may be, General
    Wayne :
' There stands old Billy Johnson, that fought at
    Lundy's Lane ! '

" And when the fight is hottest, before the traitors
    fly,
When shell and ball are screeching and bursting in
    the sky,
If any shot should hit me, and lay me on my face,
My soul would go to Washington's and not to
    Arnold's place !"

                              BAYARD TAYLOR.

ENLISTED TO-DAY.

I KNOW the sun shines, and the lilacs are blowing,
    And summer sends kisses by beautiful May ;
Oh! to see all the treasures the spring is bestowing,
    And think—my boy Willie enlisted to-day.

It seems but a day since at twilight, low humming,
    I rocked him to sleep with his cheek upon mine,
While Robby, the four-year-old, watched for the
        coming
    Of father, adown the street's indistinct line.

It is many a year since my Harry departed,
  To come back no more in the twilight or dawn ;
And Robby grew weary of watching, and started
  Alone on the journey his father had gone.

It is many a year—and this afternoon, sitting
  At Robby's old window, I heard the band play,
And suddenly ceased dreaming over my knitting,
  To recollect Willie is twenty to-day.

And that, standing beside him this soft May-day
    morning,
  The sun making gold of his wreathed cigar
    smoke,
I saw in his sweet eyes and lips a faint warning,
  And choked down the tears when he eagerly
    spoke :

" Dear mother, you know how these Northmen are
    crowing,
  They would trample the rights of the South in
    the dust ;
The boys are all fire ; and they wish I were going—"
  He stopped, but his eyes said, " Oh, say if I
    must !"

I smiled on the boy, though my heart it seemed
    breaking,
  My eyes filled with tears, so I turned them away,
And answered him, " Willie, 'tis well you are
    waking—
  Go, act as your father would bid you, to-day !"

I sit in the window, and see the flags flying,
  And drearily list to the roll of the drum,
And smother the pain in my heart that is lying,
  And bid all the fears in my bosom be dumb.

I shall sit in the window when summer is lying
  Out over the fields, and the honey-bee's hum

Lulls the rose at the porch from her tremulous sigh-
    ing,
  And watch for the face of my darling to come.

And if he should fall—his young life he has given
  For freedom's sweet sake ; and for me, I will pray
Once more with my Harry and Robby in heaven
  To meet the dear boy that enlisted to-day.

ANONYMOUS.

———

BETHEL.

[*It was in the ill-fated attack of the Union forces on Big Bethel, near Newport News, Virginia, June* 10, 1861, *that the lamented Major Theodore Winthrop lost his life.*]

WE mustered   at   midnight, in darkness we
  formed,
And the whisper went round of a fort to be
  stormed ;
But no drum-beat had called us, no trumpet we
  heard,
And no voice of command, but our colonel's low
  word—
" *Column ! Forward !*"

And out, through the mist and the murk of the
  morn,
From the beaches of Hampton our barges were
  borne ;
And we heard not a sound, save the sweep of the
  oar,
Till the word of our colonel came up from the
  shore—
" *Column ! Forward !*"

With hearts bounding bravely, and eyes all alight,
As ye dance to soft music, so trod we that night ;

Through the aisles of the greenwood, with vines
    overarched,
Tossing dew-drops, like gems, from our feet, as we
    marched—
        " Column ! Forward !"

As ye dance with the damsels, to viol and flute,
So we skipped from the shadows, and mocked their
    pursuit ;
But the soft zephyrs chased us, with scents of the
    morn,
As we passed by the hay-fields and green waving
    corn—
        " Column ! Forward !"

For the leaves were all laden with fragrance of June,
And the flowers and the foliage with sweets were in
    tune ;
And the air was so calm, and the forest so dumb,
That we heard our own heart-beats, like taps of a
    drum—
        " Column ! Forward !"

Till the lull of the lowlands was stirred by a breeze,
And the buskins of morn brushed the tops of the
    trees,
And the glintings of glory that slid from her track
By the sheen of our rifles were gayly flung back—
        " Column ! Forward !"

And the woodlands grew purple with sunshiny mist,
And the blue-crested hill-tops with rose-light were
    kissed,
And the earth gave her prayers to the sun in per-
    fumes,
Till we marched as through gardens, and trampled
    on blooms—
        " Column ! Forward !"

Ay! trampled on blossoms, and seared the sweet
　　breath
Of the greenwood with low-brooding vapors of
　　death ;
O'er the flowers and the corn we were borne like a
　　blast,
And away to the forefront of battle we passed,—
　　　　" Column ! Forward !"

For the cannon's hoarse thunder roared out from
　　the glades,
And the sun was like lightning on banners and
　　blades,
When the long line of chanting Zouaves, like a
　　flood,
From the green of the woodlands rolled, crimson
　　as blood—
　　　　" Column ! Forward !"

While the sound of their song, like the surge of the
　　seas,
With the " Star-Spangled Banner " swelled over the
　　leas ;
And the sword of Duryea, like a torch, led the
　　way,
Bearing down on the batteries of Bethel that day—
　　　　" Column ! Forward !"

Through green-tasselled cornfields our columns
　　were thrown,
And like corn by the red scythe of fire we were
　　mown ;
While the cannon's fierce ploughings new-fur-
　　rowed the plain,
That our blood might be planted for Liberty's
　　grain—
　　　　" Column ! Forward !"

Oh ! the fields of fair June have no lack of sweet
  flowers,
But their rarest and best breathe no fragrance like
  ours ;
And the sunshine of June, sprinkling gold on the
  corn,
Hath no harvest that ripeneth like Bethel's red
  morn—
        " Column ! Forward !"

When our heroes, like bridegrooms, with lips and
  with breath
Drank the first kiss of Danger and clasped her in
  death ;
And the heart of brave Winthrop grew mute with
  his lyre,
When the plumes of his genius lay moulting in
  fire—
        " Column ! Forward !"

Where he fell shall be sunshine as bright as his
  name,
And the grass where he slept shall be green as his
  fame ;
For the gold of the pen and the steel of the sword
Write his deeds—in his blood—on the land he
  adored—
        " Column ! Forward !"

And the soul of our comrade shall sweeten the
  air,
And the flowers and the grass-blades his memory
  upbear ;
While the breath of his genius, like music in leaves,
With the corn-tassels whispers, and sings in the
  sheaves—
        " Column ! Forward !"

                    A. J. H. DUGANNE.

MANASSAS.

[First Battle of Bull Run, July 21, 1861.]

THEY have met at last—as storm-clouds
    Meet in heaven ;
And the Northmen back and bleeding
    Have been driven :
And their thunders have been stilled,
And their leaders crushed or killed,
And their ranks, with terror thrilled,
    Rent and riven !

Like the leaves of Vallambrosa
    They are lying ;
In the moonlight, in the midnight,
    Dead and dying :
Like those leaves before the gale,
Swept their legions, wild and pale ;
While the host that made them quail
    Stood, defying.

When aloft in morning sunlight
    Flags were flaunted,
And " swift vengeance on the Rebel "
    Proudly vaunted :
Little did they think that night
Should close upon their shameful flight,
And rebels, victors in the fight,
    Stand undaunted.

But peace to those who perished
    In our passes !
Light be the earth above them ;
    Green the grasses !
Long shall Northmen rue the day
When they met our stern array,
And shrunk from battle's wild affray
    At Manassas !

CATHERINE M. WARFIELD.

THE DEATH OF LYON.

*[General Nathaniel Lyon was killed in the battle of
Wilson's Creek, Missouri, while in command of the Union
forces, August 10, 1861. His last words were : " Come on,
my brave boys ! I will lead you !"]*

SING, bird, on green Missouri's plain,
   The saddest song of sorrow ;
Drop tears, O clouds, in gentlest rain
   Ye from the winds can borrow ;
Breathe out, ye winds, your softest sigh,
   Weep, flowers, in dewy splendor,
For him who knew well how to die,
   But never to surrender.

Up rose serene the August sun
   Upon that day of glory ;
Up curled from musket and from gun
   The war-cloud, gray and hoary ;
It gathered like a funeral pall,
   Now broken, and now blended,
Where rang the bugle's angry call,
   And rank with rank contended.

Four thousand men, as brave and true
   As e'er went forth in daring,
Upon the foe that morning threw
   The strength of their despairing.
They feared not death—men bless the field
   That patriot soldiers die on ;
Fair Freedom's cause was sword and shield,
   And at their head was Lyon.

Their leader's troubled soul looked forth
   From eyes of troubled brightness ;
Sad soul ! the burden of the North
   Had pressed out all its lightness.
He gazed upon the unequal fight,
   His ranks all rent and gory,

And felt the shadows close like night
  Round his career of glory.

"General, come lead us !" loud the cry
  From a brave band was ringing—
"Lead us, and we will stop, or die,
  That battery's awful singing!"
He spurred to where his heroes stood—
  Twice wounded, no one knowing—
The fire of battle in his blood
  And on his forehead glowing.

Oh ! cursed for aye that traitor's hand,
  And cursed that aim so deadly,
Which smote the bravest of the land,
  And dyed his bosom redly !
Serene he lay, while past him pressed
  The battle's furious billow,
As calmly as a babe may rest
  Upon its mother's pillow.

So Lyon died ; and well may flowers
  His place of burial cover,
For never had this land of ours
  A more devoted lover.
Living, his country was his bride ;
  His life he gave her, dying ;
Life, fortune, love, he nought denied
  To her, and to her sighing.

Rest, patriot, in thy hillside grave,
  Beside her form who bore thee !
Long may the land thou diedst to save
  Her bannered stars wave o'er thee !
Upon her history's brightest page,
  And on fame's glowing portal,
She'll write thy grand, heroic age,
  And grave thy name immortal.

                              ANONYMOUS,

MOVE ON THE COLUMNS!

[*Autumn*, 1861.]

MOVE on the columns! Why delay?
  Our soldiers sicken in their camps ;
  The summer heats, the autumn damps,
Have sapped their vigor day by day;
  And now the winter comes apace,
  With death-chills in its cold embrace,
More fatal than the battle-fray.

Move on the columns! Hesitate
  No longer what to plan or do :
  Our cause is good—our men are true—
This fight is for the flag, the State,
  The Union, and the hopes of man ;
  And Right will end what Wrong began,
For God the right will vindicate.

Move on the columns! If the land
  Is locked by winter, take the sea ;
  No possible barrier can be
So fatal to a rightful stand,
  As wavering purpose when at bay ;
  This way, or that—"At once! to-day !"
Were worth ten thousand men at hand.

Move on the columns! With the sweep
  Of eagles let them strike the foe.
  The hurricane lays the forest low ;
Momentum wings the daring leap
  That clears the chasm ; the lightning stroke
  Shivers the wind-defying oak ;
The earthquake rocks the eternal steep.

Move on the columns! Why have sprung
  Our myriad hosts from hill and plain?
  Leaving the sickle in the grain—

Closing the harvest-hymn half sung—
  Half-filled the granary and the mow,
  Unturned the sod, untouched the plough,
Scythes rusting where they last were swung.

Move on the columns ! They are here
  To found anew a people's faith ;
  To save from treason and from death
A nation which they all revere ;
  And on each manly brow is set
  A purpose such as never yet
Was thwarted, when, as now, sincere.

Move on the columns ! Earth contains
  No guerdon for the good and free
  Like that which blessed our Liberty ;
And while its banner still remains
  The symbol of united power,
  Nor man nor fiend can tell the hour
In which its star-lit glory wanes.

Move on the columns—strong and bright !
  Strike down the sacrilegious hands
  That clutch and wield the battle-brands
Which menace with their Wrong our Right !
  Words now are wasted : glittering steel
  Alone can make this last appeal :
They've willed it so—and we must fight.

Move on the columns ! If they go
  By ways they had not thought to take,
  To fields we had not meant to make,
Or if they bring unthought-of woe,
  Let that which woke the fiery wrath
Fall, scorched and blackening, in its path ;
Not man, but God, may stay the blow :
    Move on the columns !
           W. D. GALLAGHER.

THE WASHERS OF THE SHROUD.

[*October*, 1861.]

ALONG a river-side, I know not where,
I walked one night in mystery of dream ;
A chill creeps curdling yet beneath my hair,
To think what chanced me by the pallid gleam
Of a moon-wraith that waned through haunted air.

Pale fireflies pulsed within the meadow-mist
Their halos, wavering thistledowns of light ;
The loon, that seemed to mock some goblin tryst,
Laughed ; and the echoes, huddling in affright,
Like Odin's hounds, fled baying down the night.

Then all was silent, till there smote my ear
A movement in the stream that checked my breath :
Was it the slow plash of a wading deer?
But something said, "This water is of Death !
The Sisters wash a shroud—ill thing to hear !"

I, looking then, beheld the ancient Three
Known to the Greek's and to the Northman's creed,
That sit in shadow of the mystic tree,
Still crooning, as they weave their endless brede,
One song : "Time was, Time is, and Time shall
        be."

No wrinkled crones were they, as I had deemed,
But fair as yesterday, to-day, to-morrow,
To mourner, lover, poet, ever seemed ;
Something too high for joy, too deep for sorrow,
Thrilled in their tones, and from their faces gleamed.

"Still men and nations reap as they have strawn,"
So sang they, working at their task the while ;
"The fatal raiment must be cleansed ere dawn ;
For Austria? Italy? the Sea-Queen's isle ?
O'er what quenched grandeur must our shroud be
        drawn ?

" Or is it for a younger, fairer corse,
That gathered States for children round his knees,
That tamed the wave to be his posting-horse,
Feller of forests, linker of the seas,
Bridge-builder, hammerer, youngest son of Thor's ?

" What make we, murmur'st thou ? and what are
    we ?
When empires must be wound, we bring the shroud,
The time-old web of the implacable Three :
Is it too coarse for him, the young and proud ?
Earth's mightiest deigned to wear it—why not he ?"

" Is there no hope ?" I moaned, " so strong, so fair !
Our Fowler whose proud bird would brook ere-
    while
No rival's swoop in all our western air !
Gather the ravens, then, in funeral file
For him, life's morn yet golden in his hair ?

" Leave me not hopeless, ye unpitying dames !
I see, half seeing.   Tell me, ye who scanned
The stars, Earth's elders, still must noblest aims
Be traced upon oblivious ocean-sand ?
Must Hesper join the wailing ghosts of names ?"

" When grass-blades stiffen with red battle-dew,
Ye deem we choose the victor and the slain :
Say, choose we them that shall be leal and true
To the heart's longing, the high faith of brain ?
Yet there the victory lies, if ye but knew.

" Three roots bear up Dominion : Knowledge.
    Will—
These twain are strong, but stronger yet the third—
Obedience—'tis the great tap-root that still,
Knit round the rock of Duty, is not stirred,
Though Heaven-loosed tempests spend their utmost
    skill.

" Is the doom sealed for Hesper ?   'Tis not we
Denounce it, but the Law before all time :
The brave makes danger opportunity ;
The waverer, paltering with the chance sublime,
Dwarfs it to peril : which shall Hesper be ?

" Hath he let vultures climb his eagle's seat
To make Jove's bolts purveyors of their maw ?
Hath he the Many's plaudits found more sweet
Than Wisdom ? held Opinion's wind for Law ?
Then let him hearken for the doomster's feet !

" Rough are the steps, slow-hewn in flintiest rock,
States climb to power by ; slippery those with gold
Down which they stumble to eternal mock :
No chafferer's hand shall long the sceptre hold,
Who, given a Fate to shape, would sell the block.

" We sing old Sagas, songs of weal and woe,
Mystic because too cheaply understood ;
Dark sayings are not ours ; men hear and know,
See Evil weak, see strength alone in Good,
Yet hope to stem God's fire with walls of tow.

" Time Was unlocks the riddle of Time Is,
That offers choice of glory or of gloom ;
The solver makes Time Shall Be surely his.
But hasten, Sisters ! for even now the tomb
Grates its slow hinge and calls from the abyss."

" But not for him," I cried, "not yet for him,
Whose large horizon, westering, star by star
Wins from the void to where on Ocean's rim
The sunset shuts the world with golden bar,
Not yet his thews shall fail, his eye grow dim !

" His shall be larger manhood, saved for those
That walk unblenching through the trial-fires ;
Not suffering, but faint heart, is worst of woes,
And he no base-born son of craven sires,
Whose eye need blench confronted with his foes.

Tears may be ours, but proud, for those who win
Death's royal purple in the foeman's lines ;
Peace, too, brings tears ; and 'mid the battle-din
The wiser ear some text of God divines,
For the sheathed blade may rust with darker sin.

" God give us peace !—not such as lulls to sleep,
But sword on thigh, and brow with purpose knit !
And let our Ship of State to harbor sweep,
Her ports all up, her battle-lanterns lit,
And her leashed thunders gathering for their leap !"

So cried I with clenched hands and passionate pain,
Thinking of dear ones by Potomac's side ;
Again the loon laughed mocking, and again
The echoes bayed far down the night and died,
While, waking, I recalled my wandering brain.

                        JAMES RUSSELL LOWELL.

IN STATE.

I.

O KEEPER of the sacred Key,
And the Great Seal of Destiny,
Whose eye is the blue canopy,
Look down upon the warring world, and tell us what
    the end will be.

" Lo, through the wintry atmosphere,
On the white bosom of the sphere,
A cluster of five lakes appear ;
And all the land looks like a couch, or warrior's
    shield, or sheeted bier.

" And on that vast and hollow field,
With both lips closed and both eyes sealed,
A mighty figure is revealed—
Stretched at full length, and stiff and stark, as in
  the hollow of a shield.

" The winds have tied the drifted snow
Around the face and chin ; and lo,
The sceptred giants come and go,
And shake their shadowy crowns and say : ' We
  always feared it would be so ! '

" She came of an heroic race :
A giant's strength, a maiden's grace,
Like two in one seem to embrace,
And match, and blend, and thorough-blend, in her
  colossal form and face.

" Where can her dazzling falchion be ?
One hand is fallen in the sea ;
The Gulf Stream drifts it far and free ;
And in that hand her shining brand gleams from
  the depths resplendently.

" And by the other, in its rest,
The starry banner of the West
Is clasped forever to her breast ;
And of her silver helmet, lo ! a soaring eagle is the
  crest.

" And on her brow a softened light,
As of a star concealed from sight
By some thin veil of fleecy white,
Or of the rising moon behind the rainy vapors of the
  night.

" The sisterhood that was so sweet,
The starry system sphered complete,
Which the mazed Orient used to greet,

The four-and-thirty fallen stars glimmer and glitter
 at her feet.

 " And over her—and over all,
For panoply and coronal—
The mighty Immemorial,
And everlasting canopy, and starry arch, and shield
 of all.

II.

 " Three cold bright moons have marched and
 wheeled,
And the white cerement that revealed
A figure stretched upon a shield,
Is turned to verdure ; and the land is now one
 mighty battle-field.

 " And lo ! the children which she bred,
And more than all else cherishéd,
To make them true in heart and head,
Stand face to face, as mortal foes, with their swords
 crossed above the dead.

 " Each hath a mighty stroke and stride :
One true, the more that he is tried ;
The other dark and evil-eyed ;
And by the hand of one of them his own dear
 mother surely died !

 " A stealthy step, a gleam of hell,—
It is the simple truth to tell :
The son stabbed, and the mother fell ;
And so she lies, all mute and pale, and pure and
 irreproachable !

 " And then the battle-trumpet blew ;
And the true brother sprang and drew
His blade to smite the traitor through ;
And so they clashed above the bier, and the night
 sweated bloody dew.

" And all their children, far and wide,
That are so greatly multiplied,
Rise up in frenzy and divide ;
And choosing each whom he will serve, unsheathe
    the sword and take their side.

" And in the low sun's bloodshot rays,
Portentous of the coming days,
The two great oceans blush and blaze,
With the emergent continent between them, wrapt
    in crimson haze.

" Now whichsoever stand or fall,
As God is great, and man is small,
The truth shall triumph over all :
Forever and forevermore, the truth shall triumph
    over all !

III.

" I see the champion sword-strokes flash ·
I see them fall and hear them clash ;
I hear the murderous engines crash ;
I see a brother stoop to loose a foeman-brother's
    bloody sash.

" I see the torn and mangled corse,
The dead and dying heaped in scores,
The headless rider by his horse,
The wounded captive bayoneted through and
    through without remorse.

" I hear the dying sufferer cry,
With his crushed face turned to the sky ;
I see him crawl in agony
To the foul pool, and bow his head into the bloody
    slime, and die.

" I see the assassin crouch and fire ;
I see his victim fall—expire ;
I see the murderer creeping nigher

To strip the dead.   He turns the head—the face !
    The son beholds his sire !

  " I hear the curses and the thanks ;
  I see the mad charge on the flanks,
  The rents, the gaps, the broken ranks,
The vanquished squadrons driven headlong down
    the river's bridgeless banks.

  " I see the death-gripe on the plain,
  The grappling monsters on the main,
  The tens of thousands that are slain,
And all the speechless suffering and agony of heart
    and brain.

  " I see the dark and bloody spots,
  The crowded rooms and crowded cots,
  The bleaching bones, the battle blots,—
And writ on many a nameless grave, a legend of
    forget-me-nots.

  " I see the gorgéd prison-den,
  The dead-line and the pent-up pen,
  The thousands quartered in the fen,
The living deaths of skin and bone that were the
    goodly shapes of men.

  " And still the bloody dew must fall !
  And His great darkness with the pall
  Of His dread Judgment cover all,
Till the dead nation rise transformed by truth to
    triumph over all !

  " And last—and last I see—the deed."
  Thus saith the Keeper of the key,
  And the Great Seal of Destiny,
  Whose eye is the blue canopy,
And leaves the pall of His great darkness over all
    the land and sea.

              FORCEYTHE WILLSON.

THE HOPES OF MAN.

OUR past is bright and grand
  In the purpling tints of time,
And the present of our land
  Points to glories more sublime.
For our destiny is won,
  And 'tis ours to lead the van
Of the nations marching on,
  Of the moving hosts of Man.
          Yes, the Starry Flag alone
          Shall wave above the van
          Of the nations sweeping on,
          Of the moving hosts of Man.

We are sprung from noble sires
  As were ever sung in song ;
We are bold with Freedom's fires,
  We are rich, and wise, and strong.
On us are freely showered
  The gifts of every clime,
And we're the richest dowered
  Of all the heirs of Time.
          Brothers, then, in Union strong,
          We shall ever lead the van,
          As the nations sweep along
          To fulfil the hopes of Man.

We are brothers, and we know
  That our Union is a tower,
When the fiercest whirlwinds blow
  And the darkest tempests lower.
We shall sweep the land and sea
  While we march in Union great—
Thirty millions of the free,
  With the steady stride of fate.
          Brothers, then, in Union strong,
          Let us ever lead the van,
          As the nations sweep along
          To fulfil the hopes of Man.

See our prairies, sky-surrounded!
  See our hills with golden veins!
See our waving woods unbounded,
  And our cities on the plains!
See the oceans kiss our strand—
  Oceans stretched from pole to pole!
See our mighty lakes expand,
  And our giant rivers roll!
      Such a land, and such alone,
        Should be leader of the van
      Of the nations sweeping on
        To fulfil the hopes of Man.

Yes, the spirit of our land,
  The young giant of the West,
With the waters in his hand,
  With the forests for his crest,
To our hearts' quick, proud pulsations,
  To our shouts that still increase,
Shall yet lead on the nations
  To their brotherhood of peace.
      Yes, Columbia, great and strong,
        Shall forever lead the van,
      As the nations sweep along
        To fulfil the hopes of Man.

                    JOSEPH O'CONNOR.

GOD SAVE THE NATION!

THOU who ordainest, for the land's salvation,
Famine, and fire, and sword, and lamentation,
Now unto Thee we lift our supplication—
      God save the Nation!

By the great sign, foretold, of Thy appearing,
Coming in clouds, while mortal men stand fearing,
Show us, amid this smoke of battle, clearing,
      Thy chariot nearing!

By the brave blood that floweth like a river,
Hurl Thou a thunderbolt from out Thy quiver!
Break Thou the strong gates! Every fetter shiver!
        Smite and deliver!

Slay Thou our foes, or turn them to derision!—
Then, in the blood-red Valley of Decision,
Make the land green with Peace, as in a vision
        Of fields elysian!

                    THEODORE TILTON.

BATTLE-HYMN OF THE REPUBLIC.

[*November*, 1861.]

MINE eyes have seen the glory of the coming of
    the Lord;
He is trampling out the vintage where the grapes
    of wrath are stored;
He hath loosed the fateful lightning of His terrible
    swift sword:
        His truth is marching on.

I have seen Him in the watchfires of a hundred cir-
    cling camps;
They have builded Him an altar in the evening
    dews and damps;
I have read His righteous sentence by the dim and
    flaring lamps:
        His day is marching on.

I have read a fiery gospel writ in burnished rows
    of steel:
" As ye deal with my contemners, so with you my
    grace shall deal;
Let the Hero, born of woman, crush the serpent
    with his heel,
        Since God is marching on."

He has sounded forth the trumpet that shall never
    call retreat ;
He is sifting out the hearts of men before His judg-
    ment-seat ;
Oh, be swift, my soul, to answer Him ! be jubilant,
    my feet !
        Our God is marching on.

In the beauty of the lilies Christ was born across
    the sea,
With a glory in His bosom that transfigures you
    and me ;
As He died to make men holy, let us die to make
    men free,
        While God is marching on.

                JULIA WARD HOWE.

ALL QUIET ALONG THE POTOMAC.

[*This piece, sometimes printed with the less character-
istic title of " The Picket Guard," has been claimed for
several authors, Northern and Southern. It appeared in
the "Southern Literary Messenger," February, 1863, as
" written by Lamar Fontaine, private of Company I, Sec-
ond Regiment Virginia Cavalry, while on picket, on the
bank of the Potomac, in 1861." More recently, it has been
claimed for another Southern soldier, named Thad Oliver.
But it is now known to have been written by Mrs. Ethel
Lynn (or Ethelinda) Beers, of New York, and first pub-
lished in " Harper's Weekly" in 1861. The phrase " All
quiet along the Potomac" was a familiar one in the fall of
that year; and in the indifferent announcement that was
one day added, " A picket shot," the author found the
inspiration of her poem.*]

  " ALL quiet along the Potomac," they say,
    " Except now and then a stray picket
  Is shot, as he walks on his beat to and fro,
    By a rifleman hid in the thicket ;

'Tis nothing—a private or two now and then
  Will not count in the news of the battle ;
Not an officer lost—only one of the men,
  Moaning out, all alone, his death-rattle."

All quiet along the Potomac to-night,
  Where the soldiers lie peacefully dreaming ;
Their tents in the rays of the clear autumn moon,
  Or the light of the watch-fires, are gleaming.
A tremulous sigh, as the gentle night-wind
  Through the forest-leaves softly is creeping ;
While stars up above, with their glittering eyes,
  Keep guard—for the army is sleeping.

There's only the sound of the lone sentry's tread,
  As he tramps from the rock to the fountain,
And thinks of the two in the low trundle-bed
  Far away in the cot on the mountain.
His musket falls slack—his face, dark and grim,
  Grows gentle with memories tender,
As he mutters a prayer for the children asleep,
  For their mother—may Heaven defend her !

The moon seems to shine just as brightly as then,
  That night, when the love yet unspoken
Leaped up to his lips—when low-murmured vows
  Were pledged to be ever unbroken.
Then drawing his sleeve roughly over his eyes,
  He dashes off tears that are welling,
And gathers his gun closer up to its place,
  As if to keep down the heart-swelling.

He passes the fountain, the blasted pine-tree—
  The footstep is lagging and weary ;
Yet onward he goes, through the broad belt of light,
  Toward the shades of the forest so dreary.
Hark ! was it the night-wind that rustled the leaves ?
  Was it moonlight so suddenly flashing ?
It looked like a rifle . . . . " Ha ! Mary, good-by !"
  And the life-blood is ebbing and plashing.

All quiet along the Potomac to-night;
  No sound save the rush of the river;
While soft falls the dew on the face of the dead—
  The picket's off duty forever!

ETHEL LYNN BEERS.

———

ONLY A PRIVATE.

ONLY a private—and who will care
  When I may pass away,
Or how, or why I perish, or where
  I mix with the common clay?
They will fill my empty place again
  With another as bold and brave;
And they'll blot me out ere the autumn rain
  Has freshened my nameless grave.

Only a private—it matters not
  That I did my duty well,
That all through a score of battles I fought,
  And then, like a soldier, fell.
The country I died for never will heed
  My unrequited claim;
And History cannot record the deed,
  For she never has heard my name.

Only a private—and yet I know
  When I heard the rallying-call
I was one of the very first to go,
  And . . . I'm one of the many who fall:
But as here I lie, it is sweet to feel
  That my honor's without a stain,—
That I only fought for my country's weal,
  And not for glory or gain.

Only a private—yet He who reads
  Through the guises of the heart,
Looks not at the splendor of the deeds,
  But the way we do our part;

And when He shall take us by the hand,
And our small service own,
There'll a glorious band of privates stand
As victors around the throne!

MARGARET J. PRESTON (*Southern*).

THE FANCY SHOT.

[*This is the title by which this famous piece is more gen-
erally known, although " Civil War " is perhaps the more
authentic one. The poem appeared early in the war, in the
London " Once a Week," with the caption " Civile Bellum,"
and dated " From the Once United States." Its author-
ship is not clearly settled, but is commonly attributed to
Charles Dawson Shanly, who died in* 1876.]

" RIFLEMAN, shoot me a fancy shot
Straight at the heart of yon prowling vidette;
Ring me a ball in the glittering spot
That shines on his breast like an amulet!"

" Ah, Captain! here goes for a fine-drawn bead;
There's music around when my barrel's in
tune!"
Crack! went the rifle, the messenger sped,
And dead from his horse fell the ringing dra-
goon.

" Now, Rifleman, steal through the bushes, and
snatch
From your victim some trinket to handsel first
blood—
A button, a loop, or that luminous patch
That gleams in the moon like a diamond stud."

" O Captain! I staggered, and sunk on my track,
When I gazed on the face of that fallen vidette;
For he looked so like you as he lay on his back
That my heart rose upon me, and masters me yet.

" But I snatched off the trinket—this locket of gold ;
 An inch from the centre my lead broke its way,
Scarce grazing the picture, so fair to behold,
 Of a beautiful lady in bridal array."

"Ha ! Rifleman, fling me the locket !—'tis she,
 My brother's young bride, and the fallen dragoon
Was her husband— Hush ! soldier, 'twas Heaven's
 decree ;
We must bury him here, by the light of the moon !

" But, hark ! the far bugles their warnings unite ;
 War is a virtue—weakness a sin ;
There's lurking and loping around us to-night ;
 Load again, Rifleman, keep your hand in !"

CHARLES DAWSON SHANLY.

THE COUNTERSIGN.

[*There has been no little dispute as to the authorship of
this poem. The Philadelphia "Press," in 1861, said it was
"written by a private in Company G, Stuart's Engineer
Regiment, at Camp Lesley, near Washington." But it
may now be stated positively that it was written by a Con-
federate soldier, still living. The poem is usually printed
in a very imperfect form, with the fourth, fifth, and sixth
stanzas omitted. The third line of the fifth stanza affords
internal evidence of Southern origin.*]

ALAS ! the weary hours pass slow,
 The night is very dark and still ;
And in the marshes far below
 I hear the bearded whippoorwill ;
I scarce can see a yard ahead,
 My ears are strained to catch each sound ;
I hear the leaves about me shed,
 And the spring's bubbling through the ground.

Along the beaten path I pace,
   Where white rags mark my sentry's track ;
In formless shrubs I seem to trace
   The foeman's form with bending back,
I think I see him crouching low :
   I stop and list—I stoop and peer,
Until the neighboring hillocks grow
   To groups of soldiers far and near.

With ready piece I wait and watch,
   Until my eyes, familiar grown,
Detect each harmless earthern notch,
   And turn guerrillas into stone ;
And then, amid the lonely gloom,
   Beneath the tall old chestnut trees,
My silent marches I resume,
   And think of other times than these.

Sweet visions through the silent night !
   The deep bay-windows fringed with vine,
The room within, in softened light,
   The tender milk-white hand in mine ;
The timid pressure, and the pause
   That often overcame our speech—
That time when by mysterious laws
   We each felt all in all to each.

And then that bitter, bitter day,
   When came the final hour to part ;
When, clad in soldier's honest gray,
   I pressed her weeping to my heart ;
Too proud of me to bid me stay,
   Too fond of me to let me go,—
I had to tear myself away,
   And left her, stolid in my woe.

So rose the dream—so passed the night—
   When, distant in the darksome glen,
Approaching up the sombre height
   I heard the solid march of men ;

Till over stubble, over sward,
  And fields where lay the golden sheaf,
I saw the lantern of the guard
  Advancing with the night relief.

" Halt !   Who goes there ?"   My challenge cry,
  It rings along the watchful line ;
" Relief !" I hear a voice reply ;
  " Advance, and give the countersign !"
With bayonet at the charge I wait—
  The corporal gives the mystic spell ;
With arms aport I charge my mate,
  Then onward pass, and all is well.

But in the tent that night awake,
  I ask, if in the fray I fall,
Can I the mystic answer make
  When the angelic sentries call ?
And pray that Heaven may so ordain,
  Where'er I go, what fate be mine,
Whether in pleasure or in pain,
  I still may have the countersign.
                    ANONYMOUS (*Southern*).

THE BRAVE AT HOME.

THE maid who binds her warrior's sash,
  With smile that well her pain dissembles,
The while beneath her drooping lash
  One starry tear-drop hangs and trembles,
Though Heaven alone records the tear,
  And fame shall never know her story,
Her heart has shed a drop as dear
  As e'er bedewed the field of glory !

The wife who girds her husband's sword,
  'Mid little ones who weep or wonder,
And bravely speaks the cheering word,
  What though her heart be rent asunder,
Doomed nightly in her dreams to hear
  The bolts of death around him rattle,
Hath shed as sacred blood as e'er
  Was poured upon the field of battle!

The mother who conceals her grief,
  While to her breast her son she presses,
Then breathes a few brave words and brief,
  Kissing the patriot brow she blesses,
With no one but her secret God
  To know the pain that weighs upon her,
Sheds holy blood as e'er the sod
  Received on freedom's field of honor!

THOMAS BUCHANAN READ.

BOY BRITTAN.

[Battle of Fort Henry, Tenn., February 6, 1862.]

I.

BOY BRITTAN—only a lad—a fair-haired boy—six-
    teen,
        In his uniform,
Into the storm—into the roaring jaws of grim Fort
    Henry—
  Boldly bears the Federal flotilla—
      Into the battle storm!

II.

Boy Brittan is master's mate aboard of the Essex—
  There he stands, buoyant and eager-eyed,
      By the brave captain's side;

Ready to do and dare. *Aye, aye, sir!* always
 ready—
   In his country's uniform.
Boom! Boom! and now the flag-boat sweeps, and
 now the Essex,
   Into the battle storm!

III.

Boom! Boom! till river and fort and field are over-
 clouded
 By battle's breath; then from the fort a gleam
And a crashing gun, and the Essex is wrapt and
 shrouded
   In a scalding cloud of steam!

IV.

   But victory! victory!
Unto God all praise be ever rendered,
 Unto God all praise and glory be!
 See, boy Brittan! see, boy, see!
They strike!   Hurrah! the fort has just surren-
 dered!
 Shout!   Shout! my boy, my warrior boy!
And wave your cap and clap your hands for joy!
 Cheer answer cheer and bear the cheer about—
Hurrah! Hurrah! for the fiery fort is ours;
 And " Victory!" " Victory!" " Victory!"
   Is the shout.
Shout—for the fiery fort, and the field, and the day
 are ours—
 The day is ours—thanks to the brave endeavor
   Of heroes, boy, like thee!
 The day is ours—the day is ours!
Glory and deathless love to all who shared with
 thee,
And bravely endured and dared with thee—
 The day is ours—the day is ours—
   Forever!

Glory and Love for one and all ; but — but — for
   thee—
  Home ! Home ! a happy "Welcome—welcome
    home " for thee !
      And kisses of love for thee—
And a mother's happy, happy tears, and a virgin's
   bridal wreath of flowers—
      For thee !

v.

     Victory ! Victory ! . . . .
But suddenly wrecked and wrapt in seething steam,
   the Essex
  Slowly drifted out of the battle's storm ;
Slowly, slowly down—laden with the dead and the
   dying ;
And there, at the captain's feet, among the dead
   and the dying,
The shot-marred form of a beautiful boy is lying—
    There in his uniform !

VI.

    Laurels and tears for thee, boy,
    Laurels and tears for thee !
Laurels of light, moist with the precious dew
  Of the inmost heart of the nation's loving heart,
And blest by the balmy breath of the beautiful and
   the true ;
Moist—moist with the luminous breath of the sing-
   ing spheres
     And the nation's sta'ry tears !
And tremble-touched by the pulse-like gush and
   start
Of the universal music of the heart,
     And all deep sympathy
Laurels and tears for thee, boy,
     Laurels and tears for thee—
Laurels of light and tears of love forevermore—
    For thee !

VII.

And laurels of light, and tears of truth,
    And the mantle of immortality;
And the flowers of love and immortal youth,
And the tender heart-tokens of all true ruth—
    And the everlasting victory!
  And the breath and bliss of Liberty;
  And the loving kiss of Liberty;
And the welcoming light of heavenly eyes,
  And the over-calm of God's canopy;
And the infinite love-span of the skies
That cover the valleys of Paradise—
  For all of the brave who rest with thee;
  And for one and all who died with thee,
  And now sleep side by side with thee;
And for every one who lives and dies,
  On the solid land or the heaving sea,
    Dear warrior-boy—like thee.

VIII.

    O the victory—the victory
    Belongs to thee!
God ever keeps the brightest crown for such as
  thou—
    He gives it now to thee!
O young and brave, and early and thrice blest—
    Thrice, thrice, thrice blest!
Thy country turns once more to kiss thy youthful
  brow,
  And takes thee—gently—gently to her breast;
And whispers lovingly, "God bless thee—bless thee
  now—
    My darling. thou shalt rest!"

              FORCEYTHE WILLSON.

LITTLE GIFFEN OF TENNESSEE.

Out of the focal and foremost fire,
Out of the hospital walls as dire,
Smitten of grape-shot and gangrene,
(Eighteenth battle, and he sixteen!)
Spectre such as we seldom see,
Little Giffen of Tennessee!

" Take him—and welcome!" the surgeon said;
" Much your doctor can help the dead!"
And so we took him and brought him where
The balm was sweet on the summer air;
And we laid him down on a wholesome bed—
Utter Lazarus, heel to head!

Weary war with the bated breath,
Skeleton boy against skeleton Death.
Months of torture, how many such!
Weary weeks of the stick and crutch!
Still a glint in the steel-blue eye
Spoke of the spirit that would not die,

And didn't! nay, more! in death's despite
The crippled skeleton learned to write!
" Dear mother " at first, of course: and then,
" Dear captain "—inquiring about " the men."
Captain's answer—" Of eighty and five,
Giffen and I are left alive!"

" Johnston's pressed at the front, they say!"
Little Giffen was up and away.
A tear, his first, as he bade good-by,
Dimmed the glint of his steel-blue eye;
" *I'll write, if spared.*" There was news of a
        fight,
But none of Giffen.   He did not write!

I sometimes fancy that were I king
Of the princely knights of the Golden Ring,

With the song of the minstrel in mine ear,
And the tender legend that trembles here,
I'd give the best, on his bended knee,
The whitest soul of my chivalry,
For little Giffen of Tennessee !

FRANCIS O. TICKNOR.

—————

GENERAL ALBERT SIDNEY JOHNSTON.

[*Fell in the Battle of Pittsburgh Landing, Tenn., March* 2,
1862.]

IN thickest fight triumphantly he fell,
  While into victory's arms he led us on ;
A death so glorious our grief should quell :
  We mourn him, yet his battle-crown is won.

No slanderous tongue can vex his spirit now,
  No bitter taunts can stain his blood-bought
    fame ;
Immortal honor rests upon his brow,
  And noble memories cluster round his name.

For hearts shall thrill and eyes grow dim with
    tears,
  To read the story of his touching fate ;
How in his death the gallant soldier wears
  The crown that came for earthly life too late.

Ye people ! guard his memory—sacred keep
  The garlands green above his hero-grave ;
Yet weep, for praise can never wake his sleep,
  To tell him he is shrined among the brave !

MARY JERVEY.

THE CUMBERLAND.

[*The United States war-ship* Cumberland, *commanded by Captain Morris, was sunk, with her crew of a hundred men, by the Confederate ram* Merrimac, *in the famous naval battle at Hampton Roads, Va., March* 9, 1862. *After sinking, the flag at her mainmast still floated above the water.*]

AT anchor in Hampton Roads we lay,
　　On board of the Cumberland, sloop-of-war ;
And at times from the fortress across the bay
　　　　The alarum of drums swept past,
　　　　Or a bugle blast
　　From the camp on the shore.

Then far away to the south uprose
　　A little feather of snow-white smoke,
And we knew that the iron ship of our foes
　　　　Was steadily steering its course
　　　　To try the force
　　Of our ribs of oak.

Down upon us heavily runs,
　　Silent and sullen, the floating fort ;
Then comes a puff of smoke from her guns,
　　　　And leaps the terrible death,
　　　　With fiery breath,
　　From each open port.

We are not idle, but send her straight
　　Defiance back in a full broadside !
As hail rebounds from a roof of slate,
　　　　Rebounds our heavier hail
　　　　From each iron scale
　　Of the monster's hide.

" Strike your flag !" the rebel cries,
　　In his arrogant old plantation strain.
" Never !" our gallant Morris replies ;
　　　　" It is better to sink than to yield !"
　　　　And the whole air pealed
　　With the cheers of our men.

THE MONITOR AND THE MERRIMAC.
(See page 8o.—"Like a kraken, huge and black.")

STONEWALL JACKSON AT BULL RUN.
(See page 89.—"Stonewall Jackson's Way.")

Then, like a kraken huge and black,
　　She crushed our ribs in her iron grasp !
Down went the Cumberland all a-wrack,
　　　　With a sudden shudder of death,
　　　　And the cannon's breath
　　For her dying gasp.

Next morn, as the sun rose over the bay,
　　Still floated our flag at the mainmast head.
Lord, how beautiful was Thy day !
　　　　Every waft of the air
　　　　Was a whisper of prayer,
　　Or a dirge for the dead.

Ho ! brave hearts that went down in the seas !
　　Ye are at peace in the troubled stream ;
Ho ! brave land with hearts like these,
　　　　Thy flag, that is rent in twain,
　　　　Shall be one again,
　　And without a seam !
　　　　　　HENRY WADSWORTH LONGFELLOW.

THE RIVER FIGHT.

[*In April*, 1862, *Admiral Farragut ran his squadron past the Confederate batteries defending the Lower Mississippi, encountering and defeating a fleet of steamers, rams, and fire-rafts.*]

　　　　*　　　*　　　*　　　*　　　*

　　WOULD you hear of the River Fight ?
　　It was two, of a soft spring night—
　　　　God's stars looked down on all,
　　And all was clear and bright
　　But the low fog's chilling breath ;
　　Up the river of Death
　　　　Sailed the Great Admiral.

On our high poop-deck he stood,
   And round him ranged the men
Who have made their birthright good
   Of manhood, once and agen—
Lords of helm and of sail,
Tried in tempest and gale,
   Bronzed in battle and wreck—
Bell and Bailey grandly led
Each his line of the blue and red—
Wainwright stood by our starboard rail,
   Thornton fought the deck.

And I mind me of more than they,
   Of the youthful, steadfast ones,
   That have shown them worthy sons
Of the seamen passed away—
(Tyson conned our helm that day,
   Watson stood by his guns).

What thought our Admiral then,
Looking down on his men ?
   Since the terrible day
     (Day of renown and tears !)
   When at anchor the Essex lay,
   Holding her foes at bay,
When, a boy, by Porter's side he stood
Till deck and plank-sheer were dyed with blood,
    'Tis half a hundred years—
   Half a hundred years, to-day !

Who could fail, with him ?
Who reckon of life or limb ?
   Not a pulse but beat the higher !
There had you seen, by the star-light dim,
Five hundred faces strong and grim—
   The Flag is going under fire !
Right up by the fort, with her helm hard a-port,
   The Hartford is going under fire !

The way to our work was plain :
Caldwell had broken the chain
(Two hulks swung down amain,
　Soon as 'twas sundered)—
Under the night's dark blue,
Steering steady and true,
Ship after ship went through—
Till, as we hove in view,
　Jackson out-thundered.

Back echoed Philip ! Ah, then—
Could you have seen our men,
　How they sprung, in the dim night haze,
To their work of toil and of clamor !
How the loaders, with sponge and rammer,
And their captains, with cord and hammer,
　Kept every muzzle ablaze !
How the guns, as with cheer and shout
Our tackle-men hurled them out,
　Brought up on the water-ways !

First, as we fired at their flash,
　'Twas lightning and black eclipse,
With a bellowing roll and crash ;
But soon, upon either bow,
　What with forts, and fire-rafts, and ships—
(The whole fleet was hard at it now,
All pounding away !) and Porter
Still thundering with shell and mortar—
'Twas the mighty sound and form
Of an equatorial storm !

(Such you see in the far south,
After long heat and drouth,
　As day draws nigh to even—
Arching from north to south,
　Blinding the tropic sun,
　The great black bow comes on—
Till the thunder-veil is riven,
When all is crash and levin,

And the cannonade of heaven
  Rolls down the Amazon !)

But as we worked along higher,
  Just where the river enlarges,
Down came a pyramid of fire—
  It was one of your long coal barges.
  (We had often had the like before)—
'Twas coming down on us to larboard,
  Well in with the eastern shore—
  And our pilot, to let it pass round
  (You may guess we never stopped to sound),
Giving us a rank sheer to starboard,
  Ran the Flag hard and fast aground !

'Twas nigh abreast of the Upper Fort ;
  And straightway a rascal ram
  (She was shaped like the devil's dam)
Puffed away for us, with a snort,
  And shoved it, with spiteful strength,
Right alongside of us, to port—
  It was all of our ship's length,
A huge crackling cradle of the pit !
  Pitch-pine knots to the brim,
  Belching flame red and grim—
What a roar came up from it !

Well, for a little it looked bad—
  But these things are, somehow, shorter
In the acting than the telling—
There was no singing-out nor yelling,
Nor any fussing and fretting,
  No stampede, in short—
But there we were, my lad,
  All a-fire on our port quarter !
Hammocks a-blaze in the netting,
  Flame spouting in at every port—
Our fourth cutter burning at the davit
(No chance to lower away and save it).

In a twinkling, the flames had risen
Halfway to maintop and mizzen,
  Darting up the shrouds like snakes !
  Ah ! how we clanked at the brakes,
  And the deep steam-pumps throbbed under,
  Sending a ceaseless flow !
Our top-men, a dauntless crowd,
Swarmed in rigging and shroud—
  There ('twas a wonder !)
The burning ratlins and strands
They quenched with their bare hard hands—
  But the great guns below
  Never silenced their thunder !

At last, by backing and sounding,
When we were clear of grounding,
  And under headway once more,
The whole rebel fleet came rounding
  The point.   If we had it hot before,
  'Twas now, from shore to shore,
  One long, loud, thundering roar—
Such crashing, splintering, and pounding,
  And smashing as you never heard before !

But that we fought foul wrong to wreck,
  And to save the land we loved so well,
You might have deemed our long gun-deck
  Two hundred feet of hell !

For all above was battle,
Broadside, and blaze, and rattle,
  Smoke and thunder alone—
(But down in the sick-bay,
Where our wounded and dying lay,
  There was scarce a sob or a moan.)
And at last, when the dim day broke,
And the sullen sun awoke,
  Drearily blinking
O'er the haze and the cannon-smoke,

That ever such morning dulls—
There were thirteen traitor hulls
   On fire and sinking !

Now, up the river !—though mad Chalmette
Sputters a vain resistance yet.
Small helm we gave her, our course to steer—
   'Twas nicer work than you well would dream,
With cant and sheer to keep her clear
   Of the burning wrecks that cumbered the stream.

The Louisiana, hurled on high,
Mounts in thunder to meet the sky !
Then down to the depths of the turbid flood
Fifty fathom of rebel mud !
The Mississippi comes floating down,
A mighty bonfire, from off the town—
And along the river, on stocks and ways,
A half-hatched devil's brood is ablaze ;
The great Anglo-Norman is all in flames,
(Hark to the roar of her tumbling frames !)
And the smaller fry that Treason would spawn
Are lighting Algiers like an angry dawn !

From stem to stern, how the pirates burn,
   Fired by the furious hands that built !
So to ashes forever turn
   The suicide wrecks of wrong and guilt !

But as we neared the city,
   By field and vast plantation,
   (Ah, millstone of our nation !)
With wonder and with pity
   What crowds we there espied
Of dark and wistful faces,
Mute in their toiling-places,
   Strangely and sadly eyed—
Haply, 'mid doubt and fear,
Deeming deliverance near—
(One gave the ghost of a cheer !)

And on that dolorous strand,
  To greet the victor-brave
  One flag did welcome wave—
Raised, ah me! by a wretched hand
All outworn on our cruel land—
  The withered hand of a slave!
But all along the levee,
  In a dark and drenching rain
(By this, 'twas pouring heavy),
  Stood a fierce and sullen train—

A strange and a frenzied time!
  There were scowling rage and pain,
    Curses, howls, and hisses,
    Out of hate's black abysses—
Their courage and their crime
  All in vain—all in vain!

For from the hour that the rebel stream,
With the Crescent City lying abeam,
  Shuddered under our keel,
Smit to the heart with self-struck sting,
Slavery died in her scorpion-ring,
  And Murder fell on his steel.

'Tis well to do and dare—
But ever may grateful prayer
Follow, as aye it ought,
When the good fight is fought,
  When the true deed is done;
Aloft in heaven's pure light
(Deep azure crossed on white),
Our fair Church-Pennant waves
O'er a thousand thankful braves,
  Bareheaded in God's bright sun.

Lord of mercy and frown,
Ruling o'er sea and shore,
Send us such scene once more!
  All in Line of Battle

When the black ships bear down
On tyrant fort and town,
   'Mid cannon cloud and rattle—
And the great guns once more
Thunder back the roar
Of the traitor walls ashore,
And the traitor flags come down !

                    HENRY HOWARD BROWNELL.

ASHBY.

[*General Turner Ashby, a noted Confederate cavalry
officer fell in an engagement at Harrisburg, Va., June,
1862.*]

To the brave all homage render ;
   Weep, ye skies of June !
With a radiance pure and tender,
   Shine, O saddened moon !
" *Dead upon the field of glory !*"—
Hero fit for song and story—
   Lies our bold dragoon !

Well they learned, whose hands have slain him,
   Braver, knightlier foe
Never fought 'gainst Moor or Paynim—
   Rode at Templestowe :
With a mien how high and joyous,
'Gainst the hordes that would destroy us
   Went he forth, we know.

Nevermore, alas ! shall sabre
   Gleam around his crest—
Fought his fight, fulfilled his labor,
   Stilled his manly breast—
All unheard sweet nature's cadence,
Trump of fame and voice of maidens ;
   Now he takes his rest.

Earth, that all too soon hath bound him,
  Gently wrap his clay !
Linger lovingly around him,
  Light of dying day !
Softly fall, ye summer showers ;
Birds and bees, among the flowers
  Make the gloom seem gay.

Then, throughout the coming ages,
  When his sword is rust,
And his deeds in classic pages—
  Mindful of her trust—
Shall Virginia, bending lowly,
Still a ceaseless vigil holy
  Keep above his dust !

             JOHN R. THOMPSON.

STONEWALL JACKSON'S WAY.

[These verses, says Mr. William Gilmore Simms, "were found, stained with blood, in the breast of a dead soldier of the old Stonewall Brigade, after one of Jackson's battles in the Shenandoah Valley." Though widely copied and justly admired, their authorship long remained a well-kept secret ; but the compiler of the present volume has been so fortunate as to discover that they were unquestionably written by Dr. J. W. Palmer, of Maryland.]

COME, stack arms, men ! Pile on the rails,
  Stir up the camp-fire bright;
No growling if the canteen fails,
  We'll make a roaring night.
Here Shenandoah brawls along,
There burly Blue Ridge echoes strong,
To swell the Brigade's rousing song
  Of " Stonewall Jackson's way."

We see him now—the queer slouched hat
   Cocked o'er his eye askew;
The shrewd, dry smile; the speech so pat,
   So calm, so blunt, so true.
The "Blue-Light Elder" knows 'em well;
Says he, "That's Banks—he's fond of shell;
Lord save his soul! we'll give him—"; well!
   That's "Stonewall Jackson's way."

Silence! ground arms! kneel all! caps off!
   Old Massa's goin' to pray.
Strangle the fool that dares to scoff!
   Attention! it's his way.
Appealing from his native sod,
In forma pauperis to God:
"Lay bare Thine arm; stretch forth Thy rod!
   Amen!" That's "Stonewall's way."

He's in the saddle now. Fall in!
   Steady! the whole brigade!
Hill's at the ford, cut off; we'll win
   His way out, ball and blade!
What matter if our shoes are worn?
What matter if our feet are torn?
"Quick step! we're with him before morn!"
   That's "Stonewall Jackson's way."

The sun's bright lances rout the mists
   Of morning, and, by George!
Here's Longstreet, struggling in the lists,
   Hemmed in an ugly gorge.
Pope and his Dutchmen, whipped before;
"Bay'nets and grape!" hear Stonewall roar;
"Charge, Stuart! Pay off Ashby's score!"
   In "Stonewall Jackson's way."

Ah! Maiden, wait and watch and yearn
   For news of Stonewall's band!
Ah! Widow, read, with eyes that burn,
   That ring upon thy hand.

Ah! Wife, sew on, pray on, hope on ;
Thy life shall not be all forlorn ;
The foe had better ne'er been born
   That gets in " Stonewall's way."

                 J. W. PALMER.

THE BAREFOOTED BOYS.

I.

BY the sword of St. Michael
   The old dragon through ;
By David his sling
   And the giant he slew ;
Let us write us a rhyme,
   As a record to tell
How the South on a time
   Stormed the ramparts of Hell
      With her barefooted boys !

II.

Had the South in her border
   A hero to spare,
Or a heart at her altar,
   Lo ! its life's blood was there !
And the black battle-grime
   Might never disguise
The smile of the South
   On the lips and the eyes
      Of her barefooted boys !

III.

There's a grandeur in fight,
   And a terror the while,
But none like the light
   Of that terrible smile—

The smile of the South,
When the storm-cloud unrolls
The lightning that loosens
The wrath in the souls
 Of her barefooted boys!

IV.

It withered the foe
Like the red light that runs
Through the dead forest leaves,
And he fled from his guns!
Grew the smile to a laugh,
Rose the laugh to a yell,
As the iron-clad hoofs
Clattered back into Hell
 From our barefooted boys!

ANONYMOUS.

REVEILLE.

[Written by a sergeant in the 140th Regiment of New York Volunteers, who died at Potomac Station, Va., December 28, 1862, aged twenty-five years. An eminent authority says of this poem, that it contains " almost the finest lyric line in the language."]

THE morning is cheery, my boys, arouse!
The dew shines bright on the chestnut boughs,
And the sleepy mist on the river lies,
Though the east is flushing with crimson dyes.
 Awake! awake! awake!
 O'er field and wood and brake,
 With glories newly born,
 Comes on the blushing morn.
 Awake! awake!

You have dreamed of your homes and friends all
 night;
You have basked in your sweethearts' smiles so
 bright;

Come, part with them all for a while again,—
Be lovers in dreams; when awake, be men.
  Turn out! turn out! turn out!
  You have dreamed full long, I know.
  Turn out! turn out! turn out!
  The east is all aglow.
   Turn out! turn out!

From every valley and hill there come
The clamoring voices of fife and drum;
And out in the fresh, cool morning air
The soldiers are swarming everywhere.
  Fall in! fall in! fall in!
  Every man in his place.
  Fall in! fall in! fall in!
  Each with a cheerful face.
   Fall in! fall in!

     MICHAEL O'CONNOR.

SPRING IN WAR-TIME

SPRING, with that nameless pathos in the air
Which dwells with all things fair,
Spring, with her golden suns and silver rain,
Is with us once again.

Out in the lonely woods the jasmine burns
Its fragrant lamps, and turns
Into a royal court with green festoons
The banks of dark lagoons.

In the deep heart of every forest tree
The blood is all aglee,
And there's a look about the leafless bowers
As if they dreamed of flowers.

Yet still on every side appears the hand
Of Winter in the land,

Save where the maple reddens on the lawn,
Flushed by the season's dawn ;

Or where, like those strange semblances we find
That age to childhood bind,
The elm puts on, as if in Nature's scorn,
The brown of Autumn corn.

As yet the turf is dark, although you know
That, not a span below,
A thousand germs are groping through the gloom,
And soon will burst their tomb.

Already, here and there, on frailest stems
Appear some azure gems,
Small as might deck, upon a gala day,
The forehead of a fay.

In gardens you may see, amid the dearth,
The crocus breaking earth ;
And near the snowdrop's tender white and green,
The violet in its screen.

But many gleams and shadows needs must pass
Along the budding grass,
And weeks go by, before the enamored South
Shall kiss the rose's mouth.

Still there's a sense of blossoms yet unborn
In the sweet airs of morn ;
One almost looks to see the very street
Grow purple at his feet.

At times a fragrant breeze comes floating by,
And brings, you know not why,
A feeling as when eager crowds await
Before a palace gate

Some wondrous pageant ; and you scarce would start,
If from a beech's heart
A blue-eyed Dryad, stepping forth, should say—
" Behold me ! I am May !"

Ah, who would couple thoughts of war and crime
With such a blessed time !
Who in the west-wind's aromatic breath
Could hear the call of Death !

Yet not more surely shall the Spring awake
The voice of wood and brake,
Than she shall rouse, for all her tranquil charms
A million men to arms.

There shall be deeper hues upon her plains
Than all her sunlight rains,
And every gladdening influence around
Can summon from the ground.

Oh ! standing on this desecrated mould,
Methinks that I behold,
Lifting her bloody daisies up to God,
Spring, kneeling on the sod,

And calling with the voice of all her rills
Upon the ancient hills
To fall and crush the tyrants and the slaves
Who turn her meads to graves.

Henry Timrod.

SPRING AT THE CAPITAL.

The poplar drops beside the way
Its tasselled plumes of silver gray ;
The chestnut points its great brown buds, impa-
tient for the laggard May.

The honeysuckles lace the wall ;
The hyacinths grow fair and tall ;
And mellow sun and pleasant wind and odorous
bees are over all.

Down-looking in this snow-white bud,
How distant seems the war's red flood!
How far remote the streaming wounds, the sicken-
    ing scent of human blood!

For Nature does not recognize
This strife that rends the earth and skies;
No war-dreams vex the winter sleep of clover-
    heads and daisy-eyes.

She holds her even way the same,
Though navies sink or cities flame;
A snow-drop is a snow-drop still, despite the Na-
    tion's joy or shame.

When blood her grassy altar wets,
She sends the pitying violets
To heal the outrage with their bloom, and cover it
    with soft regrets.

O crocuses with rain-wet eyes,
O tender-lipped anemones,
What do you know of agony, and death, and blood-
    won victories?

No shudder breaks your sunshine trance,
Though near you rolls, with slow advance,
Clouding your shining leaves with dust, the anguish-
    laden ambulance.

Yonder a white encampment hums;
The clash of martial music comes;
And now your startled stems are all a-tremble with
    the jar of drums.

Whether it lessen or increase,
Or whether trumpets shout or cease,
Still deep within your tranquil hearts the happy
    bees are humming "Peace!"

O flowers! the soul that faints or grieves
New comfort from your lips receives;
Sweet confidence and patient faith are hidden in
your healing leaves.

Help us to trust, still on and on,
That this dark night will soon be gone,
And that these battle-stains are but the blood-red
trouble of the dawn—

Dawn of a broader, whiter day
Than ever blessed us with its ray—
A dawn beneath whose purer light all guilt and
wrong shall fade away.

Then shall our nation break its bands,
And, silencing the envious lands,
Stand in the searching light unshamed, with spot-
less robe and clean white hands.

ELIZABETH AKERS ALLEN.

AT PORT ROYAL.

[1862.]

THE tent-lights glimmer on the land,
The ship-lights on the sea;
The night-wind smooths with drifting sand
Our track on lone Tybee.

At last our grating keels outslide,
Our good boats forward swing;
And while we ride the land-locked tide,
Our negroes row and sing.

For dear the bondman holds his gifts
Of music and of song:

The gold that kindly Nature sifts
  Among his sands of wrong;

The power to make his toiling days
  And poor home-comforts please;
The quaint relief of mirth that plays
  With sorrow's minor keys.

Another glow than sunset's fire
  Has filled the West with light,
Where field and garner, barn and byre,
  Are blazing through the night.

The land is wild with fear and hate,
  The rout runs mad and fast;
From hand to hand, from gate to gate,
  The flaming brand is passed.

The lurid glow falls strong across
  Dark faces broad with smiles:
Not theirs the terror, hate, and loss
  That fire yon blazing piles.

With oar-strokes timing to their song,
  They weave in simple lays
The pathos of remembered wrong,
  The hope of better days,—

The triumph-note that Miriam sung,
  The joy of uncaged birds:
Softening with Afric's mellow tongue
  Their broken Saxon words.

SONG OF THE NEGRO BOATMEN.

Oh, praise an' tanks!   De Lord he come
  To set de people free;
An' massa tink it day ob doom,
  An' we ob jubilee.

De Lord dat heap de Red Sea waves
  He jus' as 'trong as den;
He say de word: we las' night slaves;
  To-day, de Lord's freemen.
    De yam will grow, de cotton blow,
      We'll hab de rice an' corn:
    Oh, nebber you fear, if nebber you hear
      De driver blow his horn!

Ole massa on he trabbels gone;
  He leaf de land behind:
De Lord's breff blow him furder on,
  Like corn-shuck in de wind.
We own de hoe, we own de plough,
  We own de hands dat hold;
We sell de pig, we sell de cow,
  But nebber chile be sold.
    De yam will grow, de cotton blow,
      We'll hab de rice an' corn:
    Oh, nebber you fear, if nebber you hear
      De driver blow his horn!

We pray de Lord: he gib us signs
  Dat some day we be free;
De norf-wind tell it to de pines,
  De wild-duck to de sea:
We tink it when de church-bell ring,
  We dream it in de dream;
De rice-bird mean it when he sing,
  De eagle when he scream.
    De yam will grow, de cotton blow,
      We'll hab de rice an' corn:
    Oh, nebber you fear, if nebber you hear
      De driver blow his horn!

We know de promise nebber fail,
  An' nebber lie de word;
So like de 'postles in de jail,
  We waited for de Lord:

An' now he open ebery door,
　An' trow away de key;
He tink we lub him so before,
　We lub him better free.
　　　De yam will grow, de cotton blow,
　　　　He'll gib de rice an' corn :
　　　Oh, nebber you fear, if nebber you hear
　　　De driver blow his horn !

So sing our dusky gondoliers;
　And with a secret pain,
And smiles that seem akin to tears,
　We hear the wild refrain.

We dare not share the negro's trust,
　Nor yet his hope deny;
We only know that God is just,
　And every wrong shall die.

Rude seems the song ; each swarthy face,
　Flame-lighted, ruder still :
We start to think that hapless race
　Must shape our good or ill;

That laws of changeless justice bind
　Oppressor with oppressed ;
And, close as sin and suffering joined,
　We march to Fate abreast.

Sing on, poor hearts ! your chant shall be
　Our sign of blight or bloom,—
The Vala-song of Liberty,
　Or death-rune of our doom !

　　　　　JOHN GREENLEAF WHITTIER.

CAROLINA.

I.

THE despot treads thy sacred sands,
Thy pines give shelter to his bands,
Thy sons stand by with idle hands,
      Carolina!
He breathes at ease thy airs of balm,
He scorns the lances of thy palm;
Oh, who shall break thy craven calm,
      Carolina!
Thy ancient fame is growing dim,
A spot is on thy garment's rim;
Give to the winds thy battle-hymn,
      Carolina!

II.

Call on thy children of the hill,
Wake swamp and river, coast and rill,
Rouse all thy strength and all thy skill,
      Carolina!
Cite wealth and science, trade and art,
Touch with thy fire the cautious mart,
And pour thee through the people's heart,
      Carolina!
Till even the coward spurns his fears,
And all thy fields and fens and meres
Shall bristle like thy palm with spears,
      Carolina!

III.

Hold up the glories of thy dead;
Say how thy elder children bled,
And point to Eutaw's battle-bed,
      Carolina!
Tell how the patriot's soul was tried,
And what his dauntless breast defied;
How Rutledge ruled and Laurens died,
      Carolina!

Cry! till thy summons, heard at last,
Shall fall like Marion's bugle-blast
Re-echoed from the haunted Past,
   Carolina!

IV.

I hear a murmur as of waves
That grope their way through sunless caves,
Like bodies struggling in their graves,
   Carolina!
And now it deepens; slow and grand
It swells, as, rolling to the land
An ocean broke upon thy strand,
   Carolina!
Shout! let it reach the startled Huns,
And roar with all thy festal guns;
It is the answer of thy sons,
   Carolina!

V.

They will not wait to hear the call;
From Sachem's Head to Sumter's wall
Resounds the voice of hut and hall,
   Carolina!
No! thou hast not a stain, they say,
Or none save what the battle-day
Shall wash in seas of blood away,
   Carolina!
Thy skirts indeed the foe may part,
Thy robe be pierced with sword and dart,
They shall not touch thy noble heart,
   Carolina!

VI.

Ere thou shalt own the tyrant's thrall
Ten times ten thousand men must fall;
Thy corpse may hearken to his call,
   Carolina!

When, by thy bier, in mournful throngs
The women chant thy mortal wrongs,
'Twill be their own funereal songs,
   Carolina!
From thy dead breast by ruffians trod
No helpless child shall look to God ;
All shall be safe beneath thy sod,
   Carolina !

VII.

Girt with such wills to do and bear,
Assured in right, and mailed in prayer,
Thou wilt not bow thee to despair,
   Carolina !
Throw thy bold banner to the breeze !
Front with thy ranks the threatening seas
Like thine own proud armorial trees,
   Carolina !
Fling down thy gauntlet to the Huns,
And roar the challenge from thy guns ;
Then leave the future to thy sons,
   Carolina !

      HENRY TIMROD.

VOYAGE OF THE GOOD SHIP UNION.

[1862.]

'TIS midnight : through my troubled dream
 Loud wails the tempest's cry ;
Before the gale, with tattered sail,
 A ship goes plunging by.
What name ? Where bound ?—The rocks around
 Repeat the loud halloo.
—The good ship Union, southward bound :
 God help her and her crew !

And is the old flag flying still
   That o'er your fathers flew,
With bands of white and rosy light,
   And field of starry blue?
—Ay! look aloft! its folds full oft
   Have braved the roaring blast,
And still shall fly when from the sky
   This black typhoon has past!

Speak, pilot of the storm-tost bark!
   May I thy peril share?
 O landsmen, these are fearful seas
   The brave alone may dare!
 -Nay, ruler of the rebel deep,
   What matters wind or wave?
The rocks that wreck your reeling deck
   Will leave me nought to save!

O landsman, art thou false or true?
   What sign hast thou to show?
   The crimson stains from loyal veins
   That hold my heart-blood's flow!
   Enough! what more shall honor claim?
   I know the sacred sign;
Above thy head our flag shall spread,
   Our ocean path be thine!

The bark sails on : the Pilgrim's Cape
   Lies low along her lee,
Whose headland crooks its anchor-flukes
   To lock the shore and sea.
No treason here! it cost too dear
   To win this barren realm!
And true and free the hands must be
   That hold the whaler's helm!

Still on! Manhattan's narrowing bay
   No Rebel cruiser scars;
Her waters feel no pirate's keel
   That flaunts the fallen stars!

.-But watch the light on yonder height,—
   Ay, pilot, have a care !
Some lingering cloud in mist may shroud
   The Capes of Delaware !

Say, pilot, what this fort may be
   Whose sentinels look down
From moated walls that show the sea
   Their deep embrasures' frown ?
The Rebel host claims all the coast,
   But these are friends, we know,
Whose footprints spoil the " sacred soil,"
   And this is ?——Fort Monroe !

The breakers roar,—how bears the shore ?
   —The traitorous wreckers' hands
Have quenched the blaze that poured its rays
   Along the Hatteras sands.
   Ha ! say not so !   I see its glow !
   Again the shoals display
The beacon light that shines by night,
   The Union Stars by day !

The good ship flies to milder skies,
   The wave more gently flows ;
The softening breeze wafts o'er the seas
   The breath of Beaufort's rose.
What fold is this the sweet winds kiss,
   Fair-striped and many-starred,
Whose shadow palls these orphaned walls,
   The twins of Beauregard ?

What ! heard you not Port Royal's doom ?
   How the black war-ships came
And turned the Beaufort roses' bloom
   To redder wreaths of flame ?
How from Rebellion's broken reed
   We saw his emblem fall,
As soon his cursèd poison-weed
   Shall drop from Sumter's wall ?

On ! on ! Pulaski's iron hail
  Falls harmless on Tybee !
The good ship feels the freshening gale,—
  She strikes the open sea ;
She rounds the point, she threads the keys
  That guard the Land of Flowers,
And rides at last where firm and fast
  Her own Gibraltar towers !

The good ship Union's voyage is o'er,
  At anchor safe she swings,
And loud and clear with cheer on cheer
  Her joyous welcome rings :
Hurrah ! Hurrah ! it shakes the wave,
  It thunders on the shore,—
One flag, one land, one heart, one hand,
  One Nation, evermore !

OLIVER WENDELL HOLMES.

THE VIRGINIANS OF THE VALLEY.

THE knightliest of the knightly race,
  Who, since the days of old,
Have kept the lamp of chivalry
  Alight in hearts of gold ;
The kindliest of the kindly band,
  Who, rarely hunting ease,
Yet rode with Spotswood round the land,
  And Raleigh round the seas ;

Who climbed the blue Virginian hills,
  Against embattled foes,
And planted there in valleys fair
  The lily and the rose ;
Whose fragrance lives in many lands,
  Whose beauty stars the earth,

And lights the hearts of many homes
   In loveliness and worth.

We thought they slept—the sons who kept
   The names of noble sires,
And slumbered while the darkness crept
   Around the vigil fires.
But still the Golden Horseshoe knights
   Their old dominion keep,
Whose foes have found enchanted ground,
   But not a knight asleep.
                 FRANCIS O. TICKNOR.

KEARNEY AT SEVEN PINES.

[*May* 31, 1862.]

So that soldierly legend is still on its journey—
   That story of Kearney who knew not to yield!
'Twas the day when with Jameson, fierce Berry, and
      Birney,
   Against twenty thousand he rallied the field.
Where the red volleys poured, where the clamor rose
      highest,
   Where the dead lay in clumps through the dwarf
      oak and pine,
Where the aim from the thicket was surest and
      nighest,—
   No charge like Phil Kearney's along the whole line.

When the battle went ill, and the bravest were
      solemn,
   Near the dark Seven Pines, where we still held
      our ground,
He rode down the length of the withering column,
   And his heart at our war-cry leapt up with a bound.

He snuffed, like his charger, the wind of the pow-
    der,—
His sword waved us on, and we answered the sign ;
Loud our cheer as we rushed, but his laugh rang the
    louder :
"There's the devil's own fun, boys, along the
    whole line !"

How he strode his brown steed ! How we saw his
    blade brighten
In the one hand still left—and the reins in his
    teeth !
He laughed like a boy when the holidays heighten,
    But a soldier's glance shot from his visor beneath.
Up came the reserves to the mellay infernal,
    Asking where to go in—through the clearing or
    pine ?
"O, anywhere ! Forward ! 'Tis all the same, Colonel :
    You'll find lovely fighting along the whole line !"

O, evil the black shroud of night at Chantilly,[1]
    That hid him from sight of his brave men and
    tried !
Foul, foul sped the bullet that clipped the white lily,
    The flower of our knighthood, the whole army's
    pride !
Yet we dream that he still—in that shadowy region
    Where the dead form their ranks at the wan
    drummer's sign—
Rides on, as of old, down the length of his legion,
    And the word still is *Forward!* along the whole
    line.

                        EDMUND CLARENCE STEDMAN.

[1] General Philip Kearney lost his life at the battle of Chantilly,
Va., Sept. 1, 1862, by becoming separated from his men and riding
by mistake into the Confederate line. It was growing dark and
raining heavily, when Kearney, coming suddenly upon some skir-
mishers, asked what troops they were ; but perceiving they were
Confederates, he wheeled his horse and dashed away. Half-a-
dozen shots rang out, and he fell dead.

DIRGE FOR A SOLDIER.

[In Memory of General Philip Kearney.]

CLOSE his eyes, his work is done !
　What to him is friend or foeman,
Rise of moon, or set of sun,
　Hand of man, or kiss of woman ?
　　　Lay him low, lay him low,
　　　In the clover or the snow !
　　　What cares he ? he cannot know :
　　　　Lay him low !

As man may, he fought his fight,
　Proved his truth by his endeavor ;
Let him sleep in solemn night,
　Sleep forever and forever.
　　　Lay him low, lay him low,
　　　In the clover or the snow !
　　　What cares he ? he cannot know :
　　　　Lay him low !

Fold him in his country's stars,
　Roll the drum and fire the volley !
What to him are all our wars,
　What but death bemocking folly ?
　　　Lay him low, lay him low,
　　　In the clover or the snow !
　　　What cares he ? he cannot know :
　　　　Lay him low !

Leave him to God's watching eye,
　Trust him to the hand that made him.
Mortal love weeps idly by :
　God alone has power to aid him.
　　　Lay him low, lay him low,
　　　In the clover or the snow !
　　　What cares he ? he cannot know :
　　　　Lay him low !

　　　　　　　　GEORGE H. BOKER.

MALVERN HILL.

[*July* 1, 1862.]

WAS there ever message sweeter
    Than that one from Malvern Hill,
From a grim old fellow—you remember?
    Dying in the dark at Malvern Hill.
With his rough face turned a little,
    On a heap of scarlet sand,
They found him, just within the thicket,
    With a picture in his hand,—

With a stained and crumpled picture
    Of a woman's aged face;
Yet there seemed to leap a wild entreaty,
    Young and living—tender—from the face
When they flashed the lantern on it,
    Gilding all the purple shade,
And stooped to raise him softly,—
    "That's my mother, sir," he said.

" Tell her "—but he wandered, slipping
    Into tangled words and cries—
Something about Mac and Hooker,
    Something dropping through the cries
About the kitten by the fire,
    And mother's cranberry-pies, and there
The words fell, and an utter
    Silence brooded in the air.

Just as he was drifting from them,
    Out into the dark, alone,
(Poor old mother, waiting for your message,
    Waiting with the kitten, all alone!)
Through the hush his voice broke: " Tell her—
    Thank you, Doctor—when you can,
Tell her that I kissed her picture,
    And wished I'd been a better man,"

Ah, I wonder if the red feet
Of departed battle-hours
May not leave for us their searching
Message from those distant hours.
Sisters, daughters, mothers, think you,
Would your heroes, now or then,
Dying, kiss your pictured faces,
Wishing they'd been better men ?

ELIZABETH STUART PHELPS.

THREE HUNDRED THOUSAND MORE.

[In answer to President Lincoln's call, issued July 2, 1862, for 300,000 additional men, to serve three years.]

WE are coming, Father Abraham, three hundred
thousand more,
From Mississippi's winding stream and from New
England's shore ;
We leave our ploughs and workshops, our wives
and children dear,
With hearts too full for utterance, with but a silent
tear ;
We dare not look behind us, but steadfastly before :
We are coming, Father Abraham, three hundred
thousand more !

If you look across the hill-tops that meet the
northern sky,
Long moving lines of rising dust your vision may
descry ;
And now the wind, an instant, tears the cloudy
veil aside,
And floats aloft our spangled flag in glory and in
pride,
And bayonets in the sunlight gleam, and bands
brave music pour :
We are coming, Father Abraham, three hundred
thousand more !

If you look all up our valleys where the growing
  harvests shine,
You may see our sturdy farmer boys fast form-
  ing into line;
And children from their mother's knees are pull-
  ing at the weeds,
And learning how to reap and sow against their
  country's needs;
And a farewell group stands weeping at every cot-
  tage door:
We are coming, Father Abraham, three hundred
  thousand more!

You have called us, and we're coming, by Rich-
  mond's bloody tide
To lay us down, for Freedom's sake, our brothers'
  bones beside,
Or from foul treason's savage grasp to wrench the
  murderous blade,
And in the face of foreign foes its fragments to
  parade.
Six hundred thousand loyal men and true have
  gone before:
We are coming, Father Abraham, three hundred
  thousand more!

ANONYMOUS.

OUR PRIVILEGE.

[*Owing to the remoteness of California from the scenes
of the war, and the difficulty of transporting troops, that
State sent but eleven regiments to the field; although it is
probable that many Californians joined organizations from
other States and Territories, or enlisted in the regular
army.*]

NOT ours, where battle-smoke upcurls,
  And battle-dews lie wet,
To meet the charge that treason hurls
  By sword and bayonet;

Not ours to guide the fatal scythe
  The fleshless Reaper wields ;
The harvest-moon looks calmly down
  Upon our peaceful fields.

The long grass dimples on the hill,
  The pines sing by the sea,
And Plenty, from her golden horn,
  Is pouring far and free.

O brothers by the farther sea !
  Think still our faith is warm ;
The same bright flag above us waves
  That swathed our baby form.

The same red blood that dyes your fields
  Here throbs in patriot pride ;
The blood that flowed where Lander fell,
  And Baker's crimson tide.

And thus apart our hearts keep time
  With every pulse ye feel ;
And Mercy's ringing gold shall chime
  With Valor's clashing steel.

BRET HARTE.

THE VOLUNTEER.

" AT dawn," he said, " I bid them all farewell,
  To go where bugles call and rifles gleam."
And with the restless thought, asleep he fell
    And glided into dream.

A great hot plain from sea to mountain spread—
  Through it a level river slowly drawn ;
He moved with a vast crowd, and at its head
    Streamed banners like the dawn.

There came a blinding flash, a deafening roar—
    And dissonant cries of triumph and dismay ;
Blood trickled down the river's reedy shore,
    And with the dead he lay.

The morn broke in upon his solemn dreams,
    And still, with steady pulse and deepening eye,
" Where bugles call," he said, " and rifles gleam,
    I follow, though I die ! "

Wise youth ! By few is glory's wreath attained ;
    But death, or late or soon, awaiteth all.
To fight in Freedom's cause is something gained—
    And nothing lost, to fall.

                    ELBRIDGE JEFFERSON CUTLER.

THE BURIAL OF LATANÉ.

[*Captain Latané, of Stuart's Confederate Cavalry, fell,
at the head of his squadron, in the Pamunkey expedition,
in Virginia, in 1862. A private letter, written at the time,
thus describes his burial : "A few ladies, a fair-haired
little girl with her apron filled with white flowers, and
a few faithful slaves, stood reverently near while a pious
Virginia matron read the solemn and beautiful burial
service for the dead."*]

THE combat raged not long, but ours the day ;
    And, through the hosts that compassed us around,
Our little band rode proudly on its way,
        Leaving one gallant comrade, glory-crowned,
            Unburied on the field he died to gain—
            Single of all his men, amid the hostile slain.

One moment on the battle's edge he stood—
    Hope's halo, like a helmet, round his hair ;
The next beheld him, dabbled in his blood,
        Prostrate in death—and yet, in death how fair !

Even thus he passed through the red gates of
strife,
From earthly crowns and palms, to an immor-
tal life.

A brother bore his body from the field,
And gave it unto strangers' hands, that closed
The calm blue eyes, on earth forever sealed,
And tenderly the slender limbs composed :
Strangers, yet sisters, who, with Mary's love,
Sat by the open tomb, and, weeping, looked
above.

A little child strewed roses on his bier—
Pale roses, not more stainless than his soul,
Nor yet more fragrant than his life sincere,
That blossomed with good actions — brief, but
whole :
The aged matron and the faithful slave
Approached, with reverent feet, the hero's
lowly grave.

No man of God might say the burial rite
Above the " rebel "—thus declared the foe
That blanched before him in the deadly fight ;
But woman's voice, with accents soft and low,
Trembling with pity—touched with pathos—
read
Over his hallowed dust the ritual for the dead.

" '*Tis sown in weakness, it is raised in power !*"
Softly the promise floated on the air,
While the low breathings of the sunset hour
Came back responsive to the mourner's prayer.
Gently they laid him underneath the sod,
And left him with his fame, his country, and
his God !

Let us not weep for him, whose deeds endure !
So young, so brave, so beautiful ! He died

As he had wished to die; the past is sure;
 Whatever yet of sorrow may betide
  Those who still linger by the stormy shore,
  Change cannot harm him now, nor fortune
   touch him more.
       JOHN R. THOMPSON.

KILLED AT THE FORD.

HE is dead, the beautiful youth,
The heart of honor, the tongue of truth—
He, the life and light of us all,
Whose voice was blithe as a bugle-call,
Whom all eyes followed with one consent,
The cheer of whose laugh and whose pleasant word
Hushed all murmurs of discontent.

Only last night, as we rode along
Down the dark of the mountain gap,
To visit the picket-guard at the ford,
Little dreaming of any mishap,
He was humming the words of some old song:
" Two red roses he had on his cap,
And another he bore at the point of his sword."

Sudden and swift, a whistling ball
Came out of a wood, and the voice was still;
Something I heard in the darkness fall,
And for a moment my blood grew chill;
I spake in a whisper, as he who speaks
In a room where some one is lying dead;
But he made no answer to what I said.

We lifted him up on his saddle again,
And through the mire and the mist and the rain
Carried him back to the silent camp,
And laid him as if asleep on his bed;
And I saw by the light of the surgeon's lamp

Two white roses upon his cheeks,
And one, just over his heart, blood-**red.**

And I saw in a vision how far and fleet
That fatal bullet went speeding forth,
Till it reached a town in the distant **North,**
Till it reached a house in a sunny street,
Till it reached a heart that ceased to beat,
Without a murmur, without a cry ;
And a bell was tolled in that far-off town
For one who had passed from cross to crown ;
And the neighbors wondered that she should **die.**

HENRY WADSWORTH LONGFELLOW.

THE CAPTAIN'S WIFE.

WE gathered roses, Blanche and I, for little Madge
    one morning ;
    " Like every soldier's wife," said Blanche," I dread
    a soldier's fate."
Her voice a little trembled then, as under some
    forewarning. . . .
    A soldier galloped up the lane, and halted at the
    gate.

" Which house is Malcolm Blake's ?" he cried ; " a
    letter for his sister !"
    And when I thanked him, Blanche inquired, " But
    none for me, his wife ?"
The soldier played with Madge's curls, and, stoop-
    ing over, kissed her :
    " Your father was my captain, child !—I loved
    him as my life !"

Then suddenly he galloped off and left the rest un-
    spoken.
    I burst the seal, and Blanche exclaimed, " What
    makes you tremble so ?"

What answer did I dare to speak? How ought
     the news be broken?
  I could not shield her from the stroke, yet tried
     to ease the blow.

" A battle in the swamps," I said ; " our men were
     brave, but lost it."
  And, pausing there—" The note," I said, " is not
     in Malcolm's hand."
And first a flush flamed through her face, and then
     a shadow crossed it.
  " Read quick, dear May!—read all, I pray—and
     let me understand !"

I did not read it as it stood—but tempered so the
     phrases
  As not at first to hint the worst—held back the
     fatal word,
And half retold his gallant charge, his shout, his
     comrades' praises—
  Till like a statue carved in stone, she neither
     spoke nor stirred !

Oh, never yet a woman's heart was frozen so com-
     pletely !
  So unbaptized with helping tears !—so passion-
     less and dumb !
Spellbound she stood, and motionless—till little
     Madge spoke sweetly :
  " Dear mother, is the battle done? and will my
     father come ?"

I laid my finger on her lips, and set the child to
     playing.
  Poor Blanche ! the winter in her cheek was
     snowy like her name !
What could she do but kneel and pray—and lin-
     ger at her praying ? . . . .
  O Christ ! when other heroes die, moan other
     wives the same ?

Must other women's hearts yet break, to keep the
    Cause from failing ?
  God pity our brave lovers, then, who face the
    battle's blaze !
And pity wives in widowhood !—But is it unavail-
    ing ?
  O Lord ! give Freedom first, then Peace !—and
    unto Thee be praise !

THEODORE TILTON.

"OUR LEFT."

[*Manassas, August* 30, 1862.]

FROM dawn to dark they stood
  That long midsummer day,
    While fierce and fast
    The battle blast
  Swept rank on rank away.

From dawn to dark they fought,
  With legions torn and cleft;
    And still the wide
    Black battle tide
  Poured deadlier on " Our Left."

They closed each ghastly gap;
  They dressed each shattered rank;
    They knew—how well—
    That freedom fell
  With that exhausted flank.

" Oh, for a thousand men
  Like these that melt away !"
    And down they came,
    With steel and flame,
  Four thousand to the fray !

Right through the blackest cloud
　　Their lightning path they cleft ;
　　　And triumph came
　　　With deathless fame
　　To our unconquered " Left."

Ye of your sons secure,
　　Ye of your dead bereft—
　　　Honor the brave
　　　Who died to save
　　Your all upon " Our Left."

FRANCIS O. TICKNOR.

WANTED —— A MAN.

[This poem so impressed President Lincoln, that he read it to his Cabinet at the crisis referred to, in 1862, when the great want of the North was a fit leader for its armies.]

BACK from the trebly crimsoned field
　　Terrible words are thunder-tost ;
Full of the wrath that will not yield,
　　Full of revenge for battles lost !
　　Hark to their echo, as it crost
The Capital, making faces wan ;
　　" End this murderous holocaust ;
Abraham Lincoln, give us a MAN !

" Give us a man of God's own mould,
　　Born to marshal his fellow-men ;
One whose fame is not bought and sold
　　At the stroke of a politician's pen ;
　　Give us the man of thousands ten,
Fit to do as well as to plan ;
　　Give us a rallying-cry, and then,
Abraham Lincoln, give us a MAN !

" No leader to shirk the boasting foe,
    And to march and countermarch our brave,
Till they fall like ghosts in the marshes low,
    And swamp-grass covers each nameless grave;
    Nor another, whose fatal banners wave
Aye in Disaster's shameful van;
    Nor another, to bluster, and lie, and rave,—
Abraham Lincoln, give us a MAN !

" Hearts are mourning in the North,
    While the sister rivers seek the main,
Red with our life-blood flowing forth—
    Who shall gather it up again ?
    Though we march to the battle-plain
Firmly as when the strife began,
    Shall all our offering be in vain ?—
Abraham Lincoln, give us a MAN !

" Is there never one in all the land,
    One on whose might the Cause may lean ?
Are all the common ones so grand,
    And all the titled ones so mean ?
    What if your failure may have been
In trying to make good bread from bran,
    From worthless metal a weapon keen ?—
Abraham Lincoln, find us a MAN !

" O, we will follow him to the death,
    Where the foeman's fiercest columns are !
O, we will use our latest breath,
    Cheering for every sacred star !
    His to marshal us high and far;
Ours to battle, as patriots can
    When a Hero leads the Holy War !—
Abraham Lincoln, give us a MAN !"

                    EDMUND CLARENCE STEDMAN.

BEYOND THE POTOMAC.

[Lee's first invasion of Maryland, September, 1862.]

THEY slept on the fields which their valor had won,
But arose with the first early blush of the sun,
For they knew that a great deed remained to be done,
     When they passed o'er the river.

They rose with the sun, and caught life from his
    light—
Those giants of courage, those Anaks in fight—
And they laughed out aloud in the joy of their might,
     Marching swift for the river.

On! on! like the rushing of storms thro' the hills—
On! on! with a tramp that is firm as their wills—
And the one heart of thousands grows buoyant,
    and thrills,
     At the thought of the river!

Oh, the sheen of their swords! the fierce gleam of
    their eyes!
It seemed as on earth a new sunlight would rise,
And king-like flash up to the sun in the skies,
     O'er the path to the river.

But their banners, shot-scarred, and all darkened
    with gore,
On a strong wind of morning streamed wildly be-
    fore,
Like the wings of death-angels swept fast to the
    shore,
     The green shore of the river!

As they march from the hillside, the hamlet, the
    stream,
Gaunt throngs whom the foeman had manacled.
    teem,
Like men just aroused from some terrible dream
     To pass over the river.

They behold the broad banners, blood-darkened,
    yet fair,
And a moment dissolves the last spell of despair,
While a peal as of victory swells on the air,
        Rolling out to the river.

And that cry, with a thousand strange echoings
    spread,
Till the ashes of heroes seemed stirred in their bed,
And the deep voice of passion surged up from the
    dead—
        Aye! press on to the river!

On! on! like the rushing of storms through the
    hills,
On! on! with a tramp that is firm as their wills,
And the one heart of thousands grows buoyant,
    and thrills,
        As they pause by the river.

Then the wan face of Maryland, haggard and worn,
At that sight lost the touch of its aspect forlorn,
And she turned on the foeman full statured in
    scorn,
        Pointing stern to the river.

And Potomac flowed calm, scarcely heaving her
    breast,
With her low-lying billows all bright in the west,
For a charm as from God lulled the waters to rest
        Of the fair rolling river.

Passed! passed! the glad thousands march safe
    through the tide.
(Hark, despot! and hear the dread knell of your
    pride,
Ringing weird-like and wild, pealing up from the side
        Of the calm flowing river!)

'Neath a blow swift and mighty the tyrant may fall,
Vain ! vain ! to his God swells a desolate call,
For his grave has been hóllowed, and woven his pall,
    Since they passed o'er the river !
                    PAUL HAMILTON HAYNE.

BARBARA FRIETCHIE.

[*The incidents which gave rise to this poem are said to
have occurred during Stonewall Jackson's march through
Frederick City, Maryland, just before the battle of South
Mountain, in September,* 1862. *Some of the facts narrated
having been called in question, Mr. Whittier has furnished
the editor of this volume (November* 15, 1885) *with the fol-
lowing particulars:* " *Of the substantial truth of the
heroism of Barbara Frietchie I can have no doubt. Mrs.
E. D. N. Southworth, the novelist, of Washington, sent me
a slip from a newspaper, stating the circumstance as it is
given in the poem, and assured me of its substantial cor-
rectness. Dorothea L. Dix, the philanthropic worker in
the Union hospitals, confirmed it. From half a dozen
other sources I had the account, and all agree in the main
facts. Barbara Frietchie was the boldest and most out-
spoken Unionist in Frederick, and manifested it to the
Rebel army in an unmistakable manner.*"]

UP from the meadows rich with corn,
Clear in the cool September morn,

The clustered spires of Frederick stand
Green-walled by the hills of Maryland.

Round about them orchards sweep,
Apple and peach tree fruited deep,

Fair as a garden of the Lord
To the eyes of the famished rebel horde,

On that pleasant morn of the early fall
When Lee marched over the mountain wall—

BARBARA FRIETCHIE.

(See page 123. "Shook it forth with a royal will.")

Over the mountains, winding down,
Horse and foot into Frederick town.

Forty flags with their silver stars,
Forty flags with their crimson bars,

Flapped in the morning wind : the sun
Of noon looked down, and saw not one.

Up rose old Barbara Frietchie then,
Bowed with her fourscore years and ten ;

Bravest of all in Frederick town,
She took up the flag the men hauled down ;

In her attic window the staff she set,
To show that one heart was loyal yet.

Up the street came the rebel tread,
Stonewall Jackson riding ahead.

Under his slouched hat left and right
He glanced : the old flag met his sight.

" Halt !"—the dust-brown ranks stood fast ;
" Fire !"—out blazed the rifle-blast.

It shivered the window, pane and sash ;
It rent the banner with seam and gash.

Quick, as it fell, from the broken staff
Dame Barbara snatched the silken scarf ;

She leaned far out on the window-sill,
And shook it forth with a royal will.

" Shoot, if you must, this old gray head,
But spare your country's flag," she said.

A shade of sadness, a blush of shame,
Over the face of the leader came ;

The nobler nature within him stirred
To life at that woman's deed and word :

" Who touches a hair of yon gray head
Dies like a dog !   March on !" he said.

All day long through Frederick street
Sounded the tread of marching feet ;

All day long that free flag tost
Over the heads of the rebel host.

Ever its torn folds rose and fell
On the loyal winds that loved it well ;

And through the hill-gaps sunset light
Shone over it with a warm good-night.

Barbara Frietchie's work is o'er,
And the Rebel rides on his raids no more.

Honor to her ! and let a tear
Fall, for her sake, on Stonewall's bier.

Over Barbara Frietchie's grave,
Flag of Freedom and Union, wave !

Peace and order and beauty draw
Round thy symbol of light and law ;

And ever the stars above look down
On thy stars below in Frederick town !

JOHN GREENLEAF WHITTIER.

THE HEART OF THE WAR.

PEACE in the clover-scented air,
    And stars within the dome ;
And underneath, in dim repose,
    A plain New England home.
Within, a murmur of low tones
    And sighs from hearts oppressed,
Merging in prayer at last, that brings
    The balm of silent rest.

"I've closed a hard day's work, Marty,
    The evening chores are done ;
And you are weary with the house,
    And with the little one.
But he is sleeping sweetly now,
    With all our pretty brood ;
So come and sit upon my knee,
    And it will do me good.

"Oh, Marty ! I must tell you all
    The trouble in my heart,
And you must do the most you can
    To take and bear your part.
You've seen the shadow on my face,
    You've felt it day and night ;
For it has fill'd our little home,
    And banished all its light.

"I did not mean it should be so,
    And yet I might have known
That hearts that live as close as ours
    Can never keep their own.
But we are fallen on evil times,
    And, do whate'er I may,
My heart grows sad about the war,
    And sadder every day.

"I think about it when I work,
    And when I try to rest,
And never more than when your head
    Is pillowed on my breast ;
For then I see the camp-fires blaze,
    And sleeping men around,
Who turn their faces toward their homes,
    And dream upon the ground.

"I think about the dear, brave boys,
    My mates in other years,
Who pine for home and those they love,
    Till I am choked with tears.

With shouts and cheers they marched away
    On glory's shining track ;
But, ah ! how long, how long they stay,—
    How few of them come back !

"One sleeps beside the Tennessee,
    And one beside the James,
And one fought on a gallant ship
    And perished in its flames.
And some, struck down by fell disease,
    Are breathing out their life ;
And others, maimed by cruel wounds,
    Have left the deadly strife.

"Ah, Marty ! Marty ! only think
    Of all the boys have done
And suffered in this weary war,—
    Brave heroes, every one !
Oh, often, often, in the night,
    I hear their voices call :
*'Come on and help us ! Is it right
    That we should bear it all ?'*

"And when I kneel and try to pray,
    My thoughts are never free,
But cling to those who toil and fight
    And die for you and me.
And when I pray for victory,
    It seems almost a sin
To fold my hands and ask for what
    I will not help to win.

"Oh, do not cling to me and cry,
    For it will break my heart ;
I'm sure you'd rather have me die
    Than not to bear my part.
You think that some should stay at home
    To care for those away ;
But still I'm helpless to decide
    If I should go or stay.

" For, Marty, all the soldiers love,
  And all are loved again ;
And I am loved, and love, perhaps,
  No more than other men.
I cannot tell—I do not know—
  Which way my duty lies,
Or where the Lord would have me build
  My fire of sacrifice.

" I feel—I know—I am not mean ;
  And though I seem to boast,
I'm sure that I would give my life
  To those who need it most.
Perhaps the Spirit will reveal
  That which is fair and right ;
So, Marty, let us humbly kneel
  And pray to Heaven for light." . . .

Peace in the clover-scented air,
  And stars within the dome ;
And, underneath, in dim repose,
  A plain New England home.
Within, a widow in her weeds
  From whom all joy is flown,
Who kneels among her sleeping babes,
  And weeps and prays alone !

JOSIAH GILBERT HOLLAND.

CLARIBEL'S PRAYER.

THE day, with cold gray feet, clung shivering to
    the hills,
  While o'er the valley still night's rain-fringed cur-
    tains fell ;
But waking Blue-eyes smiled : " 'Tis ever as God
    wills ;
  He knoweth best, and be it rain or shine, 'tis well ;
Praise God !" cried always little Claribel.

Then sunk she on her knees ; with eager, lifted
    hands
  Her rosy lips made haste some dear request to
    tell :
" O Father, smile, and save this fairest of all lands,
  And make her free, whatever hearts rebel ;
  Amen ! Praise God !" cried little Claribel.

" And, Father," still arose another pleading prayer,
  " O save my brother, in the rain of shot and shell !
Let not the death-bolt, with its horrid streaming
    hair,
  Dash light from those sweet eyes I love so well ;
  Amen ! Praise God !" wept little Claribel.

" But, Father, grant that when the glorious fight is
    done,
  And up the crimson sky the shouts of freemen
    swell,
Grant that there be no nobler victor 'neath the sun
  Than he whose golden hair I love so well ;
  Amen ! Praise God !" cried little Claribel.

When the gray and dreary day shook hands with
    grayer night,
  The heavy air was filled with clangor of a bell ;
" Oh, shout !" the Herald cried, his worn eyes
    brimmed with light ;
  " 'Tis victory ! Oh, what glorious news to tell !"
  " Praise God ! He heard my prayer," cried Clar-
    ibel.

" But pray you, soldier, was my brother in the fight
  And in the fiery rain ? Oh, fought he brave and
    well ?"
" Dear child," the Herald said, " there was no
    braver sight
  Than his young form, so grand 'mid shot and
    shell ;"
  " Praise God !" cried trembling little Claribel.

"And rides he now with victor's plume of red,
  While trumpets' golden throats his coming steps
      foretell?"
The Herald dropped a tear. "Dear child," he
    softly said,
  "Thy brother evermore with conquerors shall
      dwell."
  "Praise God! He heard my prayer," cried Clar-
      ibel.

"With victors, wearing crowns and bearing palms,"
    he said,
And snow of sudden fear upon the rose lips fell;
"Oh, sweetest Herald, say my brother lives!" she
    plead;
  "Dear child, he walks with angels, who in
      strength excel;
  Praise God, who gave this glory, Claribel."

The cold gray day died sobbing on the weary hills,
  While bitter mourning on the night winds rose
      and fell.
"O child," the Herald wept, "'tis as the dear Lord
    wills;
  He knoweth best, and be it life or death, 'tis well."
  "Amen! Praise God!" sobbed little Claribel.

M. L. PARMELEE.

"PICCIOLA."

IT was a sergeant old and gray,
  Well singed and bronzed from siege and pillage,
Went tramping in an army's wake,
  Along the turnpike of the village.

For days and nights the winding host
  Had through the little place been marching,
And ever loud the rustics cheered,
  Till every throat was hoarse and parching.

The squire and farmer, maid and dame,
   All took the sight's electric stirring,
And hats were waved, and staves were sung,
   And 'kerchiefs white were countless whirling

They only saw a gallant show
   Of heroes stalwart under banners,
And in the fierce heroic glow
   'Twas theirs to yield but wild hosannahs.

The sergeant heard the shrill hurrahs,
   Where he behind in step was keeping ;
But glancing down beside the road
   He saw a little maid sit weeping.

" And how is this ?" he gruffly said,
   A moment pausing to regard her ;
" Why weepest thou, my little chit ?"
   And then she only cried the harder.

" And how is this, my little chit ?"
   The sturdy trooper straight repeated—
" When all the village cheers us on,
   That you, in tears, apart are seated ?

" We march two hundred thousand strong !
   And that's a sight, my baby beauty,
To quicken silence into song,
   And glorify the soldier's duty."

" It's very, very grand, I know,"
   The little maid gave soft replying ;
" And father, mother, brother, too,
   All say ' hurrah ' while I am crying.

" But think—O Mr. Soldier, think
   How many little sisters' brothers
Are going all away to fight,
   Who may be killed, as well as others !"

"Why, bless thee, child," the sergeant said,
   His brawny hand her curls caressing,
" 'Tis left for little ones like you
   To find that war's not all a blessing."

And "bless thee !" once again he cried ;
   Then cleared his throat and looked indignant,
And marched away with wrinkled brow
   To stop the straggling tear benignant.

And still the ringing shouts went up
   From doorway, thatch, and fields of tillage ;
The pall behind the standard seen
   By one alone, of all the village.

The oak and cedar bend and writhe
   When roars the wind through gap and braken ;
But 'tis the tenderest reed of all
   That trembles first when earth is shaken.

ANONYMOUS.

COME UP FROM THE FIELDS, FATHER.

COME up from the fields, father, here's a letter from
      our Pete ;
And come to the front door, mother, here's a letter
      from thy dear son.

Lo, 'tis autumn.
Lo, where the trees, deeper green, yellower and
      redder,
Cool and sweeten Ohio's villages with leaves flutter-
      ing in the moderate wind,
Where apples ripe in the orchards hang and grapes
      on the trellis'd vines,
(Smell you the smell of the grapes on the vines ?
Smell you the buckwheat where the bees were lately
      buzzing ?)

Above all, lo, the sky so calm, so transparent after
    the rain, and with wondrous clouds,
Below too, all calm, all vital and beautiful, and
    the farm prospers well.

Down in the fields all prospers well;
But now from the fields come, father, come at the
    daughter's call,
And come to the entry, mother, to the front door
    come right away.

Fast as she can she hurries, something ominous,
    her steps trembling,
She does not tarry to smooth her hair nor adjust
    her cap.

Open the envelope quickly!
O this is not our son's writing, yet his name is sign'd,
O a strange hand writes for our dear son. O stricken
    mother's soul!
All swims before her eyes, flashes with black, she
    catches the main words only,
Sentences broken, *gunshot wound in the breast,
    cavalry skirmish, taken to hospital,*
At present low, but will soon be better.

Ah, now the single figure to me,
Amid all teeming and wealthy Ohio, with all its cities
    and farms,
Sickly white in the face and dull in the head, very
    faint,
By the jamb of a door leans.

Grieve not so, dear mother (the just-grown daughter
    speaks through her sobs,
The little sisters huddle around speechless and dis-
    may'd),
*See, dearest mother, the letter says Pete will soon
    be better!*

Alas! poor boy, he will never be better (nor maybe
  needs to be better, that brave and simple soul),
While they stand at home at the door he is dead
  already,
The only son is dead.

But the mother needs to be better,
She with thin form presently drest in black,
By day her meals untouch'd, then at night fitfully
  sleeping, often waking,
In the midnight waking, weeping, longing with one
  deep longing,
O that she might withdraw unnoticed, silent from
  life escape and withdraw,
To follow, to seek, to be with her dear dead son.

WALT WHITMAN.

NOT YET.

O COUNTRY, marvel of the earth!
  O realm to sudden greatness grown!
The age that gloried in thy birth,
  Shall it behold thee overthrown?
Shall traitors lay that greatness low?
No, land of Hope and Blessing, No!

And we who wear thy glorious name,
  Shall we, like cravens, stand apart,
When those whom thou hast trusted aim
  The death-blow at thy generous heart?
Forth goes the battle-cry, and lo!
Hosts rise in harness, shouting, No!

And they who founded, in our land,
  The power that rules from sea to sea,
Bled they in vain, or vainly planned
  To leave their country great and free?
Their sleeping ashes, from below,
Send up the thrilling murmur, No!

Knit they the gentle ties which long
   These sister States were proud to wear,
And forged the kindly links so strong
   For idle hands in sport to tear—
For scornful hands aside to throw?
No, by our fathers' memory, No!

Our humming marts, our iron ways,
   Our wind-tossed woods on mountain crest,
The hoarse Atlantic, with his bays,
   The calm, broad Ocean of the West,
And Mississippi's torrent-flow,
And loud Niagara, answer, No!

Not yet the hour is nigh when they
   Who deep in Eld's dim twilight sit,
Earth's ancient kings, shall rise and say,
   " Proud country, welcome to the pit!
So soon art thou, like us, brought low!"
No, sullen groups of shadows, No!

For now, behold, the arm that gave
   The victory in our fathers' day,
Strong, as of old, to guard and save—
   That mighty arm which none can stay—
On clouds above and fields below,
Writes, in men's sight, the answer, No!
              WILLIAM CULLEN BRYANT.

THE BATTLE AUTUMN OF 1862.

THE flags of war like storm-birds fly,
   The charging trumpets blow;
Yet rolls no thunder in the sky,
   No earthquake strives below.

And calm and patient Nature keeps
   Her ancient promise well,

Though o'er her bloom and greenness sweeps
    The battle's breath of hell.

And still she walks in golden hours
    Through harvest-happy farms,
And still she wears her fruits and flowers
    Like jewels on her arms.

What mean the gladness of the plain,
    This joy of eve and morn,
The mirth that shakes the beard of grain,
    And yellow locks of corn?

Ah! eyes may well be full of tears,
    And hearts with hate are hot;
But even-paced come round the years,
    And Nature changes not.

She meets with smiles our bitter grief,
    With songs our groans of pain;
She mocks with tint of flower and leaf
    The war-field's crimson stain.

Still in the cannon's pause we hear
    Her sweet thanksgiving psalm;
Too near to God for doubt or fear,
    She shares the eternal calm.

She knows the seed lies safe below
    The fires that blast and burn;
For all the tears of blood we sow,
    She waits the rich return.

She sees, with clearer eye than ours,
    The good of suffering born—
The hearts that blossom like her flowers,
    And ripen like her corn.

Oh, give to us, in times like these,
    The vision of her eyes;
And make her fields and fruited trees
    Our golden prophecies!

Oh, give to us her finer ear!
Above this stormy din
We too would hear the bells of cheer
Ring peace and freedom in.

JOHN GREENLEAF WHITTIER.

NEVER OR NOW.

[1862.]

LISTEN, young heroes! your country is calling!
Time strikes the hour for the brave and the true!
Now, while the foremost are fighting and falling,
Fill up the ranks that have opened for you!

You whom the fathers made free and defended,
Stain not the scroll that emblazons their fame!
You whose fair heritage spotless descended,
Leave not your children a birthright of shame!

Stay not for questions while Freedom stands gasp-
ing!
Wait not till Honor lies wrapped in his pall!
Brief the lips' meeting be, swift the hands' clasping:
" Off for the wars!" is enough for them all.

Break from the arms that would fondly caress you!
Hark! 'tis the bugle-blast, sabres are drawn!
Mothers shall pray for you, fathers shall bless you,
Maidens shall weep for you when you are gone!

Never or now! cries the blood of a nation,
Poured on the turf where the red rose should
bloom;
Now is the day and the hour of salvation,—
Never or now! peals the trumpet of doom!

Never or now ! roars the hoarse-throated cannon
   Through the black canopy blotting the skies ;
Never or now ! flaps the shell-blasted pennon
   O'er the deep ooze where the Cumberland lies !

From the foul dens where our brothers are dying,
   Aliens and foes in the land of their birth,—
From the rank swamps where our martyrs are lying,
   Pleading in vain for a handful of earth,—

From the hot plains where they perish outnumbered,
   Furrowed and ridged by the battle-field's plough,
Comes the loud summons ; too long you have slum-
      bered,
   Hear the last Angel-trump—Never or Now !
            OLIVER WENDELL HOLMES.

CLOUDS IN THE WEST.

HARK ! on the wind that whistles from the West
   A manly shout for instant succor comes,
From men who fight, outnumbered, breast to breast,
   With rage-indented drums ;

Who dare for child, wife, country, stream and strand,
   Though but a fraction to the swarming foe,
There, at the flooded gateways of the land,
   To stem a torrent's flow.

To arms ! brave sons of each embattled State,
   Whose queenly standard is a Southern star :
Who would be free must ride the lists of Fate
   On Freedom's victor-car !

Forsake the field, the shop, the mart, the hum
   Of craven traffic, for the mustering clan :

The dead themselves are pledged that you shall
    come
  And prove yourself a man.

Blow, summoning trumpets, a compulsive stave
  Through all the bounds from Beersheba to Dan ;
Come out ! come out ! who scorns to be a slave,
  Or claims to be a man !

Hark ! on the breezes whistling from the West
  A manly shout for instant succor comes,
From men who fight, outnumbered, breast to breast,
  With rage-indented drums ;

Who charge and cheer amid the murderous din,
  Where still your battle-flags unbended wave,
Dying for what your fathers died to win,
  And you must fight to save.

                              A. J. REQUIER.

———

A WORD WITH THE WEST.

[*On the appointment of General Joseph E. Johnston to
the command of the Confederate armies in the West,
November*, 1862.]

ONCE more to the breach for the Land of the West !
And a leader we give, of our bravest and best,
  Of his State and his army the pride ;
Hope shines like the plume of Navarre on his crest,
  And gleams in the glaive at his side.

For his courage is keen and his honor is bright
As the trusty Toledo he wears to the fight,
  Newly wrought in the forges of Spain,
And this weapon, like all he has brandished for
    Right,
  Will never be dimmed by a stain.

He leaves the loved soil of Virginia behind,
Where the dust of his fathers is fitly enshrined,
  Where lie the fresh fields of his fame ;
Where the murmurous pines, as they sway in the
    wind,
  Seem ever to whisper his name.

The Johnstons have always borne wings on their
    spurs,
And their motto a noble distinction confers,
  " Ever ready "—for friend or for foe—
With a patriot's fervor the sentiment stirs
  The large manly heart of our Joe.

We recall that a former bold chief of the clan
Fell, bravely defending the West, in the van
  On Shiloh's illustrious day ;
And with reason we reckon our Johnston the man
  The dark bloody debt to repay.

There is much to be done : if not glory to seek,
There's a just and a terrible vengeance to wreak
  For crimes of a terrible dye,
While the plaint of the helpless, the wail of the weak
  In a chorus rise up to the sky.

For the Wolf of the North we once drove to his den,
That quailed in affright 'neath the stern glance of
    men,
  With his pack has returned to the spoil ;
Then come from the hamlet, the mountain, the glen,
  And drive him again from the soil !

Brave-born Tennesseans, so loyal, so true,
Who have hunted the beast in your highlands, of you
  Our leader has never a doubt ;
You will troop by the thousand the chase to renew
  The day when his bugles ring out.

But ye " Hunters" so famed " of Kentucky" of yore,
Where, where are the rifles that kept from your door
   The wolf and the robber as well ?
Of a truth, you have never been laggard before
   To deal with a savage so fell.

Has the love you once bore to your country grown
     cold ?
Has the fire on the altar died out ?   Do you hold
   Your lives than your freedom more dear ?
Can you shamefully barter your birthright for gold,
   Or basely take counsel of fear ?

We will not believe it !   Kentucky, the land
Of a Clay, will not tamely submit to the brand
   That disgraces the dastard, the slave ;
The hour of redemption draws nigh—is at hand—
   Her own sons her own honor shall save !

Mighty men of Missouri, come forth to the call,
With the rush of your rivers when tempests appall,
   And the torrents their sources unseal ;
And this be the watchword of one and of all—
   " Remember the butcher, McNiel !"

Then once more to the breach for the land of the
     West !
Strike home for your hearts—for the lips you love
     best—
   Follow on where your Leader you see !
One flash of his sword when the foe is hard pressed,
   And the Land of the West thall be free !

                JOHN R. THOMPSON.

THE BIVOUAC IN THE SNOW.

HALT !—the march is over,
  Day is almost done ;
Loose the cumbrous knapsack,
  Drop the heavy gun.
Chilled and wet and weary,
  Wander to and fro,
Seeking wood to kindle
  Fires amidst the snow.

Round the bright blaze gather,
  Heed not sleet nor cold ;
Ye are Spartan soldiers,
  Stout and brave and bold.
Never Xerxian army
  Yet subdued a foe
Who but asked a blanket
  On a bed of snow.

Shivering, 'midst the darkness,
  Christian men are found,
There devoutly kneeling
  On the frozen ground—
Pleading for their country,
  In its hour of woe—
For its soldiers marching
  Shoeless through the snow.

Lost in heavy slumbers,
  Free from toil and strife,
Dreaming of their dear ones—
  Home, and child, and wife,
Tentless they are lying,
  While the fires burn low—
Lying in their blankets,
  'Midst December's snow.

                MARGARET J. PRESTON.

FREDERICKSBURG.

[*December* 13, 1862.]

THE increasing moonlight drifts across my bed,
And on the churchyard by the road, I know
It falls as white and noiselessly as snow.
'Twas such a night two weary summers fled ;
The stars, as now, were waning overhead.
Listen ! Again the shrill-lipped bugles blow
Where the swift currents of the river flow
Past Fredericksburg : far off the heavens are red
With sudden conflagration : ou yon height,
Linstock in hand, the gunners hold their breath :
A signal-rocket pierces the dense night,
Flings its spent stars upon the town beneath :
Hark !—the artillery massing on the right,
Hark !—the black squadrons wheeling down to
     Death !

THOMAS BAILEY ALDRICH.

KILLED AT FREDERICKSBURG.

FRED MASON came beside my fire,
  But turned with light, familiar warning :
" Sleep, though your bed be cold and damp,
  And I will meet you in the morning."

For fraught with doubt the day had passed,
  And, noiselessly at dusk parading,
We slept upon the frozen hills
  That shook with Burnside's cannonading.

While through the gloom our long black guns
  Their messages of death deliver,
The word runs low from lip to lip :
  " At break of day we cross the river."

The long night passed ; ten thousand eyes
    Turned to the wintry heaven o'er them ;
Then left their painful sleep behind,
    To meet the dreamless sleep before them.

From bluff to bluff the batteries growled,
    And all day long we faced their thunder,—
But others, in their time, shall tell
    The story of that bloody blunder.

When Fredericksburg was won at last,
    Just where the bugle sounded " Forward !"
Fred Mason lay, his breast in front,
    His whitened features looking Nor'ward.

His fingers in the trampled soil,
    Convulsed and blue, were tightly clinching ;
His dead eyes, staring to the sky,
    Yet stared defiant and unflinching.

Dead eyes !—when last they flashed in mine,
    Our hearts were lighter than a feather :
Well, God forgive me ! but I wish
    We both had fallen there together.

Enough for thee, one soldier mourns
    A friend misfortune never altered,
A lip of cheer, a soul of fire,
    A head and hand that never faltered.

In peace, below the blood-stained height,
    This waving wood, this flowing river,
Shall lull at last thy restless brain
    To sleep forever and forever.

Above thy breast the quail shall glide,
    The rabbit cull his dewy clover ;
And long as heaven's wind shall blow,
    The holly bend thy slumber over.

Round rocky isle and laurelled banks
  The Rappahannock, softly dashing,
Sound sweet as on the fatal morn
  When last we listened to its plashing.

Here shall the solemn cricket slide
  And chant amid thy grassy cover ;
And Nature, like a maiden, watch
  The turf that wraps her daring lover.

Sleep on, sleep on ; no more this vale
  Wakes to the signal's hellish warning :
" Sleep, though your bed be cold and damp,
  And I will meet you in the morning."

CHAUNCEY HICKOX.

CHRISTMAS NIGHT OF '62.

[In the Army of Northern Virginia.]

THE wintry blast goes wailing by,
  The snow is falling overhead ;
  I hear the lonely sentry's tread,
And distant watch-fires light the sky.

Dim forms go flitting through the gloom ;
  The soldiers cluster 'round the blaze,
  To talk of other Christmas days,
And softly speak of home and home.

My sabre swinging overhead
  Gleams in the watch-fire's fitful glow,
  While fiercely drives the blinding snow,
And memory leads me to the dead.

My thoughts go wandering to and fro,
  Vibrating 'twixt the Now and Then ;
  I see the low-brow'd home agen,
The old hall wreathed with mistletoe.

And sweetly from the far-off years
  Comes borne the laughter faint and low,
  The voices of the Long Ago !
My eyes are wet with tender tears.

I feel agen the mother-kiss,
  I see agen the glad surprise
  That lightened up the tranquil eyes
And brimmed them o'er with tears of bliss,

As, rushing from the old hall-door,
  She fondly clasp'd her wayward boy—
  Her face all radiant with the joy
She felt to see him home once more.

My sabre swinging on the bough
  Gleams in the watch-fire's fitful glow,
  While fiercely drives the blinding snow
Aslant upon my sadden'd brow.

Those cherished faces all are gone !
  Asleep within the quiet graves
  Where lies the snow in drifting waves,—
And I am sitting here alone.

There's not a comrade here to-night
  But knows that lov'd ones far away
  On bended knees this night will pray :
" God bring our darling from the fight."

But there are none to wish me back,
  For me no yearning prayers arise,
  The lips are mute and closed the eyes—
My home is in the bivouac.

                    W. GORDON MacCabe.

BOSTON HYMN.

[Read at the Emancipation Meeting in Boston, January 1, 1863.]

THE word of the Lord by night
  To the watching Pilgrims came,
As they sat by the sea-side,
  And filled their hearts with flame.

God said, I am tired of kings,
  I suffer them no more;
Up to my ear the morning brings
  The outrage of the poor.

Think ye I made this ball
  A field of havoc and war,
Where tyrants great and tyrants small
  Might harry the weak and poor?

My angel,—his name is Freedom,—
  Choose him to be your king;
He shall cut pathways east and west,
  And fend you with his wing.

Lo! I uncover the land
  Which I hid of old time in the West,
As the sculptor uncovers his statue
  When he has wrought his best;

I show Columbia, of the rocks
  Which dip their foot in the seas
And soar to the air-borne flocks
  Of clouds and the boreal fleece.

I will divide my goods;
  Call in the wretch and slave:
None shall rule but the humble,
  And none but Toil shall have.

I will have never a noble,
  No lineage counted great :
Fishers and choppers and ploughmen
  Shall constitute a state.

Go, cut down trees in the forest,
  And trim the straightest boughs ;
Cut down trees in the forest,
  And build me a wooden house.

Call the people together,
  The young men and the sires,
The digger in the harvest-field,
  Hireling and him that hires ;

And here in a pine state-house
  They shall choose men to rule
In every needful faculty,
  In church and state and school.

Lo, now ! if these poor men
  Can govern the land and sea,
And make just laws below the sun,
  As planets faithful be.

And ye shall succor men ;
  'Tis nobleness to serve ;
Help them who cannot help again :
  Beware from right to swerve.

I break your bonds and masterships,
  And I unchain the slave :
Free be his heart and hand henceforth,
  As wind and wandering wave.

I cause from every creature
  His proper good to flow :
As much as he is and doeth,
  So much he shall bestow.

But, laying his hands on another
  To coin his labor and sweat,
He goes in pawn to his victim
  For eternal years in debt.

To-day unbind the captive,
  So only are ye unbound ;
Lift up a people from the dust,
  Trump of their rescue, sound !

Pay ransom to the owner,
  And fill the bag to the brim.
Who is the owner ?   The slave is owner,
  And ever was.   Pay him.

O North ! give him beauty for rags,
  And honor, O South ! for his shame ;
Nevada ! coin thy golden crags
  With Freedom's image and name.

Up ! and the dusky race
  That sat in darkness long,—
Be swift their feet as antelopes,
  And as behemoth strong.

Come, East and West and North,
  By races, as snow-flakes,
And carry my purpose forth,
  Which neither halts nor shakes.

My will fulfilled shall be,
  For, in daylight or in dark,
My thunderbolt has eyes to see
  His way home to the mark.

                    RALPH WALDO EMERSON.

THE OLD SERGEANT.

[This poem, which has been widely copied and is printed usually without the prelude, first appeared, in the form in which it is here given, as the Carrier's New Year's Address of the Louisville Courier-Journal, in 1863.]

The Carrier cannot sing to-day the ballads
  With which he used to go
Rhyming the glad rounds of the happy New Years
  That are now beneath the snow :

For the same awful and portentous Shadow
  That overcast the earth,
And smote the land last year with desolation,
  Still darkens every hearth.

And the Carrier hears Beethoven's mighty death-
      march
  Come up from every mart,
And he hears and feels it breathing in his bosom,
  And beating in his heart.

And to-day, a scarred and weather-beaten veteran,
  Again he comes along,
To tell the story of the Old Year's struggles
  In another New Year's song.

And the song is his, but not so with the story ;
  For the story, you must know,
Was told in prose to Assistant-Surgeon Austin,
  By a soldier of Shiloh :

By Robert Burton, who was brought up on the
      Adams,
  With his death-wound in his side ;
And who told the story to the Assistant-Surgeon
  On the same night that he died.

But the singer feels it will better suit the ballad,
  If all should deem it right,
To tell the story as if what it speaks of
  Had happened but last night.

" Come a little nearer, Doctor—thank you; let me
      take the cup :
Draw your chair up—draw it closer; just another
      little sup !
Maybe you may think I'm better; but I'm pretty
      well used up—
Doctor, you've done all you could do, but I'm just
      a-going up !

" Feel my pulse, sir, if you want to, but it ain't much
      use to try,"—
" Never say that," said the Surgeon, as he smothered
      down a sigh ;
" It will never do, old comrade, for a soldier to say
      die !"
" What you *say* will make no difference, Doctor,
      when you come to die.

" Doctor, what has been the matter ?"   " You were
      very faint, they say ;
You must try to get to sleep now."   " Doctor, have
      I been away ?"
" Not that anybody knows of !"   " Doctor—Doctor,
      please to stay !
There is something I must tell you, and you won't
      have long to stay !

" I have got my marching orders, and I'm ready
      now to go ;
Doctor, did you say I fainted ?—but it couldn't ha'
      been so,
For as sure as I'm a Sergeant, and was wounded at
      Shiloh,
I've this very night been back there, on the old field
      of Shiloh !

" This is all that I remember : The last time the
  Lighter came,
And the lights had all been lowered, and the noises
  much the same,
He had not been gone five minutes before something
  called my name :
' ORDERLY SERGEANT—ROBERT BURTON ! '—just
  that way it called my name.

" And I wondered who could call me so distinctly
  and so slow,
Knew it couldn't be the Lighter, he could not have
  spoken so,
And I tried to answer, ' Here, sir ! ' but I couldn't
  make it go ;
For I couldn't move a muscle, and I couldn't make
  it go.

" Then I thought : it's all a nightmare, all a hum-
  bug and a bore ;
Just another foolish *grape-vine*—and it won't come
  any more ;
But it came, sir, notwithstanding, just the same way
  as before :
' ORDERLY SERGEANT—ROBERT BURTON ! '—even
  louder than before.

" That is all that I remember, till a sudden burst of
  light,
And I stood beside the river, where we stood that
  Sunday night,
Waiting to be ferried over to the dark bluffs oppo-
  site,
When the river was perdition, and all hell was
  opposite !

" And the same old palpitation came again in all its
  power,
And I heard a Bugle sounding, as from some celes-
  tial Tower ;

And the same mysterious voice said : 'IT IS THE
  ELEVENTH HOUR!
ORDERLY SERGEANT—ROBERT BURTON—IT IS
  THE ELEVENTH HOUR!'

"Dr. Austin!—what day is this?"   "It is Wednes-
  day night, you know."
"Yes—to-morrow will be New Year's, and a right
  good time below!
What time is it, Dr. Austin?"   "Nearly twelve."
  " Then don't you go!
Can it be that all this happened—all this—not an
  hour ago?

"There was where the gunboats opened on the dark
  rebellious host;
And where Webster semi-circled his last guns upon
  the coast ;
There were still the two log-houses, just the same,
  or else their ghost—
And the same old transport came and took me
  over—or its ghost!

"And the old field lay before me, all deserted, far
  and wide :
There was where they fell on Prentiss—there
  McClernand met the tide ;
There was where stern Sherman rallied, and where
  Hurlbut's heroes died—
Lower down, where Wallace charged them, and
  kept charging till he died.

"There was where Lew Wallace showed them he
  was of the canny kin,
There was where old Nelson thundered, and where
  Rousseau waded in ;
There McCook sent 'em to breakfast, and we all
  began to win,—
There was where the grape-shot took me, just as
  we began to win.

"Now, a shroud of snow and silence over every-
thing was spread;
And but for this old blue mantle and the old hat on
my head,
I should not have even doubted, to this moment, I
was dead,—
For my footsteps were as silent as the snow upon
the dead!

"Death and silence!—Death and silence! all
around me as I sped!
And behold, a mighty Tower, as if builded to the
dead,
To the Heaven of the heavens lifted up its mighty
head,
Till the Stars and Stripes of Heaven all seemed
waving from its head!

"Round and mighty-based it towered up into the
infinite—
And I knew no mortal mason could have built a
shaft so bright;
For it shone like solid sunshine, and a winding
stair of light
Wound around it and around it till it wound clear
out of sight!

"And, behold, as I approached it—with a rapt and
dazzled stare—
Thinking that I saw old comrades just ascending
the great stair—
Suddenly the solemn challenge broke of—'Halt!'
and 'Who goes there?'
'I'm a friend,' I said, 'if you are!' 'Then advance,
sir, to the Stair!'

"I advanced! That sentry, Doctor, was Elijah
Ballantyne!
First of all to fall on Monday, after we had formed
the line!

'Welcome, my old Sergeant, welcome ! Welcome
    by that countersign !'
And he pointed to the scar there, under this old
    cloak of mine.

" As he grasped my hand I shuddered, thinking
    only of the grave ;
But he smiled, and pointed upward, with a bright
    and bloodless glaive :
'That's the way, sir, to Headquarters.' ' What
    Headquarters ? ' ' Of the Brave !'
' But the great Tower ? ' ' That was builded of the
    great deeds of the Brave !'

" Then a sudden shame came o'er me at his uniform
    of light ;
At my own so old and battered, and at his so new
    and bright ;
' Ah !' said he, ' you have forgotten the new uniform
    to-night !
' Hurry back—for you must be here at just twelve
    o'clock to-night !'

" And the next thing I remember, you were sitting
    there, and I ———
Doctor—did you hear a footstep ? Hark !--God
    bless you all ! Good-by !
Doctor, please to give my musket and my knap-
    sack, when I die,
To my son—my son that's coming—he won't get
    here till I die !

" Tell him his old father blessed him—as he never
    did before—
And to carry that old musket "——— Hark ! a knock
    is at the door ! ———
" Till the Union "——— See ! it opens ! ———
    " Father ! Father ! speak once more !"
" *Bless you !*"—gasped the old gray Sergeant. And
    he lay and said no more.

FORCEYTHE WILLSON.

READY.

L<small>OADED</small> with gallant soldiers,
 A boat shot in to the land,
And lay at the right of Rodman's Point,
 With her keel upon the sand.

Lightly, gayly, they came to shore,
 And never a man afraid;
When sudden the enemy opened fire
 From his deadly ambuscade.

Each man fell flat on the bottom
 Of the boat; and the captain said:
"If we lie here, we all are captured,
 And the first who moves is dead!"

Then out spoke a negro sailor,
 No slavish soul had he:
"Somebody's got to die, boys,
 And it might as well be me!"

Firmly he rose, and fearlessly
 Stepped out into the tide;
He pushed the vessel safely off,
 Then fell across her side:

Fell, pierced by a dozen bullets,
 As the boat swung clear and free;
But there wasn't a man of them that day
 Who was fitter to die than he!

P<small>HŒBE</small> C<small>ARY.</small>

THE DEAD CANNONEER.

[General Pelham, C. S. A., killed at Kelly's Ford, Va., March 17, 1863.]

JUST as the spring came laughing through the strife,
    With all its gorgeous cheer,
In the bright April of historic life,
    Fell the great cannoneer.

The wondrous lulling of a hero's breath
    His bleeding country weeps ;
Hushed in the alabaster arms of Death,
    Our young Marcellus sleeps.

Nobler and grander than the Child of Rome
    Curbing his chariot steeds,
The knightly scion of a Southern home
    Dazzled the land with deeds.

Gentlest and bravest in the battle-brunt,
    The champion of the truth,
He bore his banner to the very front
    Of our immortal youth.

A clang of sabres 'mid Virginian snow,
    The fiery pang of shells,—
And there's a wail of immemorial woe
    In Alabama dells.

The pennon drops that led the sacred band
    Along the crimson field ;
The meteor blade sinks from the nerveless hand
    Over the spotless shield.

We gazed and gazed upon that beauteous face ;
    While round the lips and eyes,
Couched in their marble slumber, flashed the grace
    Of a divine surprise.

O mother of a blessed soul on high !
    Thy tears may soon be shed ;
Think of thy boy with princes of the sky,
    Among the Southern dead !

How must he smile on this dull world beneath,
    Fevered with swift renown,—
He, with the martyr's amaranthine wreath
    Twining the victor's crown !

JAMES R. RANDALL.

THE BAND IN THE PINES.

[Heard after Pelham died.]

OH, band in the pine-wood, cease !
    Cease with your splendid call ;
The living are brave and noble,
    But the dead were bravest of all !

They throng to the martial summons,
    To the loud triumphant strain ;
And the dear bright eyes of long-dead friends
    Come to the heart again !

They come with the ringing bugle,
    And the deep drum's mellow roar ;
Till the soul is faint with longing
    For the hands we clasp no more !

Oh, band in the pine-wood, cease !
    Or the heart will melt in tears,
For the gallant eyes and the smiling lips,
    And the voices of old years !

JOHN ESTEN COOKE.

CHARLESTON.

[*April*, 1863.]

CALM as that second summer which precedes
    The first fall of the snow,
In the broad sunlight of heroic deeds,
    The city bides the foe.

As yet, behind their ramparts, stern and proud,
    Her bolted thunders sleep,--
Dark Sumter, like a battlemented cloud,
    Looms o'er the solemn deep.

No Calpe frowns from lofty cliff or scaur
    To guard the holy strand ;
But Moultrie holds in leash her dogs of war,
    Above the level sand.

And down the dunes a thousand guns lie couched,
    Unseen, beside the flood,—
Like tigers in some Orient jungle crouched,
    That wait and watch for blood.

Meanwhile, through streets still echoing with trade,
    Walk grave and thoughtful men,
Whose hands may one day wield the patriot's blade
    As lightly as the pen.

And maidens, with such eyes as would grow dim
    Over a bleeding hound,
Seem each one to have caught the strength of him
    Whose sword she sadly bound.

Thus girt without and garrisoned at home,
    Day patient following day,
Old Charleston looks from roof and spire and dome,
    Across her tranquil bay.

Ships, through a hundred foes, from Saxon lands
   And spicy Indian ports,
Bring Saxon steel and iron to her hands,
   And summer to her courts.

But still, along yon dim Atlantic line,
   The only hostile smoke
Creeps like a harmless mist above the brine,
   From some frail floating oak.

Shall the Spring dawn, and she, still clad in smiles,
   And with an unscathed brow,
Rest in the strong arms of her palm-crowned isles,
   As fair and free as now?

We know not; in the temple of the Fates
   God has inscribed her doom:
And, all untroubled in her faith, she waits
   The triumph or the tomb.

HENRY TIMROD.

THE BATTLE OF CHARLESTON HARBOR.

[*Bombardment of Fort Sumter by the South Atlantic Squadron, U. S. Navy, April* 7, 1863.]

I.

Two hours, or more, beyond the prime of a blithe
   April day,
The Northman's mailed "Invincibles" steamed up
   fair Charleston Bay;
They came in sullen file and slow, low-breasted on
   the wave,
Black as a midnight front of storm, and silent as
   the grave.

II.

A thousand warrior-hearts beat high as those dread
    monsters drew
More closely to the game of death across the
    breezeless blue,
And twice ten thousand hearts of those who
    watched the scene afar,
Thrill in the awful hush that bides the battle's
    broadening star.

III.

Each gunner, moveless by his gun, with rigid aspect
    stands,
The ready lanyards firmly grasped in bold, untrem-
    bling hands,
So moveless in their marbled calm, their stern
    heroic guise,
They looked like forms of statued stone with burn-
    ing human eyes!

IV.

Our banners on the outmost walls, with stately
    rustling fold,
Flash back from arch and parapet the sunlight's
    ruddy gold,—
They mount to the deep roll of drums, and widely-
    echoing cheers,
And then—once more, dark, breathless, hushed,
    wait the grim cannoneers.

V.

Onward—in sullen file and slow, low glooming on
    the wave,
Near, nearer still, the haughty fleet glides silent as
    the grave,
When sudden, shivering up the calm, o'er startled
    flood and shore,
Burst from the sacred Island Fort the thunder-
    wrath of yore!

VI.

Ha ! brutal Corsairs ! though ye come thrice-cased
in iron mail,
Beware the storm that's opening now, God's ven-
geance guides the hail !
Ye strive, the ruffian types of Might, 'gainst law and
truth and Right :
Now quail beneath a sturdier Power, and own a
mightier Might !

VII.

No empty boast ! for while we speak, more furious,
wilder, higher,
Dart from the circling batteries a hundred tongues
of fire ;
The waves gleam red, the lurid vault of heaven
seems rent above ;
Fight on, O knightly gentlemen ! for faith and
home and love !

VIII.

There's not in all that line of flame, one soul that
would not rise
To seize the victor's wreath of blood, though death
must give the prize—
There's not in all this anxious crowd that throngs
the ancient town
A maid who does not yearn for power to strike one
despot down.

IX.

The strife grows fiercer ! ship by ship the proud
armada sweeps,
Where hot from Sumter's raging breast the vol-
leyed lightning leaps ;
And ship by ship, raked, overborne, ere burned the
sunset light,
Crawls in the gloom of baffled hate beyond the field
of fight !

X.

O glorious Empress of the Main! from out thy
    storied spires
Thou well mayst peal thy bells of joy, and light thy
    festal fires,—
Since Heaven this day hath striven for thee, hath
    nerved thy dauntless sons,
And thou in clear-eyed faith hast seen God's
    angels near the guns!
             PAUL HAMILTON HAYNE.

TWILIGHT ON SUMTER.

[*In the spring and summer of* 1863, *Fort Sumter, in
possession of the Confederates since the surrender of Major
Anderson, two years before, was bombarded by the Federal
fleet, and by the artillery on Morris Island, until reduced
almost to ruins.*]

    STILL and dark along the sea
        Sumter lay ;
    A light was overhead,
    As from burning cities shed,
    And the clouds were battle-red,
        Far away.
    Not a solitary gun
    Left to tell the fort had won
        Or lost the day !
    Nothing but the tattered rag
    Of the drooping rebel flag,
And the sea-birds screaming round it in their play.

    How it woke one April morn,
        Fame shall tell;
    As from Moultrie, close at hand,
    And the batteries on the land,
    Round its faint but fearless band
        Shot and shell

Raining hid the doubtful light ;
But they fought the hopeless fight
　　Long and well,
(Theirs the glory, ours the shame !)
Till the walls were wrapt in flame,
Then their flag was proudly struck, and Sumter fell !

Now—oh, look at Sumter now,
　　In the gloom !
Mark its scarred and shattered walls,
(Hark ! the ruined rampart falls !)
There's a justice that appalls
　　In its doom ;
For this blasted spot of earth
Where rebellion had its birth
　　Is its tomb !
And when Sumter sinks at last
From the heavens, that shrink aghast,
Hell shall rise in grim derision and make room !
　　　　RICHARD HENRY STODDARD.

KEENAN'S CHARGE.

[*At the battle of Chancellorsville, Va., May 2, 1863,
it became necessary to bring a Federal battery into posi-
tion to resist a sudden onset by Stonewall Jackson. To
gain a few minutes' time, Major Peter Keenan, of the
Eighth Pennsylvania Cavalry, was ordered to charge the
enemy ; and, with his four hundred men, he rode against
ten thousand, in a charge as gallant as that of the Light
Brigade.*]

BY the shrouded gleam of the western skies,
Brave Keenan looked in Pleasonton's eyes
For an instant—clear, and cool, and still ;
Then, with a smile, he said : " I will."

"Cavalry, charge!"   Not a man of them shrank.
Their sharp, full cheer, from rank on rank,
Rose joyously, with a willing breath—
Rose like a greeting hail to death.
Then forward they sprang, and spurred and clashed ;
Shouted the officers, crimson-sashed ;
Rode well the men, each brave as his fellow,
In their faded coats of the blue and yellow ;
And above in the air, with an instinct true,
Like a bird of war their pennon flew.

With clank of scabbards and thunder of steeds,
And blades that shine like sunlit reeds,
And strong brown faces bravely pale
For fear their proud attempt shall fail,
Three hundred Pennsylvanians close
On twice ten thousand gallant foes.

Line after line the troopers came
To the edge of the wood that was ring'd with flame ;
Rode in and sabred and shot—and fell :
Nor came one back his wounds to tell.
And full in the midst rose Keenan, tall
In the gloom, like a martyr awaiting his fall,
While the circle-stroke of his sabre, swung
'Round his head, like a halo there, luminous hung.
Line after line ; ay, whole platoons,
Struck dead in their saddles, of brave dragoons
By the maddened horses were onward borne
And into the vortex flung, trampled and torn ;
As Keenan fought with his men, side by side.

So they rode, till there were no more to ride.

But over them, lying there, shattered and mute,
What deep echo rolls ?—   'Tis a death salute
From the cannon in place ; for, heroes, you braved
Your fate not in vain : the army was saved !

Over them now—year following year—
Over their graves, the pine-cones fall,

And the whippoorwill chants his spectre-call ;
But they stir not again : they raise no cheer :
They have ceased. But their glory shall never
    cease,
Nor their light be quenched in the light of peace.
The rush of their charge is resounding still,
That saved the army at Chancellorsville.

              GEORGE PARSONS LATHROP.

DEATH OF STONEWALL JACKSON.

[*On the evening of the first day's fight at Chancellors-*
ville, Va., May 2, 1863, *where Stonewall Jackson had ac-*
complished his famous flank movement around the Union
right, he rode out to inspect the ground for the morrow's
battle, and in the darkness was surprised and shot by some
of his own pickets. He died on the 10th *of May following.*]

NOT 'mid the lightning of the stormy fight,
   Not in the rush upon the vandal foe,
Did kingly Death, with his resistless might,
   Lay the great leader low.

His warrior soul its earthly shackles broke
   In the full sunshine of a peaceful town ;
When all the storm was hushed, the trusty oak
   That propped our cause went down.

Though his alone the blood that flecks the ground,
   Recording all his grand, heroic deeds,
Freedom herself is writhing with the wound,
   And all the country bleeds.

He entered not the Nation's Promised Land
   At the red belching of the cannon's mouth;
But broke the House of Bondage with his hand—
   The Moses of the South !

O gracious God! not gainless is the loss :
A glorious sunbeam gilds thy sternest frown;
And while his country staggers with the Cross,
     He rises with the Crown.
                         HARRY L. FLASH.

"THE BRIGADE MUST NOT KNOW, SIR!"

" WHO'VE ye got there?"—" Only a dying brother,
     Hurt in the front just now."
" Good boy ! he'll do.   Somebody tell his mother
     Where he was killed, and how."

" Whom have you there?"—" A crippled courier,
     Major,
     Shot by mistake, we hear.
He was with Stonewall."—" Cruel work they've
     made here ;
     Quick with him to the rear !"

" Well, who comes next?"—" Doctor, speak low,
     speak low, sir ;
     Don't let the men find out !
It's STONEWALL !"—" God !"—" The brigade must
     not know, sir,
     While there's a foe about !"

Whom have we here—shrouded in martial manner,
     Crowned with a martyr's charm ?
A grand dead hero, in a living banner,
     Born of his heart and arm :

The heart whereon his cause hung — see how
     clingeth
     That banner to his bier !
The arm wherewith his cause struck—hark! how
     ringeth
     His trumpet in their rear !

What have we left ? His glorious inspiration,
　His prayers in council met.
Living, he laid the first stones of a nation ;
　And dead, he builds it yet.

J. W. Palmer.

UNDER THE SHADE OF THE TREES.

[*This poem is founded upon the following incident, taken
from an account of Stonewall Jackson's last hours: "A
few moments before his death, he called out in his delirium,
'Order A. P. Hill to prepare for action ; . . . pass the
infantry to the front ; . . . tell Major Hawks . . .'
Here the sentence was left unfinished. But soon after, a
sweet smile overspread his face, and he murmured quietly,
with an air of relief, 'Let us cross the river and rest
under the shade of the trees.' These were his last words."*]

What are the thoughts that are stirring his breast ?
　What is the mystical vision he sees ?
—" *Let us pass over the river, and rest
　Under the shade of the trees.*"

Has he grown sick of his toils and his tasks ?
　Sighs the worn spirit for respite or ease ?
Is it a moment's cool halt that he asks
　Under the shade of the trees ?

Is it the gurgle of waters whose flow
　Ofttime has come to him, borne on the breeze,
Memory listens to, lapsing so low,
　Under the shade of the trees ?

Nay—though the rasp of the flesh was so sore,
　Faith, that had yearnings far keener than these,
Saw the soft sheen of the Thitherward Shore,
　Under the shade of the trees ;—

Caught the high psalms of ecstatic delight—
  Heard the harps harping, like soundings of seas—
Watched earth's assoiléd ones walking in white
    Under the shade of the trees?

Oh, was it strange he should pine for release,
  Touched to the soul with such transports as these,—
He who so needed the balsam of peace,
    Under the shade of the trees?

Yea, it was noblest for him—it was best
  (Questioning naught of our Father's decrees),
There to pass over the river and rest
    Under the shade of the trees!

                          MARGARET J. PRESTON.

———

THE BLACK REGIMENT.

[Port Hudson, La., June, 1863.]

DARK as the clouds of even,
Ranked in the western heaven,
Waiting the breath that lifts
All the dread mass, and drifts
Tempest and falling brand
Over a ruined land ;—
So still and orderly,
Arm to arm, knee to knee,
Waiting the great event,
Stands the Black Regiment.

Down the long dusky line
Teeth gleam and eyeballs shine ;
And the bright bayonet,
Bristling and firmly set,
Flashed with a purpose grand,
Long ere the sharp command

Of the fierce rolling drum
Told them their time had come,
Told them what work was sent
For the Black Regiment.

"Now," the flag-sergeant cried,
"Though death and hell betide,
Let the whole nation see
If we are fit to be
Free in this land ; or bound
Down, like the whining hound,—
Bound with red stripes of pain
In our old chains again!"
Oh, what a shout there went
From the Black Regiment!

"*Charge!*" Trump and drum awoke,
Onward the bondmen broke ;
Bayonet and sabre-stroke
Vainly opposed their rush.
Through the wild battle's crush,
With but one thought aflush,
Driving their lords like chaff,
In the guns' mouths they laugh ;
Or at the slippery brands
Leaping with open hands,
Down they tear man and horse,
Down in their awful course ;
Trampling with bloody heel
Over the crashing steel,
All their eyes forward bent,
Rushed the Black Regiment.

"Freedom!" their battle-cry—
"Freedom ! or leave to die !"
Ah ! and they meant the word,
Not as with us 'tis heard,
Not a mere party shout :
They gave their spirits out ;

Trusted the end to God,
And on the gory sod
Rolled in triumphant blood.

Glad to strike one free blow,
Whether for weal or woe ;
Glad to breathe one free breath,
Though on the lips of death.
Praying—alas ! in vain !—
That they might fall again,
So they could once more see
That burst to liberty !
This was what " freedom" lent
To the Black Regiment.

Hundreds on hundreds fell ;
But they are resting well ;
Scourges and shackles strong
Never shall do them wrong.

Oh, to the living few,
Soldiers, be just and true !
Hail them as comrades tried ;
Fight with them side by side ;
Never, in field or tent,
Scorn the Black Regiment.

                         GEORGE H. BOKER.

A NAMELESS GRAVE.

"A SOLDIER of the Union mustered out,"
Is the inscription on an unknown grave
At Newport News, beside the salt-sea wave,
Nameless and dateless ; sentinel or scout
Shot down in skirmish, or disastrous rout
Of battle, when the loud artillery drave
Its iron wedges through the ranks of brave
And doomed battalions, storming the redoubt.

Thou unknown hero sleeping by the sea
In thy forgotten grave ! with secret shame
I feel my pulses beat, my forehead burn,
When I remember thou hast given for me
All that thou hadst, thy life, thy very name,
And I can give thee nothing in return.

HENRY WADSWORTH LONGFELLOW.

MISSING.

IN the cool sweet hush of a wooded nook,
   Where the May-buds sprinkle the green old
     mound,
And the winds and the birds and the limpid brook
   Murmur their dreams with a drowsy sound,
Who lies so still in the plushy moss,
   With his pale cheek pressed on a breezy pillow,
Couched where the lights and the shadows cross
   Through the flickering fringe of the willow,—
      Who lies, alas !
So still, so chill, in the whispering grass ?

A soldier, clad in the Zouave dress,
   A bright-haired man, with his lips apart,—
One hand thrown up o'er his frank, dead face,
   And the other clutching his pulseless heart,—
Lies there in the shadows cool and dim,
   His musket swept by a trailing bough,
With a careless grace in each tranquil limb,
   And a wound in his manly brow—
      A wound, alas !
Whence the warm blood drips in the quiet grass.

And the violets peer from their dusky beds,
   With a tearful dew in their great pure eyes ;
And the lilies quiver their shining heads,
   Their pale lips full of a sad surprise ;

And the lizard darts through the glistening fern,
  And the squirrel rustles the branches hoary,
Strange birds fly out with a cry, to bathe
    Their wings in the sunset glory ;
        While the shadows pass
    O'er the quiet face and the dewy grass.

God pity the bride who waits at home
  With her lily cheeks and her violet eyes,
Dreaming the sweet old dream of love,
  While her lover is walking in Paradise.
God strengthen her heart as the days go by,
  And the long, drear nights of her vigil follow ;
Nor bird nor wind nor whispering grass
  May breathe the tale of the hollow :
        Alas ! alas !
  The secret is safe in the woodland grass.

                      ANONYMOUS (*Southern*).

SOMEBODY'S DARLING.

INTO a ward of the whitewashed halls
  Where the dead and the dying lay,
Wounded by bayonets, shells, and balls,
  Somebody's darling was borne one day—
Somebody's darling, so young and brave ;
  Wearing yet on his sweet pale face—
Soon to be hid in the dust of the grave—
  The lingering light of his boyhood's grace.

Matted and damp are the curls of gold
  Kissing the snow of that fair young brow,
Pale are the lips of delicate mould—
  Somebody's darling is dying now.
Back from his beautiful blue-veined brow
  Brush his wandering waves of gold ;
Cross his hands on his bosom now—
  Somebody's darling is still and cold.

Kiss him once for somebody's sake,
  Murmur a prayer soft and low ;
One bright curl from its fair mates take—
  They were somebody's pride, you know.
Somebody's hand hath rested here—
  Was it a mother's, soft and white ?
Or have the lips of a sister fair
  Been baptized in their waves of light ?

God knows best. He has somebody's love,
  Somebody's heart enshrined him there,
Somebody wafts his name above,
  Night and morn, on the wings of prayer.
Somebody wept when he marched away,
  Looking so handsome, brave, and grand ;
Somebody's kiss on his forehead lay,
  Somebody clung to his parting hand.

Somebody's watching and waiting for him,
  Yearning to hold him again to her heart ;
And there he lies with his blue eyes dim,
  And the smiling, childlike lips apart.
Tenderly bury the fair young dead—
  Pausing to drop on his grave a tear.
Carve on the wooden slab o'er his head :
  " Somebody's darling slumbers here."
          MARIA LA COSTE (*Southern*).

" HE'LL SEE IT WHEN HE WAKES."

[*In one of the battles in Virginia, a gallant young Missis-
sippian had fallen ; and at night, just before burying him,
there came a letter from his betrothed. One of the burial-
group took the letter and laid it upon the breast of the dead
soldier, with the words : " Bury it with him. He'll see it
when he wakes."*]

AMID the clouds of battle-smoke
  The sun had died away,
And where the storm of battle broke
  A thousand warriors lay.

A band of friends upon the field
  Stood round a youthful form,
Who, when the war-cloud's thunder pealed,
  Had perished in the storm.
      Upon his forehead, on his hair,
        The coming moonlight breaks,
      And each dear brother standing there
        A tender farewell takes.

But ere they laid him in his home
  There came a comrade near,
And gave a token that had come
  From her the dead held dear.
A moment's doubt upon them pressed,
  Then one the letter takes,
And lays it low upon his breast—
  "He'll see it when he wakes."
      O thou who dost in sorrow wait,
        Whose heart with anguish breaks,
      Though thy dear message came too late,
        " He'll see it when he wakes."

No more amid the fiery storm
  Shall his strong arm be seen ;
No more his young and manly form
  Tread Mississippi's green ;
And e'en thy tender words of love—
  The words affection speaks—
Came all too late ; but oh ! thy love
  " Will see them when he wakes."
      No jars disturb his gentle rest,
        No noise his slumber breaks,
      But thy words sleep upon his breast—
        " He'll see them when he wakes."

FRANK LEE.

A GEORGIA VOLUNTEER.

FAR up the lonely mountain-side
  My wandering footsteps led ;
The moss lay thick beneath my feet,
  The pine sighed overhead.
The trace of a dismantled fort
  Lay in the forest nave,
And in the shadow near my path
  I saw a soldier's grave.

The bramble wrestled with the weed
  Upon the lowly mound,
The simple headboard, rudely writ,
  Had rotted to the ground ;
I raised it with a reverent hand,
  From dust its words to clear ;
But time had blotted all but these :
  " A Georgia Volunteer."

I saw the toad and scaly snake
  From tangled covert start,
And hide themselves among the weeds
  Above the dead man's heart ;
But undisturbed, in sleep profound,
  Unheeding, there he lay ;
His coffin but the mountain soil,
  His shroud, Confederate gray.

I heard the Shenandoah roll
  Along the vale below,
I saw the Alleghanies rise
  Toward the realms of snow.
The "Valley Campaign" rose to mind—
  Its leader's name—and then
I knew the sleeper had been one
  Of Stonewall Jackson's men.

Yet whence he came, what lip shall say—
  Whose tongue will ever tell
What desolated hearths and hearts
  Have been because he fell ?
What sad-eyed maiden braids her hair—
  Her hair which he held dear ?
One lock of which, perchance, lies with
  The Georgia Volunteer !

What mother, with long-watching eyes
  And white lips cold and dumb,
Waits with appalling patience for
  Her darling boy to come ?
Her boy ! whose mountain grave swells up
  But one of many a scar
Cut on the face of our fair land
  By gory-handed war.

What fights he fought, what wounds he wore,
  Are all unknown to fame ;
Remember, on his lonely grave
  There is not even a name !
That he fought well and bravely too,
  And held his country dear,
We know, else he had never been
  A Georgia Volunteer.

He sleeps—what need to question now
  If he were wrong or right ?
He knows, e'er this, whose cause was just
  In God the Father's sight.
He wields no warlike weapons now,
  Returns no foeman's thrust ;
Who but a coward would revile
  An honest soldier's dust ?

Roll, Shenandoah, proudly roll
  Adown thy rocky glen ;
Above thee lies the grave of one
  Of Stonewall Jackson's men.

Beneath the cedar and the pine,
  In solitude austere,
Unknown, unnamed, forgotten, lies
  A Georgia Volunteer.
MARY ASHLEY TOWNSEND.

BY THE POTOMAC.

THE soft new grass is creeping o'er the graves
By the Potomac ; and the crisp ground-flower
Lifts its blue cup to catch the passing shower ;
The pine-cone ripens, and the long moss waves
Its tangled gonfalons above our braves.
Hark, what a burst of music from yon bower !—
The Southern nightingale that, hour by hour,
In its melodious summer madness raves.
Ah, with what delicate touches of her hand,
With what sweet voices, Nature seeks to screen
The awful Crime of this distracted land,—
Sets her birds singing, while she spreads her green
Mantle of velvet where the Murdered lie,
As if to hide the horror from God's eye.
THOMAS BAILEY ALDRICH.

THE VOICES OF THE GUNS.

WITHIN a green and shadowy wood,
Circled with Spring, alone I stood :
The nook was peaceful, fair, and good.

The wild-plum blossoms lured the bees,
The birds sang madly in the trees,
Magnolia scents were on the breeze.

All else was silent ; but the ear
Caught sounds of distant bugle clear,
And heard the bullets whistle near,—

When from the winding river's shore
The Rebel guns began to roar,
And ours to answer, thundering o'er ;

And, echoed from the wooded hill,
Repeated and repeated still,
Through all my soul they seemed to thrill ;

For, as their rattling storm awoke,
And loud and fast the discord broke,
In rude and trenchant *words* they spoke :

" *We hate !*" boomed fiercely o'er the tide ;
"We fear not !" from the other side ;
" *We strike !*" the Rebel guns replied.

Quick roared our answer : " We defend !"
" *Our rights !*" the battle-sounds contend ;
" The rights of all !" we answer send.

" *We conquer !*" rolled across the wave ;
" We persevere !" our answer gave ;
" *Our chivalry !*" they wildly rave.

" *Ours are the brave !*"   " Be ours the free !"
" *Be ours the slave, the masters we !*"
" On us their blood no more shall be !"

As when some magic word is spoken
By which a wizard spell is broken,
There was a silence at that token.

The wild birds dared once more to sing,
I heard the pine bough's whispering,
And trickling of a silver spring.

Then, crashing forth with smoke and din,
Once more the rattling sounds begin ;
Our iron lips roll forth : " We win !"

And dull and wavering in the gale
That rushed in gusts across the vale
Came back the faint reply : " *We fail !*"

And then a word, both stern and sad,
From throat of huge Columbiad :
" Blind fools and traitors !   Ye are mad !"

Again the Rebel answer came,
Muffled and slow, as if in shame :
" *All, all is lost !*" in smoke and flame.

Now bold and strong and stern as Fate
The Union guns sound forth : " We wait !"
Faint comes the distant cry : " *Too late !*"

" Return, return !" our cannon said ;
And, as the smoke rolled overhead,
" *We dare not !*" was the answer dread.

Then came a sound both loud and clear,
A Godlike word of hope and cheer :
" Forgiveness !" echoed far and near ;

As when beside some death-bed still
We watch, and wait God's solemn will,
A bluebird warbles his soft trill.

I clenched my teeth at that blest word,
And, angry, muttered, " Not so, Lord !
The only answer is the sword !"

I thought of Shiloh's tainted air,
Of Richmond's prisons, foul and bare,
And murdered heroes, young and fair,—

Of block and lash and overseer,
And dark, mild faces pale with fear,
Of baying hell-hounds panting near.

But then the gentle story told
My childhood in the days of old
Rang out its lessons manifold.

O prodigal and lost ! arise,
And read the welcome blest that lies
In a kind Father's patient eyes !

Thy elder brother grudges not
The lost and found should share his lot,
And wrong in concord be forgot.

Thus mused I, as the hours went by,
Till the relieving guard drew nigh,
And there was challenge and reply.

And as I hastened back to line,
It seemed an omen half divine
That " Concord " was the countersign.

ANONYMOUS.

MUSIC IN CAMP.

Two armies covered hill and plain,
  Where Rappahannock's waters
Ran deeply crimsoned with the stain
  Of battle's recent slaughters.

The summer clouds lay pitched like tents
  In meads of heavenly azure ;
And each dread gun of the elements
  Slept in its high embrasure.

The breeze so softly blew, it made
  No forest leaf to quiver ;
And the smoke of the random cannonade
  Rolled slowly from the river.

And now where circling hills looked down
  With cannon grimly planted,
O'er listless camp and silent town
  The golden sunset slanted.

When on the fervid air there came
  A strain, now rich, now tender ;
The music seemed itself aflame
  With day's departing splendor.

A Federal band, which eve and morn
  Played measures brave and nimble,
Had just struck up with flute and horn
  And lively clash of cymbal.

Down flocked the soldiers to the banks ;
  Till, margined by its pebbles,
One wooded shore was blue with " Yanks,"
  And one was gray with " Rebels."

Then all was still ; and then the band,
  With movement light and tricksy,
Made stream and forest, hill and strand,
  Reverberate with " Dixie."

The conscious stream, with burnished glow,
  Went proudly o'er its pebbles,
But thrilled throughout its deepest flow
  With yelling of the Rebels.

Again a pause ; and then again
  The trumpet pealed sonorous,
And " Yankee Doodle" was the strain
  To which the shore gave chorus.

The laughing ripple shoreward flew
  To kiss the shining pebbles ;
Loud shrieked the swarming Boys in Blue
  Defiance to the Rebels.

And yet once more the bugle sang
  Above the stormy riot ;
No shout upon the evening rang—
  There reigned a holy quiet.

The sad, slow stream, its noiseless flood
  Poured o'er the glistening pebbles ;
All silent now the Yankees stood,
  All silent stood the Rebels.

No unresponsive soul had heard
  That plaintive note's appealing,
So deeply " Home, Sweet Home " had stirred
  The hidden founts of feeling.

Or Blue, or Gray, the soldier sees,
  As by the wand of fairy,
The cottage 'neath the live oak trees,
  The cabin by the prairie.

Or cold, or warm, his native skies
  Bend in their beauty o'er him ;
Seen through the tear-mist in his eyes,
  His loved ones stand before him.

As fades the iris after rain
  In April's tearful weather,
The vision vanished as the strain
  And daylight died together.

But Memory, waked by Music's art,
  Expressed in simple numbers,
Subdued the sternest Yankee's heart,
  Made light the Rebel's slumbers.

And fair the form of Music shines—
  That bright celestial creature—
Who still 'mid War's embattled lines
  Gave this one touch of Nature.

JOHN R. THOMPSON.

U. S. SANITARY COMMISSION WORK.

(See page 185 — "How are you, Sanitary?")

"HOW ARE YOU, SANITARY?"

[*The U. S. Sanitary Commission was a benevolent organization, supported by contributions from the Northern States, which did most efficient work for the soldiers in field and hospital, sending its trained nurses and supplies of medicines and food wherever there was sickness or suffering.*]

DOWN the picket-guarded lane
Rolled the comfort-laden wain,
Cheered by shouts that shook the plain,
    Soldier-like and merry :
Phrases such as camps may teach,
Sabre-cuts of Saxon speech,
Such as " Bully !" " Them's the peach !"
    " Wade in, Sanitary !"

Right and left the caissons drew
As the car went lumbering through,
Quick succeeding in review
    Squadrons military ;
Sunburnt men with beards like frieze,
Smooth-faced boys, and cries like these :
" U. S. San. Com." " That's the cheese !'
    " Pass in, Sanitary !"

In such cheer it struggled on
Till the battle front was won ;
Then the car, its journey done,
    Lo ! was stationary ;
And where bullets whistling fly
Came the sadder, fainter cry :
" Help us, brothers, ere we die !—
    Save us, Sanitary !"

Such the work. The phantom flies,
Wrapped in battle-clouds that rise ;
But the brave—whose dying eyes,
    Veiled and visionary,

See the jasper gates swung wide,
See the parted throng outside—
Hears the voice to those who ride:
" Pass in, Sanitary !"
                              BRET HARTE.

GETTYSBURG.

[*July* 1, 2, *and* 3, 1863.]

WAVE, wave your glorious battle-flags, brave sol-
    diers of the North,
And from the field your arms have won to-day go
    proudly forth !
For now, O comrades dear and leal—from whom
    no ills could part,
Through the long years of hopes and fears, the
    nation's constant heart—
Men who have driven so oft the foe, so oft have
    striven in vain,
Yet ever in the perilous hour have crossed his path
    again,—
At last we have our heart's desire, from them we
    met have wrung
A victory that round the world shall long be told
    and sung !
It was the memory of the past that bore us through
    the fray,
That gave the grand old Army strength to conquer
    on this day !

Oh, now forget how dark and red Virginia's rivers
    flow,
The Rappahannock's tangled wilds, the glory and
    the woe ;

The fever-hung encampments, where our dying
    knew full sore
How sweet the north-wind to the cheek it soon shall
    cool no more ;
The fields we fought, and gained, and lost ; the
    lowland sun and rain
That wasted us, that bleached the bones of our
    unburied slain !
There was no lack of foes to meet, of deaths to die
    no lack,
And all the hawks of heaven learned to follow on
    our track ;
But henceforth, hovering southward, their flight
    shall mark afar
The paths of yon retreating hosts that shun the
    northern star.

At night, before the closing fray, when all the front
    was still,
We lay in bivouac along the cannon-crested hill.
Ours was the dauntless Second Corps ; and many a
    soldier knew
How sped the fight, and sternly thought of what
    was yet to do.
Guarding the centre there, we lay, and talked with
    bated breath
Of Buford's stand beyond the town, of gallant
    Reynolds' death,
Of cruel retreats through pent-up streets by mur-
    derous valleys swept,—
How well the Stone, the Iron, brigades their bloody
    outposts kept :
'Twas for the Union, for the Flag, they perished,
    heroes all,
And we swore to conquer in the end, or even like
    them to fall.

And passed from mouth to mouth the tale of that
    grim day just done,

The fight by Round Top's craggy spur—of all the
    deadliest one ;
It saved the left : but on the right they pressed us
    back too well,
And like a field in Spring the ground was ploughed
    with shot and shell.
There was the ancient graveyard, its hummocks
    crushed and red,
And there, between them, side by side, the wounded
    and the dead :
The mangled corpses fallen above—the peaceful
    dead below,
Laid in their graves, to slumber here, a score of
    years ago ;
It seemed their waking, wandering shades were
    asking of our slain,
What brought such hideous tumult now where they
    so still had lain !

Bright rose the sun of Gettysburg that morrow
    morning-tide,
And call of trump and roll of drum from height to
    height replied.
Hark ! from the east already goes up the rattling
    din ;
The Twelfth Corps, winning back their ground,
    right well the day begin !
They whirl fierce Ewell from their front ! Now we
    of the Second pray,
As right and left the brunt have borne, the centre
    might to-day.
But all was still from hill to hill for many a breath-
    less hour,
While for the coming battle-shock Lee gathered
    in his power ;
And back and forth our leaders rode, who knew not
    rest or fear,
And along the lines, where'er they came, went up
    the ringing cheer.

'Twas past the hour of nooning ; the Summer skies
    were blue ;
Behind the covering timber the foe was hid from
    view ;
So fair and sweet with waving wheat the pleasant
    valley lay,
It brought to mind our Northern homes and mead-
    ows far away ;
When the whole western ridge at once was fringed
    with fire and smoke,
Against our lines from sevenscore guns the dread-
    ful tempest broke !
Then loud our batteries answer, and far along the
    crest,
And to and fro the roaring bolts are driven east
    and west ;
Heavy and dark around us glooms the stifling sul-
    phur-cloud,
And the cries of mangled men and horse go up
    beneath its shroud.

The guns are still: the end is nigh : we grasp our
    arms anew ;
O now let every heart be stanch and every aim be
    true !
For look ! from yonder wood that skirts the valley's
    further marge,
The flower of all the Southern host move to the final
    charge.
By Heaven ! it is a fearful sight to see their double
    rank
Come with a hundred battle-flags — a mile from
    flank to flank !
Tramping the grain to earth, they come, ten thou-
    sand men abreast ;
Their standards wave—their hearts are brave—
    they hasten not, nor rest,
But close the gaps our cannon make, and onward
    press, and nigher,

And, yelling at our very front, again pour in their
  fire !

Now burst our sheeted lightnings forth, now all
  our wrath has vent !
They die, they wither ; through and through their
  wavering lines are rent.
But these are gallant, desperate men, of our own
  race and land,
Who charge anew, and welcome death, and fight
  us hand to hand :
Vain, vain ! give way, as well ye may—the crimson
  die is cast !
Their bravest leaders bite the dust, their strength
  is failing fast ;
They yield, they turn, they fly the field : we smite
  them as they run ;
Their arms, their colors, are our spoil ; the furious
  fight is done !
Across the plain we follow far and backward push
  the fray :
Cheer ! cheer ! the grand old Army at last has won
  the day !

Hurrah ! the day has won the cause ! No gray-
  clad host henceforth
Shall come with fire and sword to tread the high-
  ways of the North !
'Twas such a flood as when ye see, along the
  Atlantic shore,
The great Spring-tide roll grandly in with swelling
  surge and roar :
It seems no wall can stay its leap or balk its wild
  desire
Beyond the bound that Heaven hath fixed to higher
  mount, and higher ;
But now, when whitest lifts its crest, most loud its
  billows call,
Touched by the Power that led them on, they fall,
  and fall, and fall.

Even thus, unstayed upon his course, to Gettysburg
the foe
His legions led, and fought, and fled, and might no
further go.

Full many a dark-eyed Southern girl shall weep her
lover dead ;
But with a price the fight was ours—we too have
tears to shed !
The bells that peal our triumph forth anon shall
toll the brave,
Above whose heads the cross must stand, the hill-
side grasses wave !
Alas ! alas ! the trampled grass shall thrive another
year,
The blossoms on the apple-boughs with each new
Spring appear,
But when our patriot-soldiers fall, Earth gives them
up to God ;
Though their souls rise in clearer skies, their forms
are as the sod ;
Only their names and deeds are ours—but, for a
century yet,
The dead who fell at Gettysburg the land shall not
forget.

God send us peace ! and where for aye the loved
and lost recline
Let fall, O South, your leaves of palm—O North,
your sprigs of pine !
But when, with every ripened year, we keep the
harvest-home,
And to the dear Thanksgiving-feast our sons and
daughters come—
When children's children throng the board in the
old homestead spread,
And the bent soldier of these wars is seated at the
head,
Long, long the lads shall listen to hear the gray-
beard tell

Of those who fought at Gettysburg and stood their
　　ground so well :
" 'Twas for the Union and the Flag," the veteran
　　shall say,
" Our grand old Army held the ridge, and won
　　that glorious day !"

Edmund Clarence Stedman.

AT GETTYSBURG.

Like a furnace of fire blazed the midsummer sun,
　　When to saddle we leaped at the order,
Spurred on by the boom of the deep-throated gun
　　That told of the foe on our border.
A mist in our rear lay Antietam's dark plain,
　　And thoughts of its carnage came o'er us ;
But smiling beyond surged the fields of ripe grain,
　　And we swore none should reap it before us.

That night, with the ensign who rode by my side,
　　On the camp's dreary edge I stood picket,
Our ears intent lest every wind-rustle hide
　　A foe's stealthy tread in the thicket ;
And there, while we watched the first arrows of
　　dawn
　　Through the veil of the rising mists quiver,
He told how the foeman had closed in upon
　　His home by the Tennessee River.

He spoke of a sire in his weakness cut down,
　　With his last breath the traitor-flag scorning ;
And his brow with the memory grew dark with a
　　frown
　　That paled the red light of the morning.

For days he had followed the cowardly band ;
  And, when one lagged to forage or trifle,
Had seared in his forehead the deep Minié brand,
  And scored a fresh notch in his rifle.

But *one* of the rangers had cheated his fate—
  For him he would search the world over :
Such cool-plotting passion, such keenness of hate,
  Ne'er saw I in woman-scorned lover.
Oh, who would have thought that beneath those
    dark curls
  Lurked vengeance as sure as death-rattle ;
Or fancied those dreamy eyes, soft as a girl's,
  Could light with the fury of battle ?

To horse ! pealed the bugle, while grape-shot and
    shell
  Overhead through the forest were crashing ;
A cheer for the flag—and the summer light fell
  On the blades from a thousand sheaths flashing.
As mad ocean-waves to the storm-revel flock,
  So on we dashed, heedless of dangers ;
A moment our long line surged back at the shock,
  Then swept through the ranks of the Rangers.

I looked for the ensign.   Ahead of his troop,
  Pressing on through the conflict infernal,
His torn flag furled round him in festoon and loop,
  He spurred to the side of his colonel.
And his clear voice rang out, as I saw his bright
    sword
  Through shako and gaudy plume shiver,
With, " This for the last of the murderous horde !"
  And, " This for the home by the river !"

At evening, returned from pursuit of the foe,
  By a shell-shattered caisson we found him ;
And we buried him there in the sunset's red glow,
  With the dear old flag knotted around him.

Yet how could we mourn, when each drum's
  muffled strain
Told of foemen hurled back in disorder,—
When we knew the North reaped her rich harvest
  of grain,
Unharmed by a foe on her border!

ANONYMOUS.

JOHN BURNS OF GETTYSBURG.

[*A Union officer who was with the Eleventh Corps in the
battle of Gettysburg says : " During the first day's fight
an old man in a swallow-tailed coat and battered cylinder
hat came stalking across the fields from the town, and
made his appearance at Colonel Stone's position. With a
musket in his hand and ammunition in his pocket, this ven-
erable citizen asked Colonel Wister's permission to fight.
Wister directed him to go over to the Iron Brigade, where
he would be sheltered by the woods ; but the old man in-
sisted on going forward to the skirmish-line. He was al-
lowed to do so, and continued firing until the skirmishers
retired, when he was the last man to leave. He afterward
fought with the Iron Brigade, where he was three times
wounded. This patriotic and heroic citizen was Constable
John Burns of Gettysburg."*]

HAVE you heard the story that gossips tell
Of Burns of Gettysburg ?— No ? Ah, well :
Brief is the glory that hero earns,
Briefer the story of poor John Burns ;
He was the fellow who won renown—
The only man who didn't back down
When the rebels rode through his native town ;
But held his own in the fight next day,
When all his townsfolk ran away.
That was in July, sixty-three,—
The very day that General Lee,
Flower of Southern chivalry,
Baffled and beaten, backward reeled
From a stubborn Meade and a barren field.

I might tell how, but the day before,
John Burns stood at his cottage-door,
Looking down the village street,
Where, in the shade of his peaceful vine,
He heard the low of his gathered kine,
And felt their breath with incense sweet ;
Or, I might say, when the sunset burned
The old farm gable, he thought it turned
The milk that fell like a babbling flood
Into the milk-pail, red as blood ;
Or, how he fancied the hum of bees
Were bullets buzzing among the trees.
But all such fanciful thoughts as these
Were strange to a practical man like Burns,
Who minded only his own concerns,
Troubled no more by fancies fine
Than one of his calm-eyed, long-tailed kine,—
Quite old-fashioned and matter-of-fact,
Slow to argue, but quick to act.
That was the reason, as some folk say,
He fought so well on that terrible day.

And it was terrible.   On the right
Raged for hours the heady fight,
Thundered the battery's double bass—
Difficult music for men to face ;
While on the left—where now the graves
Undulate like the living waves
That all the day unceasing swept
Up to the pits the rebels kept—
Round-shot ploughed the upland glades,
Sown with bullets, reaped with blades ;
Shattered fences here and there,
Tossed their splinters in the air ;
The very trees were stripped and bare ;
The barns that once held yellow grain
Were heaped with harvests of the slain ;
The cattle bellowed on the plain,
The turkeys screamed with might and main,

And brooding barn-fowl left their rest
With strange shells bursting in each nest.

Just where the tide of battle turns,
Erect and lonely, stood old John Burns.
How do you think the man was dressed?
He wore an ancient, long buff vest,
Yellow as saffron—but his best ;
And buttoned over his manly breast
Was a bright blue coat with a rolling collar,
And large gilt buttons—size of a dollar,—
With tails that the country-folk called " swaller."
He wore a broad-brimmed, bell-crowned hat,
White as the locks on which it sat.
Never had such a sight been seen
For forty years on the village green,
Since old John Burns was a country beau,
And went to the " quiltings " long ago.

Close at his elbows all that day
Veterans of the Peninsula,
Sunburnt and bearded, charged away ;
And striplings, downy of lip and chin,—
Clerks that the Home-Guard mustered in,—
Glanced, as they passed, at the hat he wore,
Then at the rifle his right hand bore ;
And hailed him, from out their youthful lore,
With scraps of a slangy *répertoire :*
" How are you, White Hat ?" " Put her through !"
" Your head's level !" and " Bully for you !"
Called him, ' Daddy,''—begged he'd disclose
The name of the tailor who made his clothes,
And what was the value he set on those ;
While Burns, unmindful of jeer and scoff,
Stood there picking the rebels off—
With his long brown rifle and bell-crown hat,
And the swallow-tails they were laughing at.

'Twas but a moment, for that respect
Which clothes all courage their voices checked ;

And something the wildest could understand
Spake in the old man's strong right hand,
And his corded throat, and the lurking frown
Of his eyebrows under his old bell-crown ;
Until, as they gazed, there crept an awe
Through the ranks in whispers, and some men saw,
In the antique vestments and long white hair,
The Past of the Nation in battle there ;
And some of the soldiers since declare
That the gleam of his old white hat afar,
Like the crested plume of the brave Navarre,
That day was their oriflamme of war.

Thus raged the battle.   You know the rest ;
How the rebels, beaten, and backward pressed,
Broke at the final charge and ran.
At which John Burns—a practical man—
Shouldered his rifle, unbent his brows,
And then went back to his bees and cows.

That is the story of old John Burns ;
This is the moral the reader learns :
In fighting the battle, the question's whether
You'll show a hat that's white, or a feather.

BRET HARTE.

READING THE LIST.

" Is there any news of the war ?" she said.
" Only a list of the wounded and dead,"
        Was the man's reply,
        Without lifting his eye
        To the face of the woman standing by.
" 'Tis the very thing I want," she said ;
" Read me a list of the wounded and dead."
He read the list—'twas a sad array
Of the wounded and killed in the fatal fray.

In the very midst, was a pause to tell
Of a gallant youth who fought so well
That his comrades asked : " Who is he, pray ?"
" The only son of the Widow Gray,"
        Was the proud reply
        Of his Captain nigh . . . .
What ails the woman standing near ?
Her face has the ashen hue of fear !

" Well, well, read on ; is he wounded ?   Quick !
O God ! but my heart is sorrow-sick !
    Is he wounded ?"   " No ; he fell, they say,
    Killed outright on that fatal day !"
    But see, the woman has swooned away !

Sadly she opened her eyes to the light ;
Slowly recalled the events of the fight ;
Faintly she murmured : " Killed outright !
    It has cost me the life of my only son ;
    But the battle is fought, and the victory won ;
    The will of the Lord, let it be done !"

God pity the cheerless Widow Gray,
And send from the halls of eternal day
The light of His peace to illumine her way.

                    ANONYMOUS (*Southern*).

———

ROLL-CALL.

"CORPORAL GREEN !" the Orderly cried ;
    " Here !" was the answer, loud and clear,
    From the lips of the soldier who stood near,--
And "Here !" was the word the next replied.

" Cyrus Drew !"—then a silence fell ;
    This time no answer followed the call ;
    Only his rear-man had seen him fall :
Killed or wounded—he could not tell.

There they stood in the failing light,
  These men of battle, with grave, dark looks,
  As plain to be read as open books,
While slowly gathered the shades of night.

The fern on the hillsides was splashed with blood,
  And down in the corn where the poppies grew
  Were redder stains than the poppies knew ;
And crimson-dyed was the river's flood.

For the foe had crossed from the other side
  That day, in the face of a murderous fire
  That swept them down in its terrible ire,
And their life-blood went to color the tide.

" Herbert Kline !" At the call there came
  Two stalwart soldiers into the line,
  Bearing between them this Herbert Kline,
Wounded and bleeding, to answer his name.

" Ezra Kerr !"—and a voice answered, " Here !"
  " Hiram Kerr !"—but no man replied.
  They were brothers, these two ; the sad winds
    sighed,
And a shudder crept through the cornfield near.

" Ephraim Deane !"—then a soldier spoke :
  " Deane carried our regiment's colors," he said ;
  " Where our ensign was shot I left him dead,
Just after the enemy wavered and broke.

" Close to the roadside his body lies ;
  I paused a moment and gave him drink ;
  He murmured his mother's name, I think,
And Death came with it, and closed his eyes."

'Twas a victory ; yes, but it cost us dear,—
  For that company's roll, when called at night,
  Of a hundred men who went into the fight,
Numbered but twenty that answered " Here !"
N. G. SHEPHERD.

BY CHICKAMAUGA RIVER.

AGAIN the wandering breezes bring
   The music of the sheaves ;
Again the crickets chirp and sing
   Among the golden leaves.
Twelve times the Springs have oped the rills,
   Twelve amber Autumns sighed,
Since hung the war-cloud o'er the hills,
   The year that Charlie died.

The Springs return ; the roses blow,
   And croon the bird and bee,
And flutes the ring-dove's love-call low,
   Along the Tennessee ;
But one dear voice, one cherished tone,
   Returns to me—ah, never !
For Charlie fills a grave unknown,
   By Chickamauga River.

Kind Nature sets her blossoms there,
   And fall the vernal rains ;
But we may lay no garlands fair
   Above his loved remains.
A white stone marks an empty grave
   Our household graves beside,
And his dear name to it we gave
   The year that Charlie died.

The winds of Fall were breathing low,
   The swallow left the eaves ;
We heard the hollow bugles blow,
   When fell the harvest sheaves.
And swift the mustering squadrons passed,—
   We thought of Charlie ever,—
And swift the blue brigades were massed
   By Chickamauga River.

Along the mountain spurs we saw
    The wreaths of smoke ascend;
And, all the Sabbath day, in awe,
    We watched the war-cloud blend
With Fall's cerulean sky, and dim
    The wooded mountain side,—
Oh, how our hearts then beat for him,
    The year that Charlie died !

How Thomas thundered past, when broke
    The wavering echelon !
How down the sky in flame and smoke
    Low sunk the copper sun ;
The still night came, and who were saved
    And who were called to sever,
We could not tell ; our banner waved
    By Chickamauga River.

And some returned with happy feet ;
    But never at our door
The fair-haired boy we used to meet
    Came back to greet us more.
But memory seems to hear the fall
    Of steps at eventide,
And all the changing years recall
    The year that Charlie died.

Yet such a gift of God as he
    'Tis blessed to have cherished ;
And they shall ever stainless be
    Who've nobly fought and perished.
He nobly died, and he can know
    No dark dishonor ever ;
But green the grass for him shall **grow**
    By Chickamauga River.

Again I see the mountains blaze
    In Autumn's amber light ;
Again I see in shimmering haze
    The valleys, long and bright.

Old Lookout Mountain towers afar
　As when, in lordly pride,
It plumed its head with flags of war
　The year that Charlie died.

On wooded Mission Ridge increase
　The fruited fields of Fall,
And Chattanooga sleeps in peace
　Beneath her mountain wall.
O Country, free from sea to sea,
　With union blest forever,
Not vainly heroes died for thee
　By Chickamauga River!

HEZEKIAH BUTTERWORTH.

THE BATTLE IN THE CLOUDS.

[" *The day had been one of dense mists and rains, and much of General Hooker's battle was fought above the clouds, on the top of Lookout Mountain.*"—*General Meigs's Report of the Battle before Chattanooga, Nov. 23-25, 1863.*]

WHERE the dews and the rains of heaven have their
　　fountain,
　Like its thunder and its lightning our brave
　　burst on the foe,
Up above the clouds on Freedom's Lookout Moun-
　　tain
　Raining life-blood like water on the valleys
　　down below.
　　O, green be the laurels that grow,
　　O, sweet be the wild-buds that blow,
　In the dells of the mountain where the brave are
　　lying low.

Light of our hope and crown of our story,
  Bright as sunlight, pure as starlight shall their
      deeds of daring glow,
While the day and the night out of heaven shed
      their glory,
  On Freedom's Lookout Mountain whence they
      routed Freedom's foe.
    O, soft be the gales where they go
   Through the pines on the summit where they
      blow,
  Chanting solemn music for the souls that passed
      below.

WILLIAM DEAN HOWELLS.

AFTER ALL.

THE apples are ripe in the orchard,
  The work of the reaper is done,
And the golden woodlands redden
  In the blood of the dying sun.

At the cottage-door the grandsire
  Sits pale in his easy-chair,
While the gentle wind of twilight
  Plays with his silver hair.

A woman is kneeling beside him ;
  A fair young head is pressed,
In the first wild passion of sorrow,
  Against his aged breast.

And far from over the distance
  The faltering echoes come
Of the flying blast of trumpet
  And the rattling roll of drum.

And the grandsire speaks in a whisper:
   " The end no man can see ;
But we give him to his country,
   And we give our prayers to Thee."

The violets star the meadows,
   The rose-buds fringe the door,
And over the grassy orchard
   The pink-white blossoms pour.

But the grandsire's chair is empty,
   The cottage is dark and still ;
There's a nameless grave in the battle-field,
   And a new one under the hill.

And a pallid, tearless woman
   By the cold hearth sits alone ;
And the old clock in the corner
   Ticks on with a steady drone.

                WILLIAM WINTER.

OUR CHRISTMAS HYMN.

"GOOD-WILL and peace, peace and good-will!"
   The burden of the Advent song,
What time the love-charmed waves grew still
   To hearken to the shining throng ;
The wondering shepherds heard the strain
   Who watched by night the slumbering fleece,
The deep skies echoed the refrain,
   " Peace and good-will, good-will and peace!"

And wise men hailed the promised sign,
   And brought their birth-gifts from the East,
Dear to that Mother as the wine
   That hallowed Cana's bridal feast ;

But what to these are myrrh or gold,
　And what Arabia's costliest gem,
Whose eyes the Child divine behold,
　The blessed Babe of Bethlehem.

" Peace and good-will, good-will and peace !"
　They sing, the bright ones overhead ;
And scarce the jubilant anthems cease
　Ere Judah wails her first-born dead ;
And Ramah's wild, despairing cry
　Fills with great dread the shuddering coast,
And Rachel hath but one reply :
　" Bring back, bring back my loved and lost !"

So down two thousand years of doom
　That cry is borne on wailing winds,
But never star breaks through the gloom,
　No cradled peace the watcher finds ;
And still the Herodian steel is driven,
　And breaking hearts make ceaseless moan,
And still the mute appeal to heaven
　Man answers back with groan for groan.

How shall we keep our Christmas-tide,
　With that dread Past, its wounds agape,
Forever walking by our side,
　A fearful shade, an awful shape !
Can any promise of the Spring
　Make green the faded Autumn leaf ?
Or who shall say that time will bring
　Fair fruit to him who sows but grief ?

Wild bells that shake the midnight air
　With those dear tones that custom loves,
You wake no sounds of laughter here,
　Nor mirth in all our silent groves ;
On one broad waste, by hill or flood,
　Of ravaged lands your music falls,
And where the happy homestead stood
　The stars look down on roofless halls.

At every board a vacant chair
　　Fills with quick tears some tender eye,
And at our maddest sports appear
　　Those well-loved forms that will not die.
We lift the glass, our hand is stayed—
　　We jest, a spectre rises up—
And weeping, though no word is said,
　　We kiss and pass the silent cup,

And pledge the gallant friend who keeps
　　His Christmas eve on Malvern's height,
And him, our fair-haired boy, who sleeps
　　Beneath Virginian snows to-night ;
While by the fire she musing broods
　　On all that was and might have been,
If Shiloh's dank and oozing woods
　　Had never drunk that crimson stain.

O happy Yules of buried years !
　　Could ye but come in wonted guise,
Sweet as love's earliest kiss appears
　　When looking back through wistful eyes
Would seem those chimes whose voices tell
　　His birth-night with melodious burst,
Who, sitting by Samaria's well,
　　Quenched the lorn widow's life-long thirst.

Ah ! yet I trust that all who weep,
　　Somewhere, at last, will surely find
His rest, if through dark ways they keep
　　The child-like faith, the prayerful mind ;
And some far Christmas morn shall bring
　　From human ills a sweet release
To loving hearts, while angels sing :
　　" Peace and good-will, good-will and peace !"
　　　　　JOHN DICKSON BRUNS (*Southern*).

NEW YEAR'S EVE.

[Libby Prison, Richmond, Va., December 31, 1863.]

'TIS twelve o'clock ! Within my prison dreary,
My head upon my hand, sitting so weary,
Scanning the future, musing on the past,
Pondering the fate that here my lot has cast,
The hoarse cry of the sentry on his beat
Wakens the echoes of the silent street—
　　　　"*All's well !*"

Ah! is it so ? My fellow-captive sleeping
Where the barred window strictest watch is keeping,
Dreaming of home and wife and prattling child,
Of the sequestered vale, the mountain wild,
Tell me, when cruel morn shall break again,
Wilt thou repeat the sentinel's refrain—
　　　　"*All's well !*"

And thou, my country! Wounded, pale, and
　　bleeding,
Thy children deaf to a fond mother's pleading,
Stabbing with cruel hate the nurturing breast
To which their infancy in love was prest,
Recount thy wrongs, thy many sorrows name,
Then to the nations, if thou canst, proclaim—
　　　　"*All's well !*"

But through the clouds the sun is slowly breaking ;
Hope from her long, deep sleep is re-awaking :
Speed the time, Father ! when the bow of peace,
Spanning the gulf, shall bid the tempest cease,
When foemen, clasping each other by the hand,
Shall shout once more, in a united land—
　　　　"*All's well !*"

　　　　　　　　　　F. A. BARTLESON.

ULRIC DAHLGREN.

[Colonel Ulric Dahlgren, son of Admiral Dahlgren, U. S. Navy, distinguished himself by his dashing exploits with the Army of the Potomac, while serving on the staffs of Generals Sigel, Hooker, and Meade, and lost a leg at Gettysburg. While still on crutches, he led an expedition to free the Union prisoners in Libby Prison at Richmond, and fell in a midnight ambush, March 2, 1864, at the age of twenty-two years.]

A FLASH of light across the night,
    An eager face, an eye afire:
O lad so true, you yet may rue
    The courage of your deep desire !

" Nay, tempt me not ; the way is plain—
'Tis but the coward checks his rein ;
        For there they lie,
        And there they cry
For whose dear sake 'twere joy to die !"

He bends unto his saddle-bow,
    The steeds they follow two and two ;
Their flanks are wet with foam and sweat,
    Their riders' locks are damp with dew.

" O comrades, haste ! the way is long,
The dirge it drowns the battle song ;
        The hunger preys,
        The famine slays,
An awful horror veils our ways !"

Beneath the pall of prison wall
    The rush of hoofs they seem to hear ;
From loathsome guise they lift their eyes,
    And beat their bars and bend their ear.

" Ah, God be thanked ! our friends are nigh ;
He wills it not that thus we die ;
        O fiends accurst
        Of Want and Thirst,
Our comrades gather—do your worst !"

A sharp affright runs through the night,
  An ambush stirred, a column reined ;
The hurrying steed has checked his speed,
  His smoking flanks are crimson-stained.

O noble son of noble sire,
Thine ears are deaf to our desire !
    O knightly grace
    Of valiant race,
Thy grave is honor's trysting-place !

O life so pure ! O faith so sure !
  O heart so brave, and true, and strong !
With tips of flame is writ your name
  In annalled deed and storied song !

It flares across the solemn night,
It glitters in the radiant light ;
    A jewel set,
    Unnumbered yet,
In our Republic's coronet !

                    KATE BROWNLEE SHERWOOD.

OBSEQUIES OF STUART.

[*General J. E. B. Stuart, the famous chief of the Confed-
erate cavalry, fell in an engagement with General Sheri-
dan's forces, at Yellow Tavern, Va., May 12, 1864.*]

WE could not pause, while yet the noon-tide air
  Shook with the cannonade's incessant pealing,
The funeral pageant fitly to prepare—
  A nation's grief revealing.

The smoke, above the glimmering woodland wide
  That skirts our southward border in its beauty,
Marked where our heroes stood and fought and died
  For love and faith and duty.

And still, what time the doubtful strife went on,
  We might not find expression for our sorrow;
We could but lay our dear dumb warrior down,
  And gird us for the morrow.

One weary year agone, when came a lull
  With victory in the conflict's stormy closes,
When the glad Spring, all flushed and beautiful,
  First mocked us with her roses,

With dirge and bell and minute-gun, we paid
  Some few poor rites—an inexpressive token
Of a great people's pain—to Jackson's shade,
  In agony unspoken.

No wailing trumpet and no tolling bell,
  No cannon, save the battle's boom receding,
When Stuart to the grave we bore, might tell,
  With hearts all crushed and bleeding.

The crisis suited not with pomp, and she
  Whose anguish bears the seal of consecration
Had wished his Christian obsequies should be
  Thus void of ostentation.

Only the maidens came, sweet flowers to twine
  Above his form so still and cold and painless,
Whose deeds upon our brightest record shine,
  Whose life and sword were stainless.

They well remembered how he loved to dash
  Into the fight, festooned from summer bowers;
How like a fountain's spray his sabre's flash
  Leaped from a mass of flowers.

And so we carried to his place of rest
  All that of our great Paladin was mortal:
The cross, and not the sabre, on his breast,
  That opes the heavenly portal.

No more of tribute might to us remain ;
   But there will come a time when Freedom's martyrs
A richer guerdon of renown shall gain
      Than gleams in stars and garters.

I hear from out that sunlit land which lies
   Beyond these clouds that gather darkly o'er us,
The happy sounds of industry arise
      In swelling peaceful chorus.

And mingling with these sounds, the glad acclaim
   Of millions undisturbed by war's afflictions,
Crowning each martyr's never-dying name
      With grateful benedictions.

In some fair future garden of delights,
   Where flowers shall bloom and song-birds sweetly
         warble,
Art shall erect the statues of our knights
      In living bronze and marble.

And none of all that bright heroic throng
   Shall wear to far-off time a semblance grander,
Shall still be decked with fresher wreaths of song,
      Than this beloved commander.

The Spanish legend tells us of the Cid,
   That after death he rode erect, sedately,
Along his lines, even as in life he did,
      In presence yet more stately :

And thus our Stuart, at this moment, seems
   To ride out of our dark and troubled story
Into the region of romance and dreams,
      A realm of light and glory ;

And sometimes, when the silver bugles blow,
   That ghostly form, in battle reappearing,
Shall lead his horsemen headlong on the foe,
      In victory careering !

                 JOHN R. THOMPSON.

THE THOUSAND AND THIRTY-SEVEN.

[A full regiment of infantry consists of a thousand men and thirty-seven commissioned officers.]

THREE years ago to-day
    We raised our hands to heaven,
And on the rolls of muster
    Our names were thirty-seven ;
There were just a thousand bayonets,
    And the swords were thirty-seven,
As we took the oath of service
    With our right hands raised to heaven.

Oh, 'twas a gallant day,
    In memory still adored,
That day of our sun-bright nuptials
    With the musket and the sword !
Shrill rang the fifes, the bugles blared,
    And beneath a cloudless heaven
Twinkled a thousand bayonets,
    And the swords were thirty-seven.

Of the thousand stalwart bayonets
    Two hundred march to-day ;
Hundreds lie in Virginia swamps,
    And hundreds in Maryland clay ;
And other hundreds, less happy, drag
    Their shattered limbs around,
And envy the deep, long, blessèd sleep
    Of the battle-field's holy ground.

For the swords—one night, a week ago,
    The remnant, just eleven,
Gathered around a banqueting board
    With seats for thirty-seven ;
There were two limped in on crutches,
    And two had each but a hand
To pour the wine and raise the cup
    As we toasted " Our flag and land !"

And the room seemed filled with whispers,
  As we looked at the vacant seats,
And, with choking throats, we pushed aside
  The rich but untasted meats ;
Then in silence we brimmed our glasses,
  As we rose up—just eleven—
And bowed as we drank to the loved and the dead
  Who had made us thirty-seven !

CHARLES G. HALPINE.

DRIVING HOME THE COWS.

OUT of the clover and blue-eyed grass
  He turned them into the river lane ;
One after another he let them pass,
  Then fastened the meadow bars again.

Under the willows, and over the hill,
  He patiently followed their sober pace ;
The merry whistle for once was still,
  And something shadowed the sunny face.

Only a boy ! and his father had said
  He never could let his youngest go ;
Two already were lying dead
  Under the feet of the trampling foe.

But after the evening work was done,
  And the frogs were loud in the meadow swamp,
Over his shoulder he slung his gun
  And stealthily followed the foot-path damp :

Across the clover and through the wheat,
  With resolute heart and purpose grim,
Though cold was the dew on his hurrying feet,
  And the blind bat's flitting startled him.

Thrice since then had the lanes been white,
  And the orchards sweet with apple-bloom ;
And now, when the cows came back at night,
  The feeble father drove them home.

For news had come to the lonely farm
  That three were lying where two had lain ;
And the old man's tremulous, palsied arm
  Could never lean on a son's again.

The summer day grew cool and late :
  He went for the cows when the work was done ;
But down the lane, as he opened the gate,
  He saw them coming one by one :

Brindle, Ebony, Speckle, and Bess,
  Shaking their horns in the evening wind,
Cropping the buttercups out of the grass ;—
  But who was it following close behind ?

Loosely swung in the idle air
  The empty sleeve of army blue ;
And worn and pale, from the crisping hair,
  Looked out a face that the father knew.

For Southern prisons will sometimes yawn,
  And yield their dead unto life again;
And the day that comes with a cloudy dawn,
  In golden glory at last may wane.

The great tears sprang to their meeting eyes ;
  For the heart must speak when the lips are
      dumb :
And under the silent evening skies
  Together they followed the cattle home.

KATE PUTNAM OSGOOD.

THE SILENT MARCH.

[In one of the campaigns of the Army of Northern Virginia, while General Lee was lying asleep by the wayside an army of fifteen thousand men passed by in silence, anxious not to disturb his rest.]

O'ERCOME with weariness and care,
    The war-worn veteran lay
On the green turf of his native land,
    And slumbered by the way.

The breeze that sighed across his brow,
    And smoothed its deepened lines,
Fresh from his own loved mountains bore
    The murmur of their pines ;

And the glad sound of waters,
    The blue rejoicing streams,
Whose sweet familiar tones were blent
    With the music of his dreams.

They brought no sound of battle's din,
    Shrill fife or clarion,
But only tenderest memories
    Of his own fair Arlington.

While thus the chieftain slumbered,
    Forgetful of his care,
The hollow tramp of thousands
    Came sounding through the air.

With ringing spur and sabre,
    And trampling feet, they come,
Gay plume and rustling banner,
    And fife and trump and drum.

But soon the foremost column
    Sees where, beneath the shade,
In slumber, calm as childhood,
    Their wearied chief is laid.

And down the line a murmur
  From lip to lip there ran,
Until the stilly whisper
  Had spread to rear from van.

And o'er the host a silence
  As deep and sudden fell,
As though some mighty wizard
  Had hushed them with a spell.

And every sound was muffled,
  And every soldier's tread
Fell lightly as a mother's
  'Round her baby's cradle-bed.

And rank and file and column,
  So softly by they swept,
It seemed a ghostly army
  Had passed him as he slept.

But mightier than enchantment
  Was that with magic wove—
The spell that hushed their voices—
  Deep reverence and love.

ANONYMOUS.

LEE TO THE REAR.

[*Founded on an incident in one of the battles of the Wilderness, when General Lee seized the colors of a Texan regiment to lead a charge against a well-nigh impregnable position. The colonel promised to carry the position if Lee would go to the rear; and when the soldiers heard the promise and expostulation, they repeated it, and "Lee to the rear!" was shouted down the line.*]

DAWN of a pleasant morning in May
Broke through the Wilderness cool and gray;
While perched in the tallest tree-tops, the birds
Were carolling Mendelssohn's "Songs without
    words."

Far from the haunts of men remote,
The brook brawled on with a liquid note;
And Nature, all tranquil and lovely, wore
The smile of the spring, as in Eden of yore.

Little by little as daylight increased,
And deepened the roseate flush in the East—
Little by little did morning reveal
Two long glittering lines of steel;

Where two hundred thousand bayonets gleam,
Tipped with the light of the earliest beam,
And the faces are sullen and grim to see
In the hostile armies of Grant and Lee.

All of a sudden, ere rose the sun,
Pealed on the silence the opening gun—
A little white puff of smoke there came,
And anon the valley was wreathed in flame.

Down on the left of the Rebel lines,
Where a breastwork stands in a copse of pines,
Before the Rebels their ranks can form,
The Yankees have carried the place by storm.

Stars and Stripes on the salient wave,
Where many a hero has found a grave,
And the gallant Confederates strive in vain
The ground they have drenched with their blood, to
    regain.

Yet louder the thunder of battle roared—
Yet a deadlier fire on the columns poured;
Slaughter infernal rode with Despair,
Furies twain, through the murky air.

Not far off, in the saddle there sat
A gray-bearded man in a black slouched hat;
Not much moved by the fire was he,
Calm and resolute Robert Lee.

Quick and watchful he kept his eye
On the bold Rebel brigades close by,—
Reserves that were standing (and dying) at ease,
While the tempest of wrath toppled over the trees.

For still with their loud, deep, bull-dog bay,
The Yankee batteries blazed away,
And with every murderous second that sped
A dozen brave fellows, alas ! fell dead.

The grand old graybeard rode to the space
Where Death and his victims stood face to face,
And silently waved his old slouched hat—
A world of meaning there was in that !

" Follow me ! Steady !   We'll save the day !"
This was what he seemed to say ;
And to the light of his glorious eye
The bold brigades thus made reply :

" We'll go forward, but you must go back"—
And they moved not an inch in the perilous track ;
" Go to the rear, and we'll send them to hell !"
And the sound of the battle was lost in their yell.

Turning his bridle, Robert Lee
Rode to the rear.   Like waves of the sea,
Bursting the dikes in their overflow,
Madly his veterans dashed on the foe.

And backward in terror that foe was driven,
Their banners rent and their columns riven,
Wherever the tide of battle rolled
Over the Wilderness, wood and wold.

Sunset out of a crimson sky
Streamed o'er a field of ruddier dye,
And the brook ran on with a purple stain,
From the blood of ten thousand foemen slain.

Seasons have passed since that day and year—
Again o'er its pebbles the brook runs clear,
And the field in a richer green is drest
Where the dead of a terrible conflict rest.

Hushed is the roll of the Rebel drum,
The sabres are sheathed, and the cannon are dumb ;
And Fate, with his pitiless hand, has furled
The flag that once challenged the gaze of the world ;

But the fame of the Wilderness fight abides ;
And down into history grandly rides,
Calm and unmoved as in battle he sat,
The gray-bearded man in the black slouched hat.

JOHN R. THOMPSON.

RUNNING THE BLOCKADE.

A CHASE IN SOUNDINGS.

HOVE in the stays, she lay,
In the blockading grounds
Of the North Carolina sounds,
Beleaguered half a day,
The good ship Heir of Lynn :
The still air shut her in
The very focus of light ;
Where the sea grows hot and white,
As if it had turned to salt
Or solid rock, with a fault
That clipped the horizon's edge
In a long irregular ledge.

In the summer of sixty-three,
As still as they could be
The sea and air ; and every
Spar lost in a revery

Over its shadow, under
The sea, in curious wonder.
Not a cat's-paw turned the streamer,
To spell at it letter by letter;
And for fifty leagues and better,
You could see the smoke of a steamer
Drifting down in the offing.
You could hear the sullen coughing,
Over sixty miles away,
At Wilmington harbor and bay,—
The pounding of cannon and mortar,
And the groan of torpedoes under
The sea, that came over her quarter,
Like the bellow of smothered thunder.

Uneasily looked the master
Now at the sea, and then
Off in a dream again
Of home, as the bo's'n cast her
Dipsy[1] lead in the shallow,
To a sort of nasal tune,
Larded with talk and tallow,
In the bight of the afternoon;
Drawling from sea-worn topics,
To sudden squalls in the tropics;
And lee shores whose hot lips
Had opened and swallowed ships,—
Till the slow talk seemed to pool
In the old Annapolis school;
And the master was "Joe" again,
With his messmate, Geordie of Maine,
Who loved, with loves like his own,
Sweethearts they never had won,—
Like the small blue flowers that live but a day,
Sweet things, in the inlets of Chesapeake Bay.

The skies got bluer and bluer,
Till the far-off gunboat knew her,

---

[1] Deep sea.

And came up, hand over hand,
With a rushing, like falling sand,
Of the coils of her screw propeller,
Like the rifles that twist out her shell, or
The leverage fold and grapple
Of the sinewy boa-constrictor,
While her stem peeled the scum as an apple,
And the plunge of her steam beat the drums of a
    victor.

But, like omens in viscera,
Old Romans sought for ;
As the stars fought with **Sisera,—**
Faster and faster,
And over and past her,
Swirled the cone of the **cyclone and fought her.**

It touched the sails of the **schooner**
The turn of a sandglass sooner ;
And, breaking in sudden bloom,—
From her foretop studding-sail,
Aft to her spanker-boom,
Down to her channel rail,
Fore to her flying jibs ;—
Like a lily when it buds
She flowers out of her ribs,
White as the salt-sea seeds ;
Bobbing about, like a cup.
Then a shout, and the hunt is **up.**

    *   *   *   *   *

" A lee shore and a squall !
There's but one of them all,"
As he steamed within hail,
Said the gunboat commander,
" Of all that I know,
That would dare carry sail
To beach her and land her,—
Annapolis Joe."

As swivels of hail
Beat tattoo on the sail,
And he looked on the sea,
Where tempests unchain
Reefs hid in white rain ;
" You'll want boots to follow me
All night," said the master,
" With your wrought-iron roster,
Old Geordie of Maine."

Ship ahoy ! Heave to !
The wind seemed to wrestle
With steam in the vessel,
Elastic and pliant,
And wrench the propeller
With the strength of a giant,
As if to compel her
To shrink from the danger
Her keel timbers ran on :
But grimly defiant,
And louder and louder,
In the bursting of powder,
Spoke the lips of her cannon.

    *   *   *   *   *

" It's Joe, to be sure,"
Said the naval commander,
" And he's got a king's ransom of stores in his keel ;
I'll sink her, or land her
Rawbones on a lee shore,
To feed the Sound fishes on his powder and steel."

A reef rose between,
Where the keel of the sea seemed to jib and careen,
And pitch on its beam ends,
About which the water ran smooth with vehemence,
Like the gates of a lock when its hinges are swung.
And the bore of the current shoots out in a tongue,
But, taut and close-lasted,
From keelson to masthead ;

Spanker vangs to spritsail-yards,
And flying jib-boom,
As true to her halyards
As belle of the room
When her feet, to the click of the castanets clip-
    ping,
Make rhymes to the music's adagios tripping,—
As dangerously quick as Herodias' daughter,—
While the wind kissed her lacings and whipped
    round her quarter,
And pitch-piped its bagpipes as shrill as a demon,
The sloop felt her tiller ;
Double banked her propeller ;
And rushed at the sluice with a full head of steam on.

       *   *   *   *   *

But the fugitive ship,
Like a wild thing at bay,
That will double and slip
From corner to panel,
Like a fox, stole away.
The nips of the channel,
In shoulder and knee,
Seemed to rise and bend over **her;**
The bellowing sea,
To open and cover her ;
And where the surf plunges
Through coral and sponges
In slings of the wind as light as a feather,
To rove the blue phosphorous frost in her shrouds,
The burst of the clouds
Mixed the sea and the sand and the sky altogether,
And the welkin cracked open with terrible bright-
    ening,
Till the bed of the sea seemed to bristle with light-
    ning ;
And over, and under
The clamor of waves, pealed the toll of the thunder.

       *   *   *   *   *

So, all through the night, in the darkness they
    grope.
In the wash of the water, and swish of the spray,
Clung the sloop to the chase, as if towed by a rope,
Till the morning gun slipped it, at breaking of day.
Tira la, sang the bugles—*a fox stole away !*
Stole away ; stole away : stole away ; stole away :
Tira la, sang the bugles—*a fox stole away !*

In Wilmington town there's a ringing of bells
As the people go down, to see her come in,
With her flag at the forepeak, as every one tells
Of the old ballad luck of the ship Heir of Lynn.

If you ever meet Josey, or Geordie of Maine,
You will run the chase over in soundings again.

                        WILL WALLACE HARNEY.

————

THE ALABAMA.

[*Sunk in the harbor of Cherbourg, France, by the United
States Steamer Kearsarge, June* 19, 1864.]

SHE has gone to the bottom ! the wrath of the tide
    Now breaks in vain insolence o'er her ;
No more the rough seas like a queen shall she ride,
    While the foe flies in terror before her !

Now captive or exiled, or silent in death,
    The forms that so bravely did man her ;
Her deck is untrod, and the gale's stirring breath
    Flouts no more the red cross of her banner !

She is down 'neath the waters, but still her bright
        name
    Is in death, as in life, ever glorious,
And a sceptre all barren the conqueror must claim,
    Though he boasts the proud title " Victorious."

Her country's lone champion, she shunned not the
    fight,
  Though unequal in strength, bold and fearless ;
And proved in her fate, though not matchless in
    might,
  In daring at least she was peerless.

No trophy hung high in the foe's hated hall
  Shall speak of her final disaster,
Nor tell of the danger that could not appall,
  Nor the spirit that nothing could master !

The death-shot has sped—she has grimly gone
    down,
  But left her destroyer no token,
And the mythical wand of her mystic renown,
  Though the waters o'erwhelm, is unbroken.

For lo ! ere she settles beneath the dark wave
  On her enemies' cheeks spreads a pallor,
As another deck summons the swords of the brave
  To gild a new name with their valor.

Her phantom will yet haunt the wild roaring breeze,
  Causing foemen to start and to shudder,
While their commerce still steals like a thief o'er the
    seas,
  And trembles from bowsprit to rudder.

The spirit that shed on the wave's gleaming crest
  The light of a legend romantic
Shall live while a sail flutters over the breast
  Of thy far-bounding billows, Atlantic !

And as long as one swift keel the strong surges
    stems,
  Or " poor Jack " loves his song and his story,
Shall shine in tradition the valor of Semmes
  And the brave ship that bore him to glory !

                       MAURICE BELL.

THE BAY FIGHT.

[*Mobile Harbor, Alabama, August* 8, 1864.]

THREE days through sapphire seas we sailed,
  The steady Trade blew strong and free,
The Northern Light his banners paled,
The Ocean Stream our channels wet,
  We rounded low Canaveral's lee,
And passed the isles of emerald set
  In blue Bahama's turquoise sea.

By reef and shoal obscurely mapped,
  And hauntings of the gray sea-wolf,
The palmy Western Key lay lapped
  In the warm washing of the Gulf.

But weary to the hearts of all
  The burning glare, the barren reach
  Of Santa Rosa's withered beach,
And Pensacola's ruined wall.

And weary was the long patrol,
  The thousand miles of shapeless strand,
From Brazos to San Blas that roll
  Their drifting dunes of desert sand.

Yet coastwise as we cruised or lay,
  The land-breeze still at nightfall bore,
By beach and fortress-guarded bay,
  Sweet odors from the enemy's shore,

Fresh from the forest solitudes,
  Unchallenged of his sentry lines,—
The bursting of his cypress buds,
  And the warm fragrance of his pines.

Ah, never braver bark and crew,
  Nor bolder Flag a foe to dare,
Had left a wake on ocean blue
  Since Lion-Heart sailed Trenc-le-mer!

But little gain by that dark ground
  Was ours, save, sometime, freer breath

For friend or brother strangely found,
  'Scaped from the drear domain of death.

And little venture for the bold,
  Or laurel for our valiant Chief,
  Save some blockaded British thief,
Full fraught with murder in his hold,

Caught unawares at ebb or flood,
  Or dull bombardment, day by day,
  With fort and earthwork, far away,
Low couched in sullen leagues of mud.

A weary time,—but to the strong
  The day at last, as ever, came;
And the volcano, laid so long,
  Leaped forth in thunder and in flame !

    " *Man your starboard battery !*"
  Kimberly shouted ;—
The ship, with her hearts of oak,
Was going, 'mid roar and smoke,
    On to victory !
  None of us doubted,
No, not our dying—
Farragut's Flag was flying !

Gaines growled low on our left,
  Morgan roared on our right ;
Before us, gloomy and fell,
With breath like the fume of hell,
Lay the Dragon of iron shell,
  Driven at last to the fight !

Ha, old ship ! do they thrill,
  The brave two hundred scars
  You got in the River-Wars ?
That were leeched with clamorous skill,
  (Surgery savage and hard,)
Splinted with bolt and beam,
Probed in scarfing and seam,
  Rudely linted and tarred
With oakum and boiling pitch,

And sutured with splice and hitch,
   At the Brooklyn Navy-Yard!

Our lofty spars were down,
To bide the battle's frown
(Wont of old renown)—
But every ship was drest
In her bravest and her best,
   As if for a July day;
Sixty flags and three,
   As we floated up the bay—
At every peak and mast-head flew
The brave Red, White, and Blue,—
   We were eighteen ships that day.

With hawsers strong and taut,
The weaker lashed to port,
   On we sailed two by two—
That if either a bolt should feel
Crash through caldron or wheel,
Fin of bronze, or sinew of steel,
   Her mate might bear her through.

Forging boldly ahead,
The great Flag-Ship led,
   Grandest of sights!
On her lofty mizzen flew
Our Leader's dauntless Blue,
   That had waved o'er twenty fights
So we went with the first of the tide,
   Slowly, 'mid the roar
   Of the rebel guns ashore
And the thunder of each full broadside.

Ah, how poor the prate
Of statute and state
   We once held with these fellows!
Here on the flood's pale-green,
   Hark how he bellows,
   Each bluff old Sea-Lawyer!
Talk to them, Dahlgren,
   Parrott, and Sawyer!

On, in the whirling shade
 Of the cannon's sulphury breath,
 We drew to the Line of Death
That our devilish Foe had laid,—
Meshed in a horrible net,
 And baited villainous well,
Right in our path were set
 Three hundred traps of hell !

And there, O sight forlorn !
There, while the cannon
  Hurtled and thundered,—
 (Ah, what ill raven
Flapped o'er the ship that morn !)—
Caught by the under-death,
In the drawing of a breath
  Down went dauntless Craven,
  He and his hundred !

A moment we saw her turret,
 A little heel she gave,
And a thin white spray went o'er her,
 Like the crest of a breaking wave ;—
In that great iron coffin,
 The channel for their grave,
 The fort their monument,
(Seen afar in the offing),
Ten fathom deep lie Craven
 And the bravest of our brave.

Then in that deadly track
A little the ships held back,
 Closing up in their stations ;—
There are minutes that fix the fate
 Of battles and of nations,
 (Christening the generations,)
When valor were all too late,
 If a moment's doubt be harbored ;—
From the maintop, bold and brief,
Came the word of our grand old chief :
 " *Go on !* "—'twas all he said,—

Our helm was put to starboard,
  And the Hartford passed ahead.

Ahead lay the Tennessee,
  On our starboard bow he lay,
With his mail-clad consorts three
  (The rest had run up the Bay);
There he was, belching flame from his bow,
And the steam from his throat's abyss
Was a Dragon's maddened hiss;
  In sooth a most cursed craft!—
In a sullen ring, at bay,
By the Middle Ground they lay,
  Raking us fore and aft.

  Trust me, our berth was hot,
  Ah, wickedly well they shot—
How their death-bolts howled and stung!
  And the water-batteries played
  With their deadly cannonade
Till the air around us rung;
So the battle raged and roared;—
Ah, had you been aboard
  To have seen the fight we made!

How they leaped, the tongues of flame,
  From the cannon's fiery lip!
How the broadsides, deck and frame,
  Shook the great ship!

  And how the enemy's shell
  Came crashing, heavy and oft,
  Clouds of splinters flying aloft
And falling in oaken showers;—
  But ah, the pluck of the crew!
Had you stood on that deck of ours,
  You had seen what men may do.

Still, as the fray grew louder,
  Boldly they worked and well—
Steadily came the powder,
  Steadily came the shell.

And if tackle or truck found hurt,
  Quickly they cleared the wreck—
And the dead were laid to port,
  All a-row, on our deck.

Never a nerve that failed,
Never a cheek that paled,
Not a tinge of gloom or pallor ;—
  There was bold Kentucky's grit,
And the old Virginian valor,
  And the daring Yankee wit.

There were blue eyes from turfy Shannon,
  There were black orbs from palmy Niger,—
But there, alongside the cannon,
  Each man fought like a tiger !

A little, once, it looked ill,
  Our consort began to burn—
They quenched the flames with a will,
But our men were falling still,
  And still the fleet was astern.

Right abreast of the Fort
  In an awful shroud they lay,
  Broadsides thundering away,
And lightning from every port ;
  Scene of glory and dread !
A storm-cloud all aglow
  With flashes of fiery red,
The thunder raging below,
  And the forest of flags o'erhead !

So grand the hurly and roar,
  So fiercely their broadsides blazed,
The regiments fighting ashore
  Forgot to fire as they gazed.

  There, to silence the Foe,
  Moving grimly and slow,
They loomed in that deadly wreath,

Where the darkest batteries frowned,—
Death in the air all round,
And the black torpedoes beneath!

And now, as we looked ahead,
All for'ard, the long white deck
Was growing a strange dull red,-
But soon, as once and again
Fore and aft we sped,
(The firing to guide or check,)
You could hardly choose but tread
On the ghastly human wreck,
(Dreadful gobbet and shred
That a minute ago were men!)

Red, from mainmast to bitts!
Red, on bulwark and wale,
Red, by combing and hatch,
Red, o'er netting and vail!

And ever, with steady con,
The ship forged slowly by,—
And ever the crew fought on,
And their cheers rang loud and high.

Grand was the sight to see
How by their guns they stood,
Right in front of our dead,
Fighting square abreast—
Each brawny arm and chest
All spotted with black and red,
Chrism of fire and blood!

Worth our watch, dull and sterile,
Worth all the weary time,
Worth the woe and the peril,
To stand in that strait sublime!

Fear? A forgotten form!
Death? A dream of the eyes!
We were atoms in God's great storm
That roared through the angry skies.

One only doubt was ours,
  One only dread we knew,—
Could the day that dawned so well
Go down for the Darker Powers?
  Would the fleet get through?
And ever the shot and shell
Came with the howl of hell,
The splinter-clouds rose and fell,
  And the long line of corpses grew,—
  Would the fleet win through?

They are men that never will fail,
  (How aforetime they've fought!)
But Murder may yet prevail,—
  They may sink as Craven sank.
Therewith one hard fierce thought,
Burning on heart and lip,
Ran like fire through the ship:
  Fight her, to the last plank!

A dimmer renown might strike
  If Death lay square alongside,—
But the Old Flag has no like,
  She must fight, whatever betide;—
When the War is a tale of old,
And this day's story is told,
  They shall hear how the Hartford died!

But as we ranged ahead,
  And the leading ships worked in,
  Losing their hope to win,
The enemy turned and fled—
And one seeks a shallow reach:
  And another, winged in her flight,
  Our mate, brave Jouett, brings in;—
  And one, all torn in the fight,
Runs for a wreck on the beach,
  Where her flames soon fire the night.

And the Ram, when well up the Bay,
  And we looked that our stems should meet,

(He had us fair for a prey,)
Shifting his helm midway,
　Sheered off, and ran for the fleet;
There, without skulking or sham,
　He fought them gun for gun ;
And ever he sought to ram,
　But could finish never a one.

From the first of the iron shower
　Till we sent our parting shell,
'Twas just one savage hour
　Of the roar and the rage of hell.

With the lessening smoke and thunder,
　Our glasses around we aim,—
What is that burning yonder?
　Our Philippi—aground and in flame!

Below, 'twas still all a-roar,
As the ships went by the shore,
　But the fire of the Fort had slacked,
(So fierce their volleys had been,)—
And now with a mighty din,
The whole fleet came grandly in,
　Though sorely battered and wracked.

So, up the Bay we ran,
　The Flag to port and ahead,—
And a pitying rain began
　To wash the lips of our dead.

A league from the Fort we lay,
　And deemed that the end must lag,—
When lo ! looking down the Bay,
　There flaunted the Rebel Rag ;—
The Ram is again under way
　And heading dead for the Flag !

Steering up with the stream,
　Boldly his course he lay,
Though the fleet all answered his fire,
And, as he still drew nigher,

Ever on bow and beam
  Our Monitors pounded away;
  How the Chickasaw hammered **away** !

Quickly breasting the wave,
  Eager the prize to win,
First of us all the brave
  Monongahela went in
Under full head of steam ;—
Twice she struck him abeam,
Till her stem was a sorry work,
  (She might have run on a crag !)
The Lackawana hit fair,
He flung her aside like cork,
  And still he held for the Flag.

High in the mizzen shroud,
  (Lest the smoke his sight o'erwhelm,)
Our Admiral's voice rang loud:
  " *Hard-a-starboard your helm !*
Starboard, and run him down ! "
  Starboard it was,—and so,
Like a black squall's lifting frown,
Our mighty bow bore down
  On the iron beak of the Foe.

We stood on the deck together,
  Men that had looked on death
In battle and stormy weather ;
  Yet a little we held our breath,
  When, with the hush of death,
The great ships drew together.

Our Captain strode to the bow,
  Drayton, courtly and wise,
  Kindly cynic, and wise,
(You hardly had known him now,
  The flame of fight in his eyes !)—
His brave heart eager to feel
How the oak would tell on the steel !

But, as the space grew short,
  A little he seemed to shun us ;
Out peered a form grim and lanky,
And a voice yelled, " *Hard-a-port !*
Hard-a-port !—here's the damned Yankee
  Coming right down on us ! "

He sheered, but the ships ran foul
With a gnarring shudder and growl :
  He gave us a deadly gun ;
But as he passed in his pride,
(Rasping right alongside !)
  The Old Flag, in thunder-tones
Poured in her port broadside,
Rattling his iron hide
  And cracking his timber-bones !

Just then, at speed on the Foe,
  With her bow all weathered and brown,
  The great Lackawana came down
Full tilt, for another blow ;—
We were forging ahead,
  She reversed—but, for all our pains,
Rammed the old Hartford, instead,
  Just for'ard the mizzen chains !

Ah ! how the masts did buckle and bend,
  And the stout hull ring and reel,
As she took us right on end !
  (Vain were engine and wheel,
  She was under full steam,)—
With the roar of a thunder-stroke
Her two thousand tons of oak
  Brought up on us, right abeam !

A wreck, as it looked, we lay,—
(Rib and plank shear gave way
  To the stroke of that giant wedge !)
Here, after all, we go—
The old ship is gone !—ah, no,
  But cut to the water's edge.

Never mind then,—at him again !
  His flurry now can't last long ;
He'll never again see land,—
Try that on *him*, Marchand !
  On him again, brave Strong !

Heading square at the hulk,
  Full on his beam we bore ;
But the spine of the huge Sea-Hog
Lay on the tide like a log,
  He vomited flame no more.

By this, he had found it hot ;—
  Half the fleet, in an angry ring,
  Closed round the hideous thing,
Hammering with solid shot,
And bearing down, bow on bow ;
  He has but a minute to choose,—
Life or renown ?—which now
  Will the Rebel Admiral lose ?

Cruel, haughty, and cold,
He ever was strong and bold ;—
  Shall he shrink from a wooden stem ?
He will think of that brave band
He sank in the Cumberland ;—
  Ay, he will sink like them.

Nothing left but to fight
Boldly his last sea-fight !
  Can he strike ?   By Heaven, 'tis true !
  Down comes the traitor Blue,
And up goes the captive White !

Up went the White !   Ah, then
The hurrahs that once and again
Rang from three thousand men
  All flushed and savage with fight !
Our dead lay cold and stark ;
But our dying, down in the dark,
  Answered as best they might,

Lifting their poor lost arms,
 And cheering for God and Right!

Ended the mighty noise,
 Thunder of forts and ships.
Down we went to the hold,-
Oh, our dear dying boys!
 How we pressed their poor brave lips
 (Ah, so pallid and cold!)
And held their hands to the last,
 (Those that had hands to hold.)

Still thee, O woman heart!
 (So strong an hour ago;)
If the idle tears must start,
 'Tis not in vain they flow.

They died, our children dear,
 On the drear berth-deck they died,—
Do not think of them here—
Even now their footsteps near
The immortal, tender sphere—
(Land of love and cheer!
 Home of the Crucified!)

And the glorious deed survives;
 Our threescore, quiet and cold,
Lie thus, for a myriad lives
 And treasure-millions untold,—
(Labor of poor men's lives,
Hunger of weans and wives,
 Such is war-wasted gold.)

Our ship and her fame to-day
 Shall float on the storied Stream
When mast and shroud have crumbled away,
 And her long white deck is a dream.

One daring leap in the dark,
 Three mortal hours, at the most,—
And hell lies stiff and stark
 On a hundred leagues of coast.

For the mighty Gulf is ours,—
  The bay is lost and won,
  An Empire is lost and won!
Land, if thou yet hast flowers,
Twine them in one more wreath
  Of tenderest white and red,
(Twin buds of glory and death!)
  For the brows of our brave dead,
    For thy Navy's noblest son.

Joy, O Land, for thy sons,
  Victors by flood and field!
The traitor walls and guns
  Have nothing left but to yield;
    (Even now they surrender!)

And the ships shall sail once more,
  And the cloud of war sweep on
To break on the cruel shore;—
  But Craven is gone,
  He and his hundred are gone.

The flags flutter up and down
  At sunrise and twilight dim,
The cannons menace and frown,—
  But never again for him,
  Him and the hundred.

The Dahlgrens are dumb,
  Dumb are the mortars;
Never more shall the drum
  Beat to colors and quarters,—
  The great guns are silent.

O brave heart and loyal!
  Let all your colors dip;—
  Mourn him, proud ship!
From main deck to royal.
  God rest our Captain,
  Rest our lost hundred!

Droop, flag and pennant!
  What is your pride for?
  Heaven, that he died for,
Rest our Lieutenant,
  Rest our brave threescore!

      *   *   *   *

O Mother Land! this weary life
  We led, we lead, is 'long of thee;
Thine the strong agony of strife,
  And thine the lonely sea.

Thine the long decks all slaughter-sprent,
  The weary rows of cots that lie
With wrecks of strong men, marred and rent,
  'Neath Pensacola's sky.

And thine the iron caves and dens
  Wherein the flame our war-fleet drives;
The fiery vaults, whose breath is men's
  Most dear and precious lives!

Ah, ever, when with storm sublime
  Dread Nature clears our murky air,
Thus in the crash of falling crime
  Some lesser guilt must share.

Full red the furnace fires must glow
  That melt the ore of mortal kind:
The mills of God are grinding slow,
  But ah, how close they grind!

To-day the Dahlgren and the drum
  Are dread Apostles of His Name;
His kingdom here can only come
  By chrism of blood and flame.

Be strong: already slants the gold
  Athwart these wild and stormy skies;
From out this blackened waste, behold
  What happy homes shall rise!

But see thou well no traitor gloze,
　No striking hands with Death and Shame,
Betray the sacred blood that flows
　So freely for thy name.

And never fear a victor foe :—
　Thy children's hearts are strong and high ;
Nor mourn too fondly ; well they know
　On deck or field to die.

Nor shalt thou want one willing breath,
　Though, ever smiling round the brave,
The blue sea bear us on to death,
　The green were one wide grave.

HENRY HOWARD BROWNELL.

BIVOUAC ON A MOUNTAIN SIDE.

I SEE before me now a travelling army halting,
Below a fertile valley spread, with barns and the
　　orchards of summer,
Behind, the terraced sides of a mountain, abrupt,
　　in places rising high,
Broken, with rocks, with clinging cedars, with tall
　　shapes dingily seen,
The numerous camp-fires scattered near and far,
　　some away up on the mountain,
The shadowy forms of men and horses, looming,
　　large-sized, flickering,
And over all the sky—the sky ! far, far out of reach,
　　studded, breaking out, the eternal stars.

WALT WHITMAN.

SHERIDAN'S RIDE.

[*During General Sheridan's temporary absence, his troops in the Shenandoah Valley were surprised and routed by the Confederates under General Early. The Union commander hurried to the front in time to rally his forces and turn defeat into victory—October* 19, 1864.]

UP from the South at break of day,
Bringing to Winchester fresh dismay,
The affrighted air with a shudder bore,
Like a herald in haste, to the chieftain's door,
The terrible grumble, and rumble, and roar,
Telling the battle was on once more,
And Sheridan twenty miles away.

And wider still those billows of war
Thundered along the horizon's bar ;
And louder yet into Winchester rolled
The roar of that red sea uncontrolled,
Making the blood of the listener cold,
As he thought of the stake in that fiery fray,
And Sheridan twenty miles away.

But there is a road from Winchester town,
A good broad highway leading down ;
And there, through the flush of the morning light,
A steed as black as the steeds of night
Was seen to pass, as with eagle flight ;
As if he knew the terrible need,
He stretched away with his upmost speed ;
Hills rose and fell ; but his heart was gay,
With Sheridan fifteen miles away.

Still sprung from those swift hoofs, thundering South,
The dust, like smoke from the cannon's mouth,
Or the trail of a comet, sweeping faster and faster,
Foreboding to traitors the doom of disaster.
The heart of the steed and the heart of the master
Were beating like prisoners assaulting their walls,
Impatient to be where the battlefield calls ;

SHERIDAN'S RIDE.
(See page 24. "*He dashed down the line 'mid a storm of huzzas.*"

SHERMAN'S MARCH TO THE SEA.

(See pages 267 and 268.)

Every nerve of the charger was strained to full play,
With Sheridan only ten miles away.

Under his spurning feet, the road
Like an arrowy Alpine river flowed,
And the landscape sped away behind
Like an ocean flying before the wind,
And the steed, like a barque fed with furnace ire,
Swept on, with his wild eye full of fire.
But lo ! he is nearing his heart's desire ;
He is snuffing the smoke of the roaring fray,
With Sheridan only five miles away.

The first that the General saw were the groups
Of stragglers, and then the retreating troops ;
What was done ? what to do ?—a glance told him
      both ;
Then, striking his spurs, with a terrible oath,
He dashed down the line, 'mid a storm of huzzas,
And the wave of retreat checked its course there,
      because
The sight of the master compelled it to pause.
With foam and with dust the black charger was gray;
By the flash of his eye, and his red nostril's play,
He seemed to the whole great army to say :
" I have brought you Sheridan all the way
From Winchester down to save the day !"

Hurrah, hurrah for Sheridan !
Hurrah, hurrah for horse and man !
And when their statues are placed on high,
Under the dome of the Union sky,—
The American soldiers' Temple of Fame,-
There with the glorious General's name
Be it said in letters both bold and bright :
" Here is the steed that saved the day
By carrying Sheridan into the fight,
From Winchester,—twenty miles away !"

THOMAS BUCHANAN READ.

THE CAVALRY CHARGE.

WITH bray of the trumpet
  And roll of the drum,
And keen ring of bugle,
  The cavalry come.
Sharp clank the steel scabbards,
  The bridle-chains ring,
And foam from red nostrils
  The wild chargers fling.

Tramp! tramp! o'er the greensward
  That quivers below,
Scarce held by the curb-bit
  The fierce horses go!
And the grim-visaged colonel,
  With ear-rending shout,
Peals forth to the squadrons
  The order,—" *Trot out!* "

One hand on the sabre,
  And one on the rein,
The troopers move forward
  In line on the plain.
As rings the word, " *Gallop!* "
  The steel scabbards clank,
And each rowel is pressed
  To a horse's hot flank :
And swift is their rush
  As the wild torrent's flow,
When it pours from the crag
  On the valley below.

" *Charge!* " thunders the leader :
  Like shaft from the bow
Each mad horse is hurled
  On the wavering foe.
A thousand bright sabres
  Are gleaming in air :
A thousand dark horses
  Are dashed on the square.

Resistless and reckless
  Of aught may betide,
Like demons, not mortals,
  The wild troopers ride.
Cut right! and cut left!—
  For the parry who needs?
The bayonets shiver
  Like wind-scattered reeds.

Vain—vain the red volley
  That bursts from the square,—
The random-shot bullets
  Are wasted in air.
Triumphant, remorseless,
  Unerring as death,—
No sabre that's stainless
  Returns to its sheath.

The wounds that are dealt
  By that murderous steel
Will never yield case
  For the surgeon to heal.
Hurrah! they are broken—
  Hurrah! boys, they fly!
None linger save those
  Who but linger to die.

Rein up your hot horses
  And call in your men,—
The trumpet sounds *"Rally
  To colors"* again.
Some saddles are empty,
  Some comrades are slain,
And some noble horses
  Lie stark on the plain;
But war's a chance game, boys,
  And weeping is vain.

FRANCIS A. DURIVAGE.

THE CAVALRY CHARGE.

HARK ! the rattling roll of the musketeers,
And the ruffled drums, and the rallying cheers,
And the rifles burn with a keen desire
Like the crackling whips of a hemlock fire,
And the singing shot and the shrieking shell
And the splintered fire of the shattered hell,
And the great white breaths of the cannon smoke
As the growling guns by batteries spoke ;
And the ragged gaps in the walls of blue
Where the iron surge rolled heavily through,
That the Colonel builds with a breath again
As he cleaves the din with his " *Close up, men !*"
And the groan torn out from the blackened lips,
And the prayer doled slow with the crimsoned drips,
And the beaming look in the dying eye
As under the cloud the Stars go by,
" *But his soul marched on !*" the Captain said,
For the Boy in Blue can never be dead !

And the troopers sit in their saddles all
Like statues carved in an ancient hall,
And they watch the whirl from their breathless
      ranks,
And their spurs are close to the horses' flanks,
And the fingers work of the sabre hand—
Oh, to bid them live, and to make them grand !
And the bugle sounds to the charge at last,
And away they plunge, and the front is passed !
And the jackets blue grow red as they ride,
And the scabbards too, that clank by their side,
And the dead soldiers deaden the strokes iron-shod
As they gallop right on o'er the plashy red sod—
Right into the cloud all spectral and dim,
Right up to the guns black-throated and grim,
Right down on the hedges bordered with steel,
Right through the dense columns,—then " *Right
      about wheel !*"

Hurrah ! a new swath through the harvest again !
Hurrah for the Flag ! To the battle, Amen !

BENJAMIN F. TAYLOR.

THE CHARGE BY THE FORD.

EIGHTY and nine with their captain
   Rode on the enemy's track,
Rode in the gray of the morning :
   Nine of the ninety came back.

Slow rose the mist from the river,
   Lighter each moment the way ;
Careless and tearless and fearless
   Galloped they on to the fray.

Singing in tune, how the scabbards
   Loud on the stirrup-irons rang,
Clinked as the men rose in saddle,
   Fell as they sank with a clang.

What is it moves by the river,
   Jaded and weary and weak ?
Gray-backs—a cross on their banner—·
   Yonder the foe whom they seek.

Silence ! They see not, they hear not,
   Tarrying there by the marge :
Forward! Draw sabre! Trot! Gallop!
   Charge! like a hurricane, *charge!*

Ah ! 'twas a man-trap infernal—
   Fire like the deep pit of hell !
Volley on volley to meet them,
   Mixed with the gray rebels' yell.

Ninety had ridden to battle,
   Tracing the enemy's track,—
Ninety had ridden to battle,
   Nine of the ninety came back.

Honor the name of the ninety ;
  Honor the heroes who came
Scathless from five hundred muskets,
  Safe from the lead-bearing flame.

Eighty and one of the troopers
  Lie on the field of the slain—
Lie on the red field of honor :
  Honor the nine who remain !

Cold are the dead there, and gory,
  There where their life-blood was spilt ;
Back come the living, each sabre
  Red from the point to the hilt.

Give them three cheers and a tiger !
  Let the flags wave as they come !
Give them the blare of the trumpet !
  Give them the roll of the drum !

THOMAS DUNN ENGLISH.

———

CAVALRY SONG.

OUR good steeds snuff the evening air,
  Our pulses with their purpose tingle ;
The foeman's fires are twinkling there ;
  He leaps to hear our sabres jingle !
    HALT !
  Each carbine sends its whizzing ball :
  Now, cling ! clang ! forward all,
    Into the fight !

Dash on beneath the smoking dome :
  Through level lightnings gallop nearer !
One look to Heaven ! No thoughts of home :
  The guidons that we bear are dearer.
    CHARGE !

Cling! clang! forward all!
Heaven help those whose horses fall!
   Cut left and right!

They flee before our fierce attack!
  They fall! they spread in broken surges!
Now, comrades, bear our wounded back,
  And leave the foeman to his dirges.
        WHEEL!
The bugles sound the swift recall:
Cling! clang! backward all!
    Home, and good-night!
     EDMUND CLARENCE STEDMAN.

THE WATCHERS.

BESIDE a stricken field I stood;
On the torn turf, on grass and wood,
Hung heavily the dew of blood.

Still in their fresh mounds lay the slain,
But all the air was quick with pain
And gusty sighs and tearful rain.

Two angels, each with drooping head,
And folded wings and noiseless tread,
Watched by that valley of the dead.

The one, with forehead saintly bland,
And lips of blessing, not command,
Leaned, weeping, on her olive wand.

The other's brows were scarred and knit,
His restless eyes were watch-fires lit,
His hands for battle-gauntlets fit.

" How long,"—I knew the voice of Peace;
" Is there no respite?—no release?—
When shall the hopeless quarrel cease?

" O Lord, how long !—One human soul
Is more than any parchment scroll,
Or any flag thy winds unroll.

" What price was Ellsworth's, young and brave ?
How weigh the gift that Lyon gave,
Or count the cost of Winthrop's grave ?

" O brother ! if thine eye can see,
Tell how and when the end shall be,
What hope remains for thee and me."

Then Freedom sternly said : " I shun
No strife nor pang beneath the sun,
When human rights are staked and won.

" I knelt with Ziska's hunted flock,
I watched in Toussaint's cell of rock,
I walked with Sidney to the block.

" The moor of Marston felt my tread,
Through Jersey snows the march I led,
My voice Magenta's charges sped.

" But now through weary day and night
I watch a vague and aimless fight,
For leave to strike one blow aright.

" On either side my foe they own :
One guards through love his ghastly throne,
And one through fear to reverence grown.

" Why wait we longer, mocked, betrayed,
By open foes, or those afraid
To speed thy coming through my aid ?

" Why watch to see who win or fall ?—
I shake the dust against them all,
I leave them to their senseless brawl."

" Nay," Peace implored : " yet longer wait ;
The doom is near, the stake is great,
God knoweth if it be too late.

"Still wait and watch ; the way prepare
Where I with folded wings of prayer
May follow, weaponless and bare."

"Too late !" the stern sad voice replied,
" Too late !" its mournful echo sighed,
In low lament the answer died.

A rustling as of wings in flight,
An upward gleam of lessening white,
So passed the vision, sound and sight.

But round me, like a silver bell
Rung down the listening sky to tell
Of holy help, a sweet voice fell.

" Still hope and trust," it sang ; " the rod
Must fall, the wine-press must be trod,
But all is possible with God !"

                    JOHN GREENLEAF WHITTIER.

MY AUTUMN WALK.

[*October*, 1864.]

ON woodlands ruddy with autumn
    The amber sunshine lies ;
I look on the beauty round me,
    And tears come into my eyes.

For the wind that sweeps the meadows
    Blows out of the far Southwest,
Where our gallant men are fighting,
    And the gallant dead are at rest.

The golden-rod is leaning,
    And the purple aster waves
In a breeze from the land of battles,
    A breath from the land of graves.

Full fast the leaves are dropping
    Before that wandering breath ;
As fast, on the field of battle,
    Our brethren fall in death.

Beautiful over my pathway
    The forest spoils are shed ;
They are spotting the grassy hillocks
    With purple and gold and red.

Beautiful is the death-sleep
    Of those who bravely fight
In their country's holy quarrel,
    And perish for the Right.

But who shall comfort the living,
    The light of whose homes is gone :
The bride that, early widowed,
    Lives broken-hearted on ;

The matron whose sons are lying
    In graves on a distant shore ;
The maiden, whose promised husband
    Comes back from the war no more ?

I look on the peaceful dwellings
    Whose windows glimmer in sight,
With croft and garden and orchard,
    That bask in the mellow light ;

And I know that, when our couriers
    With news of victory come,
They will bring a bitter message
    Of hopeless grief to some.

Again I turn to the woodlands,
    And shudder as I see
The mock-grape's blood-red banner
    Hung out on the cedar-tree ;

And I think of days of slaughter,
  And the night-sky red with flames,
On the Chattahoochee's meadows,
  And the wasted banks of the James.

Oh, for the fresh spring-season,
  When the groves are in their prime;
And far away in the future
  Is the frosty autumn-time!

Oh, for that better season,
  When the pride of the foe shall yield,
And the hosts of God and Freedom
  March back from the well-won field;

And the matron shall clasp her first-born
  With tears of joy and pride;
And the scarred and war-worn lover
  Shall claim his promised bride!

The leaves are swept from the branches;
  But the living buds are there,
With folded flower and foliage,
  To sprout in a kinder air.

WILLIAM CULLEN BRYANT.

HYMN OF THE MOTHERS OF OUR VOL-UNTEERS.

HOME calls each loved familiar name
  With precious memories stored:
Deal gently, Lord! 'Twas not for fame
  Our children took the sword.

We never thought, when each young face
  First softly touched our own,
And little hands with sweet embrace
  About our necks were thrown,

That our own veins were nursing then
    The holy cause of Right,
And that from our own bosoms men
    Would spring to Freedom's fight.

We deem not now the offering vain,
    Our dearest though we give;
Nor do we ask release from pain,
    If but the Nation live.

Still, sometimes as alone we kneel
    Where once the cradle stood,
So much comes back—'tis hard to feel
    That all our grief is good.

The rosy cheeks so round and fair,
    The pattering little feet,
The laughing eyes and silken hair
    Of those whose touch was sweet,

Rise up amid the glare and din
    Of battle's fiery tide,
And flit past prison bars, within
    Which love is crucified!

We know we bade them go, when stirred
    The land from sea to sea,
For 'twas Thy voice, O Christ, they heard
    Proclaiming liberty.

But, oh, this travail long and sore,
    Watching their woeful way,
And never able to do more
    Than serve at home and pray.

It seems as if the mother's hand
    Could soothe their sufferings best,
And that the mother ought to stand
    By children laid at rest.

Forgive, O God, our doubts and fears
 While Thy great work goes on ;
We do rejoice amid our tears,
 And pray, " Thy will be done."

Thy will—good will—its message now
 Of promised peace grows strong,
And, flashing on War's awful brow,
 Proclaims the doom of Wrong.

It is enough. Out from the gloom
 Rises a nation free.
Still, at the cross and by the tomb,
 We cling, O Lord, to Thee.

HORATIO NELSON POWERS.

WOMAN'S WAR MISSION.

FOLD away all your bright tinted dresses,
 Turn the key on your jewels to-day,
And the wealth of your tendril-like tresses
 Braid back, in a serious way :
No more delicate gloves, no more laces,
 No more trifling in boudoir and bower ;
But come with your souls in your faces—
 To meet the stern needs of the hour !

Look around ! By the torchlight unsteady,
 The dead and the dying seem one.
What ! paling and trembling already,
 Before your dear mission's begun ?
These wounds are more precious than ghastly ;
 Fame presses her lips to each scar,
As she chants of a glory which vastly
 Transcends all the horrors of war.

Pause here by this bedside—how mellow
 The light showers down on that brow !

Such a brave, brawny visage !—Poor fellow !
   Some homestead is missing him now.
Some wife shades her eyes in the clearing,
   Some mother sits moaning, distressed,—
While the loved one lies faint, but unfearing,
   With the enemy's ball in his breast.

Here's another ; a lad—a mere stripling—
   Picked up from the field, almost dead ;
With the blood through his sunny hair rippling
   From a horrible gash in the head.
They say he was first in the action,
   Gay-hearted, quick-handed, and witty ;
He fought till he fell with exhaustion,
   At the gates of our fair Southern city.

Fought and fell 'neath the guns of that city,
   With a spirit transcending his years ;
Lift him up in your large-hearted pity,
   And touch his pale lips with your tears.
Touch him gently—most sacred the duty
   Of dressing that poor shattered hand !
God spare him to rise in his beauty,
   And battle once more for the land !

Who groaned ?   What a passionate murmur—
   " In thy mercy, O God ! let me die ! "
Ha ! surgeon, your hand must be firmer,
   That grapeshot has shattered his thigh.
Fling the light on those poor furrowed features,
   Gray-haired and unknown—bless the brother !
O God ! that one of *thy* creatures
   Should e'er work such woe on another !

Wipe the sweat from his brow with your kerchief ;
   Let the stained tattered collar go wide.
See ! he stretches out blindly to search if
   The surgeon still stands at his side.
" My son's over yonder ! he's wounded—
   Oh ! this ball that has broken my thigh ! "

And again he burst out, all a-tremble,—
" *In thy mercy, O God! let me die!* "

Pass on ! It is useless to linger
  While others are claiming your care ;
There is need of your delicate finger,
  For your womanly sympathy, there !
There are sick ones athirst for caressing—
  There are dying ones raving of home—
There are wounds to be bound with a blessing—
  And shrouds to make ready for some.

They have gathered about you the harvest
  Of death, in its ghastliest view ;
The nearest as well as the farthest
  Is here with the traitor and true !
And crowned with your beautiful patience,
  Made sunny with love at the heart,
You must balsam the wounds of a nation,
  Nor falter, nor shrink from your part !

Up and down through the wards, where the fever
  Stalks noisome, and gaunt and impure,
You must go with your steadfast endeavor
  To comfort, to counsel, to cure !
I grant that the task's superhuman,
  But strength will be given to you
To do for those dear ones what woman
  Alone in her pity can do.

And the lips of the mothers will bless you
  As angels sweet visaged and pale !
And the little ones run to caress you,
  While the wives and the sisters cry " Hail !"
But e'en if you drop down unheeded,
  What matter ? God's ways are the best ;
You've poured out your life where 'twas needed,
  And He will take care of the rest.

ANONYMOUS (*Southern*).

A WOMAN OF THE WAR.

[*The story told in this poem is literally true. Its hero-
ine, Margaret Augusta Peterson, lived at Rochester,
N. Y.; and when, after the battles of the Wilderness, the
hospitals of that city were filled with wounded men, she
offered her services, and was accepted, as a nurse, at St.
Mary's Hospital. She died September 1, 1864, at the age
of twenty-three; and her grave and the surgeon's may be
seen in Mount Hope Cemetery, Rochester.*]

THROUGH the sombre arch of that gateway tower
    Where my humblest townsman rides at last,
You may spy the bells of a nodding flower,
    On a double mound that is thickly grassed.

And between the spring and the summer time,
    Or ever the lilac's bloom is shed,
When they come with banners and wreaths and
        rhyme,
    To deck the tombs of the nation's dead,

They find there a little flag in the grass,
    And fling a handful of roses down,
And pause a moment before they pass
    To the Captain's grave with the gilded crown.

But if perchance they seek to recall
    What name, what deeds, these honors declare,
They cannot tell, they are silent all
    As the noiseless harebell nodding there.

She was tall, with an almost manly grace,
    And young, with strange wisdom for one so
        young,
And fair with more than a woman's face;
    With dark, deep eyes, and a mirthful tongue.

The poor and the fatherless knew her smile;
    The friend in sorrow had seen her tears;
She had studied the ways of the rough world's
        guile,
    And read the romance of historic years.

What she might have been in these times of ours,
 At once it is easy and hard to guess;
For always a riddle are half-used powers,
 And always a power is lovingness.

But her fortunes fell upon evil days—
 If days are evil when evil dies,—
And she was not one who could stand at gaze
 Where the hopes of humanity fall and rise.

Nor could she dance to the viol's tune
 When the drum was throbbing throughout the
 land,
Or dream in the light of the summer moon
 When Treason was clenching his mailéd hand.

Through the long gray hospital's corridor
 She journeyed many a mournful league,
And her light foot fell on the oaken floor
 As if it never could know fatigue.

She stood by the good old surgeon's side,
 And the sufferers smiled as they saw her stand;
She wrote, and the mothers marvelled and cried
 At their darling soldiers' feminine hand.

She was last in the ward when the lights burned low,
 And Sleep called a truce to his foeman Pain;
At the midnight cry she was first to go,
 To bind up the bleeding wound again.

For sometimes the wreck of a man would rise,
 Weird and gaunt in the watch-lamp's gleam,
And tear away bandage and splints and ties,
 Fighting the battle all o'er in his dream.

No wonder the youngest surgeon felt
 A charm in the presence of that brave soul,
Through weary weeks, as she nightly knelt
 With the letter from home or the doctor's dole.

He heard her called, and he heard her blessed,
  With many a patriot's parting breath ;
And ere his soul to itself confessed,
  Love leaped to life in those vigils of death.

" O, fly to your home !" came a whisper dread,
  " For now the pestilence walks by night."
" The greater the need of me here," she said,
  And bared her arm for the lancet's bite.

Was there death, green death, in the atmosphere ?
  Was the bright steel poisoned ?   Who can tell !
Her weeping friends gathered beside her bier,
  And the clergyman told them all was well.

Well—alas that it should be so !
  When a nation's debt reaches reckoning-day—
Well for it to be able, but woe
  To the generation that's called to pay !

Down from the long gray hospital came
  Every boy in blue who could walk the floor ;
The sick and the wounded, the blind and the lame,
  Formed two long files from her father's door.

There was grief in many a manly breast,
  While men's tears fell as the coffin passed ;
And thus she went to the world of rest,
  Martial and maidenly up to the last.

And that youngest surgeon, was he to blame ?—
  He held the lancet—Heaven only knows.
No matter ; his heart broke all the same,
  And he laid him down, and never arose.

So Death received, in his greedy hand,
  Two precious coins of the awful price
That purchased freedom for this dear land—
  For master and bondman—yea, bought it twice.

Such fates too often such women are for !
God grant the Republic a large increase,
To match the heroes in time of war,
And mother the children in time of peace.

ROSSITER JOHNSON.

THE LAST REGIMENT.

["*In a pretty little village in Louisiana, destroyed by shells toward the end of the war, on a bayou back from the river, a great number of very old men had been left by their sons and grandsons, while they went to the war. And these old men, many of them veterans of other wars, formed themselves into a regiment, made for themselves uniforms, picked up old flint-lock guns, even mounted a rusty old cannon, and so prepared to go to battle if ever the war came within their reach. Toward the close of the war, some gunboats came down the river, shelling the shore. The old men heard the firing, and, gathering together, they set out with their old muskets and rusty old cannon to try to reach the river over the corduroy road through the cypress swamp. They marched out right merrily that hot day, shouting and bantering to encourage each other, the dim fires of their old eyes burning with desire of battle, although not one of them was young enough or strong enough to stand erect. And they never came back any more. The shells from the gunboats set the dense and sultry woods on fire. The old men were shut in by the flames—the gray beards and the gray moss and the gray smoke together.*"]

THE dying land cried; they heard her death call ;
  These bent, bearded men stopped, listened intent ;
Then rusty old muskets rushed down from the wall,
  And squirrel-guns gleamed in that regiment,
And grandsires marched, old muskets in hand,
The last men left in the whole Southland.

The gray grandsires ! They were seen to reel,
  Their rusty old muskets a wearisome load:

They marched, scarce tall as the cannon's wheel,
   Marched merrily on up the corduroy road ;
These gray old boys, all broken and bent,
Marched out, the gallant last regiment.

But, oh ! that march through the cypress trees,
   When zest and excitement had died away !
That desolate march through the marsh to the
      knees—
   These gray grandsires in their robes of gray,
These gray grandsires all broken and bent,—
The gray moss mantling the regiment.

The gray bent men and the mosses gray !
   The dull dead gray of the uniform !
The dull dead skies, like to lead that day,
   Dull, dead, heavy, and deathly warm !
Oh, what meant more than the cypress meant,
With its mournful moss, to that regiment ?

That deadly march through the marshes deep !—
   That sultry day, and the deeds in vain !
The rest on the cypress roots, the sleep—
   The sleeping never to rise again !
The rust on the guns !   The rust and the rent—
That dying and desolate regiment !

The muskets left leaning against the trees !
   The cannon wheels clogged from the moss o'er-
      head !
The cypress trees kneeling on obstinate knees
   As gray men kneeled by the gray men dead !
A lone bird rising, long-legged and gray,
Slow rising, and rising, and drifting away !

The dank dead mosses gave back no sound ;
   The drums lay silent as the drummers there ;
The sultry stillness was so profound
   You might have heard an unuttered prayer ;
And ever and ever, and far away,
Kept drifting that desolate bird in gray.

The long gray shrouds of that cypress wood,
  Like veils that sweep where the gray nuns
    weep—
That cypress moss o'er the dankness deep,
Why, the cypress roots they were running blood;
And to right and to left lay an old man dead—
A mourning cypress set foot and head.

'Twas man hunting man in the wilderness there;
  'Twas man hunting man, and hunting to slay;
  But nothing was found but death that day,
And possibly God, in that poisonous air;
And possibly God—and that bird in gray
Slow rising, and rising, and drifting away.

Now down in the swamp where the gray men fell
  The fire-flies volley and volley at night,
And black men belated are heard to tell
  Of the ghosts in gray in a mimic fight—
Of the ghosts of the gallant old men in gray
Who silently died in the swamp that day.

                                JOAQUIN MILLER.

"SHOT THROUGH THE HEART."

[*In memory of Lieutenant John R. Porter, of Alabama,
who fell, shot through the heart, at the battle of Frank-
lin, Tenn., November 30, 1864.*]

ACROSS the brown and wintry morn,
  Borne on the soft wind's wing,
The weird sweet chords of a New Year's Song
  Are struck by the coming Spring—
    Ah, would 'twere last year's Spring!

Under the leaves the violet bends,
  Laden with scented breath;
Do they bend and blow thus sweetly
  Where the wooing air is death?
    Can flowers bloom in death?

Out in the bridal robe of white
  Sweet hawthorn decks the lane;
Who tuned the windharp's thrilling string
  To the sad, sad minor strain?
    Hark! that sad minor strain!

I think, as I see the whitening bloom
  Drift down in a fleecy cloud,
Not of the mist of bridal veils,
  But the chill of an icy shroud—
    Snow is the soldier's shroud.

There's a whisper of crocus and hyacinth
  Where fairies watch their birth;
Methinks like little white babes they lie,
  Still-born on their mother-earth—
    Dead babes on the mother-earth.

Where the dear warm blood flowed out so free,
  Did the wild wind steal its moans
That fill me with anguish of unshed tears?
  'Tis the Banshee's shivering groans!—
    List! it shivers, and sobs, and groans!

O spirit of sorrow, Banshee white!
  Wail on, for I cannot sleep;
Coldness and darkness wander with me,
  The vigil of woe to keep—
    Pale woe her watch must keep.
        *   *   *   *   *
In the long, long march, did he track the snow
  With his weary bleeding feet?
Was his dear face cold in the pelting rain,
  Or numbed by the blinding sleet?
    Barefoot through the blinding sleet!

Was he pale from the pain, the hunger pain,
  Or did he step proud and strong
To the onward note from the bugle's throat
  When the boys cheered loud and long?
    Oh, the march was long, so long!

Where, where is the sword whose gleaming blade
  Flashed up against the sky,
And wrote in a broad white quivering line
  How Southern men could die!—
    Thus martyrs fighting die!

Ho! Walthalls's men, and Brantley's line!
  The good steel must not rust;
His name must be the battle-cry,
  His murderers bite the dust!
    They yet shall gnaw the dust!
      *   *   *   *   *

"*Shot through the heart!*" My own stands still,
  With its breaking, breaking pain;
All, all grows dark, but the words of fire
  That burn my reeling brain—
    Rent heart and aching brain.

Who sprang to his side in the foremost ranks,
  And over him bent the knee,
To smooth from his brow the dark damp hair,
  And kiss him again for me?
    Who kissed his dear lips for me?

Kind stranger, guard that sacred spot;
  He died to free thy land;
His name thou'lt find on rude head-board,
  Carved there by pitying hand—
    God bless that soldier's hand!

We've watched and nursed your dying ones,
  Have wreathed their graves with flowers;
Will any gentle hand thus wreathe
  That holy mound of ours?
    Oh, shield that grave of ours!

Oh, the parching thirst and numbing cold
  And the hunger-pain are o'er;
The weary feet, fresh-sandalled now,
  Rest on the golden shore—
    Fair, God-lit, healing shore.
      *   *   *   *   *

In his threadbare suit, with its honor-stains,
  They laid him down to rest ;
Did they fold our flag, with its spotless stars,
  On my poor dead brother's breast ?
    Oh, dear, dear bleeding breast !

Oh, say that I'm mad or dreaming—
  That Joy will come once more !
Then the Summer woods of the bright Southland
  May leaf as they leaved of yore !
    With Life they sprung of yore !

Then the hills may don their arabesque,
  And the Arcenciel may shine,
While the rose on the cheek of the blushing year
  Woos the roses back to mine :
    The roses have died on mine.

No ; the Spring will pass, and Summer fruit,
  And Fall sheaves gild the ground ;
But the sad weird song the Banshee sings
  Will follow the whole year round—
    Dark Winter the whole year round !

Down in the glen, the dogwood white,
  By the maple's living red,
But brings to mind the cold, cold sheet
  That shrouds the bleeding dead !—
    Snow shrouds our darling dead !

Oh, weary Winter has almost gone,
  With its Christmas berries swung ;
They seem but drops of human blood
  From human anguish wrung !
    O God, our hearts are wrung !

" *Killed outright !*"—Oh, wretched dream !
  When, when shall I awake ?
If the words ring on, thus wildly on,
  My tortured heart must break !—
    God help me ere it break !

                              INA MARIE PORTER.

SHERMAN'S MARCH TO THE SEA.

[*This popular song was written while its author, Adjutant Byers, of the Fifth Iowa Regiment, was a prisoner at Columbia, S. C. Of its origin he says : " There are hundreds of old comrades who remember the afternoon in the prison-pen at Columbia when our glee club said, ' Now we are going to sing something about Billy Sherman !' and with what rousing cheers the song and the writer were welcomed. The rebel officers ran in to see what was loose among the prisoners, and they, too, had music in their souls, and said if the glee club would sing ' Dixie Land ' they might sing ' Sherman's March to the Sea' also ; and so for weeks our glee club—the only sunshine we had in prison—made the old barrack walls ring with songs of the blue and the gray." The piece attracted the attention of General Sherman, who sent for the author and attached him to his staff.*]

OUR camp-fires shone bright on the mountain
   That frowned on the river below,
As we stood by our guns in the morning,
   And eagerly watched for the foe ;
When a rider came out of the darkness
   That hung over mountain and tree,
And shouted, "Boys, up and be ready !
   For Sherman will march to the sea !"

Then cheer upon cheer for bold Sherman
   Went up from each valley and glen,
And the bugles re-echoed the music
   That came from the lips of the men ;
For we knew that the stars in our banner
   More bright in their splendor would be,
And that blessings from Northland would greet us
   When Sherman marched down to the sea.

Then forward, boys ! forward to battle !
   We marched on our wearisome way,
We stormed the wild hills of Resaca—
   God bless those who fell on that day !
Then Kenesaw, dark in its glory,
   Frowned down on the flag of the free ;

But the East and the West bore our standard,
   And Sherman marched on to the sea.

Still onward we pressed, till our banners
   Swept out from Atlanta's grim walls,
And the blood of the patriot dampened
   The soil where the traitor-flag falls;
We paused not to weep for the fallen
   Who slept by each river and tree,
Yet we twined them a wreath of the laurel,
   As Sherman marched down to the sea.

Oh, proud was our army that morning,
   That stood where the pine darkly towers,
When Sherman said, "Boys, you are weary,
   But to-day fair Savannah is ours!"
Then sang we the song of our chieftain,
   That echoed o'er river and lea,
And the stars in our banner shone brighter
   When Sherman marched down to the sea.

                     SAMUEL H. M. BYERS.

SONG OF SHERMAN'S ARMY.

A PILLAR of fire by night,
   A pillar of smoke by day,
Some hours of march--then a halt to fight,
   And so we hold our way;
Some hours of march—then a halt to fight,
   As on we hold our way.

Over mountain and plain and stream,
   To some bright Atlantic bay,
With our arms aflash in the morning beam,
   We hold our festal way;
With our arms aflash in the morning beam,
   We hold our checkless way.

There is terror wherever we come,
  There is terror and wild dismay
When they see the Old Flag and hear the drum
  Announce us on the way;
When they see the Old Flag and hear the drum
  Beating time to our onward way.

Never unlimber a gun
  For those villainous lines in gray;
Draw sabres, and at 'em upon the run!
  'Tis thus we clear our way;
Draw sabres, and soon you will see them run,
  As we hold our conquering way.

The loyal, who long have been dumb,
  Are loud in their cheers to-day;
And the old men out on their crutches come,
  To see us hold our way;
And the old men out on their crutches come,
  To bless us on our way.

Around us in rear and flanks
  Their futile squadrons play;
With a sixty-mile front of steady ranks,
  We hold our checkless way;
With a sixty-mile front of serried ranks,
  Our banner clears the way.

Hear the spattering fire that starts
  From the woods and copses gray!
There is just enough fighting to quicken our hearts,
  As we frolic along the way;
There is just enough fighting to warm our hearts,
  As we rattle along the way.

Upon different roads abreast
  The heads of our columns gay,
With fluttering flags all forward prest,
  Hold on their conquering way;
With fluttering flags to victory prest,
  We hold our glorious way!

Ah, traitors who bragged so bold
  In the sad war's early day!
Did nothing predict you should ever behold
  The Old Flag come this way?
Did nothing predict you should yet behold
  Our banner come back this way?

By Heaven! 'tis a gala march,
  'Tis a picnic or a play;
Of all our long war, 'tis the crowning arch,—
  Hip, hip! for Sherman's way!
Of all our long war, this crowns the arch,—
  For Sherman and Grant, hurra!

                    CHARLES G. HALPINE.

ETHIOPIA SALUTING THE COLORS.

WHO are you, dusky woman, so ancient, hardly
    human,
With your woolly-white and turban'd head, and
    bare bony feet?
Why, rising by the roadside here, do you the colors
    greet?

('Tis while our army lines Carolina's sands and pines,
Forth from thy hovel door, thou, Ethiopia, com'st to
    me,
As under doughty Sherman I march toward the sea.)

*Me, master, years a hundred, since, from my par-
    ents sundered,*
*A little child, they caught me as the savage beast
    is caught,*
*Then hither me across the sea the cruel slaver
    brought.*

No further does she say, but lingering all the day,
Her high-borne turban'd head she wags, and rolls
    her darkling eye,

And courtesies to the regiments, the guidons mov-
ing by.

What is it, fateful woman, so blear, hardly human ?
Why wag your head with turban bound, yellow, red
and green ?
Are the things so strange and marvellous you see or
have seen ?

WALT WHITMAN.

SAVANNAH.

Thou hast not drooped thy stately head,
Thy woes a wondrous beauty shed !
Not like a lamb to slaughter led,
But with the lion's monarch tread,
Thou comest to thy battle bed,
  Savannah ! O Savannah !

Thine arm of flesh is girded strong;
The blue veins swell beneath thy wrong;
To thee the triple cords belong
Of woe and death and shameless wrong,
And spirit vaunted long, too long !
  Savannah ! O Savannah !

No blood-stains spot thy forehead fair;
Only the martyrs' blood is there;
It gleams upon thy bosom bier,
It moves thy deep, deep soul to prayer,
And tunes a dirge for thy sad ear,
  Savannah ! O Savannah !

Thy clean white hand is opened wide
For weal or woe, thou Freedom Bride ;
The sword-sheath sparkles at thy side,
Thy plighted troth, whate'er betide,
Thou hast but Freedom for thy guide,
  Savannah ! O Savannah !

What though the heavy storm-cloud lowers,
Still at thy feet the old oak towers;
Still fragrant are thy jessamine bowers,
And things of beauty, love, and flowers
Are smiling o'er this land of ours,
          My sunny home, Savannah!

There is no film before thy sight,—
Thou seest woe and death and night,
And blood upon thy banner bright;
But in thy full wrath's kindled might
What carest thou for woe or night?
          My rebel home, Savannah!

Come—for the crown is on thy head!
Thy woes a wondrous beauty shed;
Not like a lamb to slaughter led,
But with the lion's monarch tread,
Oh! come unto thy battle bed,
          Savannah! O Savannah!
                    ALETHEA S. BURROUGHS.

THE FOE AT THE GATES.
[*Charleston*, 1865.]

RING round her! children of her glorious skies,
    Whom she hath nursed to stature proud and great;
Catch one last glance from her imploring eyes,
    Then close your ranks and face the threatening
        fate.

Ring round her! with a wall of horrent steel
    Confront the foe, nor mercy ask nor give;
And in her hour of anguish let her feel
    That ye can die whom she has taught to live.

Ring round her! swear, by every lifted blade,
    To shield from wrong the mother who gave you
        birth;

That never violent hand on her be laid,
  Nor base foot desecrate her hallowed hearth.

Curst be the dastard who shall halt or doubt !
  And doubly damned who casts one look behind !
Ye who are men ! with unsheathed sword, and shout,
  Up with her banner ! give it to the wind !

Peal your wild slogan, echoing far and wide,
  Till every ringing avenue repeat
The gathering cry, and Ashley's angry tide
  Calls to the sea-waves beating round her feet.

Sons, to the rescue ! spurred and belted, come !
  Kneeling, with clasp'd hands, she invokes you now
By the sweet memories of your childhood's home,
  By every manly hope and filial vow,

To save her proud soul from that loathéd thrall
  Which yet her spirit cannot brook to name ;
Or, if her fate be near, and she must fall,
  Spare her—she sues—the agony and shame.

From all her fanes let solemn bells be tolled ;
  Heap with kind hands her costly funeral pyre,
And thus, with pæan sung and anthem rolled,
  Give her unspotted to the God of Fire.

Gather around her sacred ashes then,
  Sprinkle the cherished dust with crimson rain,
Die ! as becomes a race of free-born men,
  Who will not crouch to wear the bondman's chain.

So, dying, ye shall win a high renown,
  If not in life, at least by death, set free ;
And send her fame through endless ages down—
  The last grand holocaust of Liberty.

                              JOHN DICKSON BRUNS.

FLAG OF TRUCE.

LET us bury our dead:
Since we may not of vantage or victory prate;
And our army, so grand in the onslaught of late,
All crippled has shrunk to its trenches instead,—
  For the carnage was great:
  Let us bury our dead.

  Let us bury our dead:
Oh, we thought to surprise you, as, panting and
 flushed,
From our works to assault you we valiantly rushed:
But you fought like the gods—till we faltered and
 fled,
  And the earth, how it blushed!
  Let us bury our dead.

  So we bury our dead—
From the field; from the range and the crash of the
 gun;
From the kisses of love; from the face of the sun!
Oh, the silence they keep while we dig their last bed!
  Lay them in, one by one:
  So we bury our dead.

  Fast we bury our dead:
All too scanty the time, let us work as we may,
For the foe burns for strife and our ranks are at
 bay:
O'er the graves we are digging what legions will
 tread—
  Swift, and eager to slay,
  Though we bury our dead.

  See, we bury our dead!
Oh, they fought as the young and the dauntless will
 fight,
Who fancy their war is a war for the right!

Right or wrong, it was precious—this blood they
    have shed :
        Surely God will requite,
        And we bury our dead.

        Yes, we bury our dead.
If they erred as they fought, will He charge them
    with blame,
When their hearts beat aright, and the truth was
    their aim ?
Nay, never in vain has such offering bled—
        North or South, 'tis the same—
        Fast we bury our dead.

        Thus we bury our dead.
Oh, ye men of the North, with your banner that
    waves
Far and wide o'er our Southland, made rugged with
    graves,
Are ye verily right, that so well ye have sped ?
        Were we wronging our slaves ?
        Well—we bury our dead.

        Ah, we bury our dead !
And granting you all you have claimed on the
    whole—
Are we 'spoiled of our birthright and stricken in
    soul,
To be spurned at Heaven's court when its records
    are read ?
        Nay, expound not the scroll
        Till we bury our dead !

        Haste and bury our dead !
No time for revolving of right and of wrong ;
We must venture our souls with the rest of the
    throng ;
And our God must be Judge, as He sits overhead,
        Of the weak and the strong,
        While we bury our dead.

Now peace to our dead :
Fair grow the sweet blossoms of Spring where they
lie . . . .
Hark ! the musketry roars, and the rifles reply ;
Oh, the fight will be close and the carnage be
dread ;
To the ranks let us hie,—
We have buried our dead.

AMANDA T. JONES.

"STACK ARMS !"

[*Written in prison at Fort Delaware, Del., on hear-
ing of the surrender of General Lee.*]

" STACK ARMS !" I've gladly heard the cry
When, weary with the dusty tread
Of marching troops, as night drew nigh,
I sank upon my soldier bed,
And calmly slept ; the starry dome
Of heaven's blue arch my canopy,
And mingled with my dreams of home
The thoughts of Peace and Liberty.

" *Stack Arms !*" I've heard it when the shout
Exulting ran along our line,
Of foes hurled back in bloody rout,
Captured, dispersed ; its tones divine
Then came to mine enraptured ear,
Guerdon of duty nobly done,
And glistened on my cheek the tear
Of grateful joy for victory won.

" *Stack Arms !*" In faltering accents, slow
And sad, it creeps from tongue to tongue,
A broken, murmuring wail of woe,
From manly hearts by anguish wrung.

LEE SAYING FAREWELL TO HIS SOLDIERS.

(See page 276 — "Stack Arms.")

Like victims of a midnight dream,
  We move, we know not how nor why ;
For life and hope like phantoms seem,
  And it would be relief—to die !

JOSEPH BLYNTH ALSTON.

"ASHES OF GLORY."

FOLD up the gorgeous silken sun,
  By bleeding martyrs blest,
And heap the laurels it has won
  Above its place of rest.

No trumpet's note need harshly blare—
  No drum funereal roll—
Nor trailing sables drape the bier
  That frees a dauntless soul.

It lived with Lee, and decked his brow
  From Fate's empyreal palm ;
It sleeps the sleep of Jackson now,
  As spotless and as calm.

It was outnumbered—not outdone ;
  And they shall shuddering tell,
Who struck the blow, its latest gun
  Flashed ruin as it fell.

Sleep, shrouded ensign !—not the breeze
  That smote the victor tar
With death, across the heaving seas
  Of fiery Trafalgar ;—

Not Arthur's knights, amid the gloom
  Their knightly deeds have starred,
Nor Gallic Henry's matchless plume,
  Nor peerless-born Bayard ;—

Not all that antique fables feign
  And Orient dreams disgorge,
Nor yet the silver cross of Spain,
  And lion of St. George,—

Can bid thee pale.   Proud emblem, still
  Thy crimson glory shines
Beyond the lengthened shades that fill
  Their proudest kingly lines.

Sleep, in thine own historic night,—
  And be thy blazoned scroll:
A warrior's banner takes its flight
  To greet the warrior's soul!

A. J. REQUIER.

THE CONQUERED BANNER.

[*This is one of the many famous poems whose authorship has been in dispute.   Simms, in his "War Poetry of the South," credits it to "Anna Peyre Dinnies, of Louisiana;" and Longfellow's "Poems of Places" gives it as anonymous. But Father Ryan is unquestionably the author.   It appears in the complete edition of his Poems (Baltimore, 1883), and he has written the editor of the present collection: "I wrote 'The Conquered Banner' at Knoxville, Tenn., one evening soon after Lee's surrender, when my mind was engrossed with thoughts of our dead soldiers and dead cause.   It was first published in the New York 'Freeman's Journal.' I never had any idea that the poem, written in less than an hour, would attain celebrity.   No doubt the circumstances of its appearance lent it much of its fame.   In expressing my own emotions at the time, I echoed the unuttered feelings of the Southern people; and so 'The Conquered Banner' became the requiem of the Lost Cause."*]

FURL that Banner, for 'tis weary,
Round its staff 'tis drooping dreary:
  Furl it, fold it,—it is best;
For there's not a man to wave it,
And there's not a sword to save it,
And there's not one left to lave it

In the blood which heroes gave it,
And its foes now scorn and brave it :
    Furl it, hide it,—let it rest !

Take that Banner down ! 'tis tattered ;
Broken is its staff and shattered,
And the valiant hosts are scattered
    Over whom it floated high ;
Oh, 'tis hard for us to fold it,
Hard to think there's none to hold it,
Hard that those who once unrolled it
    Now must furl it with a sigh !

Furl that Banner—furl it sadly ;
Once ten thousands hailed it gladly,
And ten thousands wildly, madly,
    Swore it should forever wave—
Swore that foemen's swords could **never**
Hearts like theirs entwined dissever,
And that flag should float forever
    O'er their freedom or their grave !

Furl it !—for the hands that grasped it,
And the hearts that fondly clasped it,
    Cold and dead are lying low ;
And the Banner—it is trailing,
While around it sounds the wailing
    Of its people in their woe ;
For though conquered, they adore it—
Love the cold dead hands that bore it,
Weep for those who fell before it,
Pardon those who trailed and tore it ;
And oh, wildly they deplore it,
    Now to furl and fold it so !

Furl that Banner ! True, 'tis gory,
Yet 'tis wreathed around with glory,
And 'twill live in song and story
    Though its folds are in the dust !

For its fame on brightest pages,
Penned by poets and by sages,
Shall go sounding down the ages—
    Furl its folds though now we must !

Furl that Banner, softly, slowly;
Treat it gently—it is holy,
    For it droops above the dead ;
Touch it not—unfold it never ;
Let it droop there, furled forever,—
    For its people's hopes are fled.

                          ABRAM J. RYAN.

IN THE LAND WHERE WE WERE DREAMING.

FAIR were our visions ! Oh, they were as grand
As ever floated out of faerie land ;
    Children were we in single faith,
    But God-like children, whom nor death
Nor threat nor danger drove from honor's path,
    In the land where we were dreaming.

Proud were our men, as pride of birth could render ;
As violets, our women pure and tender ;
    And when they spoke, their voice did thrill
    Until at eve the whip-poor-will,
At morn the mocking-bird, were mute and still,
    In the land where we were dreaming.

And we had graves that covered more of glory
Than ever tracked tradition's ancient story ;
    And in our dream we wove the thread
    Of principles for which had bled
And suffered long our own immortal dead,
    In the land where we were dreaming.

Though in our land we had both bond and free,
Both were content ; and so God let them be ;—

'Till envy coveted our land,
And those fair fields our valor won ;
But little recked we, for we still slept on,
    In the land where we were dreaming.

Our sleep grew troubled and our dreams grew
        wild—
Red meteors flashed across our heaven's field ;
    Crimson the moon ; between the Twins
    Barbed arrows fly, and then begins
Such strife as when disorder's Chaos reigns,
    In the land where we were dreaming.

Down from her sun-lit heights smiled Liberty
And waved her cap in sign of Victory—
    The world approved, and everywhere,
    Except where growled the Russian bear,
The good, the brave, the just gave us their prayer
    In the land where we were dreaming.

We fancied that a Government was ours—
We challenged place among the world's great
        powers ;
    We talked in sleep of Rank, Commission,
    Until so life-like grew our vision
That he who dared to doubt but met derision,
    In the land where we were dreaming.

We looked on high : a banner there was seen,
Whose field was blanched and spotless in its sheen—
    Chivalry's cross its Union bears,
    And veterans swearing by their scars
Vowed they would bear it through a hundred wars,
    In the land where we were dreaming.

A hero came amongst us as we slept ;
At first he lowly knelt—then rose and wept ;
    Then gathering up a thousand spears
    He swept across the field of Mars ;
Then bowed farewell and walked beyond the stars,
    In the land where we were dreaming.

We looked again : another figure still
Gave hope, and nerved each individual will—
    Full of grandeur, clothed with power,
    Self-poised, erect, he ruled the hour
With stern, majestic sway—of strength a tower,
    In the land where we were dreaming.

As, while great Jove, in bronze, a warder God,
Gazed eastward from the Forum where he stood,
    Rome felt herself secure and free,
    So, " Richmond's safe," we said, while we
Beheld a bronzéd hero—God-like Lee,
    In the land where we were dreaming.

As wakes the soldier when the alarum calls—
As wakes the mother when the infant falls—
    As starts the traveller when around
    His sleeping couch the fire-bells sound—
So woke our nation with a single bound,
    In the land where we were dreaming.

Woe! woe is me! the startled mother cried—
While we have slept our noble sons have died!
    Woe! woe is me! how strange and sad
    That all our glorious vision's fled,
And left us nothing real but the dead,
    In the land where we were dreaming.

DANIEL B. LUCAS.

———

ABRAHAM LINCOLN.

A HORATIAN ODE.

NOT as when some great Captain falls
In battle, where his country calls,
    Beyond the struggling lines
    That push his dread designs

To doom, by some stray ball struck dead:
Or, in the last charge, at the head
   Of his determined men,
   Who *must* be victors then.

Nor as when sink the civic great,
The safer pillars of the State,
   Whose calm, mature, wise words
   Suppress the need of swords.

With no such tears as e'er were shed
Above the noblest of our dead
   Do we to-day deplore
   The Man that is no more.

Our sorrow hath a wider scope,
Too strange for fear, too vast for hope,
   A wonder, blind and dumb,
   That waits—what is to come!

Not more astounded had we been
If Madness, that dark night, unseen,
   Had in our chambers crept,
   And murdered while we slept.

We woke to find a mourning earth,
Our Lares shivered on the hearth,
   The roof-tree fallen, all
   That could affright, appall!

Such thunderbolts, in other lands,
Have smitten the rod from royal hands,
   But spared, with us, till now,
   Each laurelled Cæsar's brow.

No Cæsar he whom we lament,
A Man without a precedent,
   Sent, it would seem, to do
   His work, and perish, too.

Not by the weary cares of State,
The endless tasks, which will not wait,
    Which, often done in vain,
    Must yet be done again :

Not in the dark, wild tide of war,
Which rose so high, and rolled so far,
    Sweeping from sea to sea
    In awful anarchy :

Four fateful years of mortal strife,
Which slowly drained the nation's life,
    (Yet for each drop that ran
    There sprang an armêd man !)

Not then ; but when, by measures meet,
By victory, and by defeat,
    By courage, patience, skill,
    The people's fixed " *We will !*"

Had pierced, had crushed Rebellion dead,
Without a hand, without a head,
    At last, when all was well,
    He fell, O how he fell !

The time, the place, the stealing shape,
The coward shot, the swift escape,
    The wife, the widow's scream,—
    It is a hideous Dream !

A dream ? What means this pageant, then ?
These multitudes of solemn men,
    Who speak not when they meet,
    But throng the silent street ?

The flags half-mast that late so high
Flaunted at each new victory ?
    (The stars no brightness shed,
    But bloody looks the red !)

The black festoons that stretch for miles,
And turn the streets to funeral aisles?
 (No house too poor to show
 The nation's badge of woe.)

The cannon's sudden, sullen boom,
The bells that toll of death and doom,
 The rolling of the drums,
 The dreadful car that comes?

*   *   *   *   *

Peace! Let the long procession come;
For hark, the mournful muffled drum,
 The trumpet's wail afar,
 And see, the awful car!

Peace! Let the sad procession go,
While cannon boom and bells toll slow.
 And go, thou sacred car,
 Bearing our woe afar!

Go, darkly borne, from State to State,
Whose loyal, sorrowing cities wait
 To honor all they can
 The dust of that good man.

Go, grandly borne, with such a train
As greatest kings might die to gain.
 The just, the wise, the brave,
 Attend thee to the grave.

And you, the soldiers of our wars,
Bronzed veterans, grim with noble scars,
 Salute him once again,
 Your late commander—slain!

Yes, let your tears indignant fall,
But leave your muskets on the wall;
 Your country needs you now
 Beside the forge—the plough.

(When Justice shall unsheathe her brand,
If Mercy may not stay her hand,
   Nor would we have it so,
   She must direct the blow.)

And you, amid the master-race,
Who seem so strangely out of place,
   Know ye who cometh ?   He
   Who hath declared ye free.

Bow while the body passes—nay,
Fall on your knees, and weep, and pray !
   Weep, weep—I would ye might—
   Your poor black faces white !

And, children, you must come in bands,
With garlands in your little hands,
   Of blue and white and red,
   To strew before the dead.

So sweetly, sadly, sternly goes
The Fallen to his last repose.
   Beneath no mighty dome,
   But in his modest home ;

The churchyard where his children rest,
The quiet spot that suits him best,
   There shall his grave be made,
   And there his bones be laid.

And there his countrymen shall come,
With memory proud, with pity dumb,
   And strangers far and near,
   For many and many a year.

For many a year and many an age,
While History on her ample page
   The virtues shall enroll
   Of that Paternal Soul.

                RICHARD HENRY STODDARD.

WHEN LILACS LAST IN THE DOORYARD BLOOM'D.

[" *I think this poem and 'Lowell's Commemoration Ode,'
each in its own way, the most notable elegies resulting from
the war and its episodes.*"—*E. C. Stedman.*]

WHEN lilacs last in the dooryard bloom'd,
And the great star early droop'd in the western sky
 in the night,
I mourn'd, and yet shall mourn with ever-returning
 spring.

Ever-returning spring, trinity sure to me you bring,
Lilac blooming perennial and drooping star in the
 west,
And thought of him I love.

O powerful western fallen star !
O shades of night—O moody, tearful night !
O great star disappear'd—O the black murk that
 hides the star !
O cruel hands that hold me powerless—O helpless
 soul of me !
O harsh surrounding cloud that will not free my
 soul.

In the door-yard fronting an old farm-house near
 the white-wash'd palings,
Stands the lilac-bush tall-growing with heart-shap'd
 leaves of rich green,
With many a pointed blossom rising delicate, with
 the perfume strong I love,
With every leaf a miracle—and from this bush in the
 door-yard,
With delicate-color'd blossoms and heart-shaped
 leaves of rich green,
A sprig with its flower I break.

In the swamp in seclud'd recesses
A shy and hidden bird is warbling a song.

Solitary the thrush,
The hermit withdrawn to himself, avoiding the set-
    tlements,
Sings by himself a song.

Song of the bleeding throat,
Death's outlet song of life, (for well, dear brother, I
    know
If thou wast not granted to sing thou would'st surely
    die.)

Over the breast of the spring, the land, amid cities,
Amid lanes, and through old woods, where lately the
        violets peep'd from the ground, spotting the gray
        debris,
Amid the grass in the fields each side of the lanes,
        passing the endless grass,
Passing the yellow-spear'd wheat, every grain from
        its shroud in the dark-brown fields uprisen,
Passing the apple-tree blows of white and pink in
        the orchards,
Carrying a corpse to where it shall rest in the grave,
Night and day journeys a coffin.

Coffin that passes through lanes and streets,
Through day and night with the great cloud dark-
        ening the land,
With the pomp of the inloop'd flags, with the cities
        draped in black,
With the show of the States themselves as of crape-
        veil'd women standing,
With processions long and winding and the flam-
        beaus of the night,
With the countless torches lit, with the silent sea of
        faces and the unbared heads,
With the waiting depot, the arriving coffin and the
        sombre faces,
With dirges through the night, with the thousand
        voices rising strong and solemn,

With all the mournful voices of the dirges pour'd
    around the coffin,
The dim-lit churches and the shuddering organs—
    where amid these you journey,
With the tolling, tolling bells' perpetual clang,
Here, coffin that slowly passes,
I give you my sprig of lilac.

          *   *   *   *   *   *

O how shall I warble myself for the dead one there
    I loved?
And how shall I deck my song for the large sweet
    soul that has gone?
And what shall my perfume be for the grave of him
    I love?

Sea-winds blown from east and west,
Blown from the Eastern sea and blown from the
    Western sea, till there on the prairies meeting,
These and with these and the breath of my chant
I'll perfume the grave of him I love.

          *   *   *   *   *   *

To the tally of my soul,
Loud and strong kept up the gray-brown bird,
With pure deliberate notes spreading filling the
    night.

Loud in the pines and cedars dim,
Clear in the freshness moist and the swamp per-
    fume,
And I with my comrades there in the night.

While my sight that was bound in my eyes unclos'd,
As to long panoramas of visions.

And I saw askant the armies,
I saw as in noiseless dreams hundreds of battle-
    flags,
Borne through the smoke of the battles and pierc'd
    with missiles I saw them,

And carried hither and yon through the smoke, and
    torn and bloody,
And at last but a few shreds left on the staffs, (and
    all in silence,)
And the staffs all splinter'd and broken.

I saw battle-corpses, myriads of them,
And the white skeletons of young men, I saw them,
I saw the debris and debris of all the slain soldiers
    of the war,
But I saw they were not as was thought,
They themselves were fully at rest, they suffer'd not,
The living remain'd and suffer'd, the mother suffer'd,
And the wife and the child and the musing comrade
    suffer'd,
And the armies that remained suffer'd.

Passing the visions, passing the night,
Passing, unloosing the hold of my comrades' hands,
Passing the song of the hermit bird and the tallying
    song of my soul,
Victorious song, death's outlet song, yet varying
    ever-altering song,
As low and wailing, yet clear the notes, rising and
    falling, flooding the night,
Sadly sinking and fainting, as warning and warn-
    ing, and yet again bursting with joy,
Covering the earth and filling the spread of the
    heaven,
As that powerful psalm in the night I heard from
    recesses,
Passing, I leave thee lilac with heart-shap'd leaves,
I leave thee there in the door-yard, blooming, re-
    turning with spring.

I cease from my song for thee,
From my gaze on thee in the west, fronting the
    west, communing with thee,
O comrade lustrous with silver face in the night.

Yet each to keep and all, retrievements out of the
 night,
The song, the wondrous chant of the gray-brown
 bird,
And the tallying-chant, the echo arous'd in my soul,
With the lustrous and drooping star with the
 countenance full of woe,
With the holders holding my hand nearing the call
 of the bird,
Comrades mine and I in the midst, and their memory
 ever to keep, for the dead I loved so well,
For the sweetest, wisest soul of all my days and
 lands—and this for his dear sake,
Lilac and star and bird twined with the chant of my
 soul,
There in the fragrant pines and the cedars dusk and
 dim.

WALT WHITMAN.

O CAPTAIN ! MY CAPTAIN !

[*Abraham Lincoln, died April* 15, 1865.]

O CAPTAIN ! my Captain ! our fearful trip is done ;
The ship has weather'd every rack, the prize we
 sought is won ;
The port is near, the bells I hear, the people all
 exulting,
While follow eyes the steady keel, the vessel grim
 and daring :
   But O heart ! heart ! heart !
    O the bleeding drops of red,
     Where on the deck my Captain lies,
      Fallen cold and dead !

O Captain ! my Captain ! rise up and hear the bells ;
Rise up—for you the flag is flung—for you the
 bugle trills ;

For you bouquets and ribbon'd wreaths—for you
    the shores a-crowding ;
For you they call, the swaying mass, their eager
    faces turning ;
        Here Captain ! dear father !
          This arm beneath your head ;
            It is some dream that on the deck
              You've fallen cold and dead.

My Captain does not answer, his lips are pale and
    still ;
My father does not feel my arm, he has no pulse
    nor will :
The ship is anchor'd safe and sound, its voyage
    closed and done ;
From fearful trip the victor ship comes in with ob-
    ject won :
        Exult, O shores, and ring, O bells !
          But I, with mournful tread,
            Walk the deck my Captain lies,
            Fallen cold and dead.
                WALT WHITMAN.

ABRAHAM LINCOLN.

[*Summer*, 1865.]

DEAD is the roll of the drums,
    And the distant thunders die,
    They fade in the far-off sky ;
And a lovely summer comes,
    Like the smile of Him on high.

Lulled the storm and the onset ;
    Earth lies in a sunny swoon ;
    Stiller splendor of noon,
Softer glory of sunset,
    Milder starlight and moon !

ABRAHAM LINCOLN.

(See pages 291 and 293.)

For the kindly Seasons love us ;
　They smile over trench and clod,
(Where we left the bravest of us,)—
　There's a brighter green of the sod,
And a holier calm above us
　In the blessed Blue of God.

The roar and ravage were vain ;
　And Nature, that never yields,
Is busy with sun and rain
At her old sweet work again
　On the lonely battle-fields.

How the tall white daisies grow
　Where the grim artillery rolled !
(Was it only a moon ago ?
　It seems a century old,)—

And the bee hums in the clover,
　As the pleasant June comes on ;
Aye, the wars are all over,—
　But our good Father is gone.

There was tumbling of traitor fort,
　Flaming of traitor fleet,—
Lighting of city and port,
　Clasping in square and street.

There was thunder of mine and gun,
　Cheering by mast and tent,—
When—his dread work all done,
And his high fame full won—
　Died the good President.

In his quiet chair he sate,
　Pure of malice or guile,
Stainless of fear or hate,—
　And there played a pleasant smile
On the rough and careworn face ;
　For his heart was all the while
On means of mercy and grace.

The brave old Flag drooped o'er him,
  (A fold in the hard hand lay,)—
  He looked, perchance, on the play,—
But the scene was a shadow before him,
  For his thoughts were far away.

'Twas but the morn , (yon fearful
  Death-shade, gloomy and vast,
  Lifting slowly at last,)
  His household heard him say,
" 'Tis long since I've been so cheerful,
  So light of heart as to-day."

'Twas dying, the long dread clang,—
  But, or ever the blessed ray
  Of peace could brighten to-day,
  Murder stood by the way,—
Treason struck home his fang !
One throb—and, without a pang,
  That pure soul passed away.
      *   *   *   *
Kindly Spirit ! — Ah, when did treason
  Bid such a generous nature cease,
Mild by temper and strong by reason,
  But ever leaning to love and peace ?

A head how sober ! a heart how spacious !
  A manner equal with high or low ;
Rough, but gentle ; uncouth, but gracious ;
  And still inclining to lips of woe.

Patient when saddest, calm when sternest,
  Grieved when rigid for justice' sake ;
Given to jest, yet ever in earnest,
  If aught of right or truth were at stake.

Simple of heart, yet shrewd therewith ;
  Slow to resolve, but firm to hold ;
Still with parable and with myth
  Seasoning truth, like Them of old ;

Aptest humor and quaintest pith!
(Still we smile o'er the tales he told.)

Yet whoso might pierce the guise
  Of mirth in the man we mourn
Would mark, and with grieved surprise,
  All the great soul had borne,
In the piteous lines, and the kind, sad eyes
  So dreadfully wearied and worn.

   *   *   *   *   *

The Land's great lamentations,
  The mighty mourning of cannon,
    The myriad flags half-mast,—
The late remorse of the nations,
  Grief from Volga to Shannon!
    (Now they know thee at last.)

How, from gray Niagara's shore
  To Canaveral's surfy shoal,—
From the rough Atlantic roar
  To the long Pacific roll,—
    For bereavement and for dole,
Every cottage wears its weed,
  White as thine own pure soul,
And black as the traitor deed!

How, under a nation's pall,
  The dust so dear in our sight
    To its home on the prairie passed,—
The leagues of funeral,
  The myriads, morn and night,
    Pressing to look their last!

Nor alone the State's Eclipse;
  But how tears in hard eyes gather,—
And on rough and bearded lips,
Of the regiments and the ships,—
    " Oh, our dear Father!"

And methinks of all the million
   That looked on the dark dead face,
'Neath its sable-plumed pavilion,
   The crone of a humbler race
Is saddest of all to think on,
   And the old swart lips that said,
Sobbing, " Abraham Lincoln !
   Oh, he is dead, he is dead !"

Hush ! let our heavy souls
   To-day be glad ; for agen
The stormy music swells and rolls
   Stirring the hearts of men.

And under the Nation's Dome,
   They've guarded so well and long,
Our boys come marching home,
   Two hundred thousand strong.

All in the pleasant month of May,
   With war-worn colors and drums,
Still, through the livelong summer's day,
   Regiment, regiment comes.

Like the tide, yesty and barmy,
   That sets on a wild lee-shore,
Surge the ranks of an army
   Never reviewed before !

Who shall look on the like agen,
   Or see such host of the brave ?
A mighty River of marching men
     Rolls the Capital through—
   Rank on rank, and wave on wave,
     Of bayonet-crested blue !

How the chargers neigh and champ,
(Their riders weary of camp,)
   With curvet and with caracole !—
The cavalry comes with thundrous tramp,
   And the cannons heavily roll.

And ever, flowery and gay,
The Staff sweeps on in a spray
    Of tossing forelocks and manes ;
But each bridle-arm has a weed
Of funeral, black as the steed
    That fiery Sheridan reins.

Grandest of mortal sights
    The sun-browned ranks to view,—
The Colors ragg'd in a hundred fights,
    And the dusty Frocks of Blue !

And all day, mile on mile,
With cheer, and waving, and smile,
The war-worn legions defile
    Where the nation's noblest stand ;
And the Great Lieutenant looks on,
    With the Flower of a rescued Land,
For the terrible work is done,
And the Good Fight is won
    For God and for Fatherland.

So, from the fields they win,
    Our men are marching home,
    A million are marching home !
To the cannon's thundering din,
    And banners on mast and dome,—
And the ships come sailing in
    With all their ensigns dight,
    As erst for a great sea-fight.

Let every color fly,
    Every pennon flaunt in pride ;
Wave, Starry Flag, on high !
Float in the sunny sky,
    Stream o'er the stormy tide !
For every stripe of stainless hue,
And every star in the field of blue,
Ten thousand of the brave and true
    Have laid them down and died.

And in all our pride to-day
  We think, with a tender pain,
Of those so far away,
  They will not come home again.

And our boys had fondly thought,
  To-day, in marching by,
From the ground so dearly bought,
And the fields so bravely fought,
  To have met their Father's eye.

But they may not see him in place,
  Nor their ranks be seen of him ;
We look for the well-known face,
  And the splendor is strangely dim.

Perished ?—who was it said
  Our Leader had passed away ?
Dead ?   Our President dead ?—
  He has not died for a day !

We mourn for a little breath,
  Such as, late or soon, dust yields ;
But the Dark Flower of Death
  Blooms in the fadeless fields.

We looked on a cold, still brow :
  But Lincoln could yet survive ;
  He never was more alive,
Never nearer than now.

For the pleasant season found him,
  Guarded by faithful hands,
  In the fairest of Summer Lands :
With his own brave Staff around him,—
  There our President stands.

There they are all at his side,
  The noble hearts and true,
  That did all men might do,—
Then slept, with their swords, and died.

Of little the storm has reft us
    But the brave and kindly clay,
('Tis but dust where Lander left us,
    And but turf where Lyon lay.)

There's Winthrop, true to the end,
    And Ellsworth of long ago,
    (First fair young head laid low !)
There's Baker, the brave old friend,
    And Douglas, the friendly foe :

(Baker, that still stood up
    When 'twas death on either hand :
" 'Tis a soldier's part to stoop,
    But the Senator must stand.")

The heroes gather and form :—
    There's Cameron, with his scars,
Sedgwick, of siege and storm,
    And Mitchell, that joined his stars.

Winthrop, of sword and pen,
    Wadsworth, with silver hair,
Mansfield, ruler of men,
    And brave McPherson are there.

Birney, who led so long,
    Abbott, born to command,
Elliott the bold, and Strong,
    Who fell on the hard-fought strand.

Lytle, soldier and bard,
    And the Ellets, sire and son,
Ransom, all grandly scarred,
And Redfield, no more on guard,
    (But Alatoona is won !)

Reno, of pure desert,
    Kearney, with heart of flame,
And Russell, that hid his hurt
    Till the final death-bolt came.

Terrill, dead where he fought,
　　Wallace, that would not yield,
And Sumner, who vainly sought
　　A grave on the foughten field,

(But died ere the end he saw,
　　With years and battles outworn.)
There's Harmon of Kenesaw,
And Ulric Dahlgren, and Shaw,
　　That slept with his Hope Forlorn.

Bayard, that knew not fear,
　　(True as the knight of yore,)
And Putnam, and Paul Revere,
　　Worthy the names they bore.

Allen, who died for others,
　　Bryan, of gentle fame,
And the brave New-England brothers
　　That have left us Lowell's name.

Home, at last, from the wars,—
　　Stedman, the staunch and mild,
　　And Janeway, our hero-child,
Home, with his fifteen scars !

There's Porter, ever in front,
　　True son of a sea-king sire,
And Christian Foote, and Dupont,
(Dupont, who led his ships
Rounding the first Ellipse
　　Of thunder and of fire.)

There's Ward, with his brave death-wounds,
　　And Cummings, of spotless name,
And Smith, who hurtled his rounds
　　When deck and hatch were aflame ;

Wainwright, steadfast and true,
　　Rodgers, of brave sea-blood,

And Craven, with ship and crew
  Sunk in the salt sea flood.

And, a little later to part,
  Our Captain, noble and dear—
  (Did they deem thee, then, austere?
Drayton !—O pure and kindly heart !
  Thine is the seaman's tear.)

All such,—and many another,
  (Ah, list how long to name !)
That stood like brother by brother,
  And died on the field of fame.

And around—(for there can cease
  This earthly trouble)—they throng,
The friends that had passed in peace,
  The foes that have seen their wrong.

(But, a little from the rest,
  With sad eyes looking down,
  And brows of softened frown,
With stern arms on the chest,
Are two, standing abreast,—
  Stonewall and Old John Brown.)

But the stainless and the true,
  These by their President stand,
To look on his last review,
  Or march with the old command.

And lo, from a thousand fields,
  From all the old battle-haunts,
A greater Army than Sherman wields,
  A grander Review than Grant's !

Gathered home from the grave,
  Risen from sun and rain,—
Rescued from wind and wave,
  Out of the stormy main,—

The Legions of our Brave
　　Are all in their lines again !

Many a stout Corps that went,
Full-ranked, from camp and tent,
　　And brought back a brigade ;
Many a brave regiment,
　　That mustered only a squad.

The lost battalions,
　　That, when the fight went wrong,
Stood and died at their guns,—
　　The stormers steady and strong,

With their best blood that bought
　　Scarp, and ravelin, and wall—
The companies that fought
　　Till a corporal's guard was all.

Many a valiant crew,
　　That passed in battle and wreck,—
Ah, so faithful and true !
　　They died on the bloody deck,
They sank in the soundless blue.

All the loyal and bold
　　That lay on a soldier's bier,—
　　The stretchers borne to the rear,
The hammocks lowered to the hold.

The shattered wreck we hurried,
　　In death-fight, from deck and port,—
The Blacks that Wagner buried,
　　That died in the Bloody Fort !

Comrades of camp and mess,
　　Left, as they lay, to die,
In the battle's sorest stress,
　　When the storm of fight swept by :
They lay in the Wilderness—
　　Ah, where did they not lie ?

In the tangled swamp they lay,
    They lay so still on the sward !—
They rolled in the sick-bay,
Moaning their lives away ;—
    They flushed in the fevered ward.

They rotted in Libby yonder,
    They starved in the foul stockade,—
Hearing afar the thunder
    Of the Union cannonade !

But the old wounds all are healed,
    And the dungeoned limbs are free,—
The Blue Frocks rise from the field,
    The Blue Jackets out of the sea.

They've 'scaped from the torture-den,
    They've broken the bloody sod,
They're all come to life agen !—
The Third of a Million men
    That died for Thee and for God !

A tenderer green than May
    The Eternal Season wears,—
The blue of our summer's day
    Is dim and pallid to theirs,—
The Horror faded away,
    And 'twas heaven all unawares !

Tents on the Infinite Shore !
    Flags in the azuline sky,
Sails on the seas once more !
    To-day, in the heaven on high,
All under arms once more !

The troops are all in their lines,
    The guidons flutter and play :
But every bayonet shines,
    For all must march to-day.

What lofty pennons flaunt ?
What mighty echoes haunt,
  As of great guns, o'er the main?
  Hark to the sound again !
The Congress is all-ataunt !
  The Cumberland's manned again !

All the ships and their men
  Are in line of battle to-day,—
All at quarters, as when
  Their last roll thundered away,—
All at their guns, as then,
  For the Fleet salutes to-day.

The armies have broken camp
  On the vast and sunny plain,
  The drums are rolling again ;
With steady, measured tramp,
  They're marching all again.

With alignment firm and solemn,
  Once again they form
In mighty square and column,—
  But never for charge and storm.

The Old Flag they died under
  Floats above them on the shore,
And on the great ships yonder
  The ensigns dip once more,—
And once again the thunder
  Of the thirty guns and four !

In solid platoons of steel,
  Under heaven's triumphal arch,
The long lines break and wheel ;
  And the word is, " Forward, march

The colors ripple o'erhead,
  The drums roll up to the sky,

And with martial time and tread
  The regiments all pass by,—
The Ranks of our faithful Dead,
  Meeting their President's eye.

With a soldier's quiet pride
  They smile o'er the perished pain,
  For their anguish was not vain,—
For thee, O Father, we died!
  And we did not die in vain.

March on, your last brave mile!
  Salute him, Star and Lace,
Form round him, rank and file,
  And look on the kind, rough face;
But the quaint and homely smile
  Has a glory and a grace
It never had known erewhile,—
  Never, in time and space.

Close round him, hearts of pride!
Press near him, side by side,—
  Our Father is not alone!
For the Holy Right ye died,
And Christ, the Crucified,
  Waits to welcome his own.

               HENRY HOWARD BROWNELL.

PROMETHEUS VINCTUS.

[*Written while Jefferson Davis was a prisoner in Fortress Monroe, where he was confined for two years after the downfall of the Confederacy.*]

PROMETHEUS on the cold rock bound,
  The vulture at his heart,
In you, O Southern Chief, has found
  A fitting counterpart.

The Titan by his wondrous skill
  Fashioned a man from clay ;
You formed a nation at your will,
  And bent it to your sway.

He made a dull insensate thing,
  A form without a soul ;
Your spirit, with life's stirring spring,
  Electrified the whole.

Like him, your greatness did you wrong,
  Your virtue was your bane ;
Each soared above the common throng,
  Each found a prison chain !

Your aims alike were noble ; well
  Ye battled, till at length
Each, having done his utmost, fell—
  Dragged down by Force and Strength !

Ye fell, but gained a height sublime,
  And more than mortal fame,
Binding upon the breast of Time
  An ever glorious name.

No farther may the semblance go.
  O'erwhelmed by Zeus' frown,
Prometheus with supernal woe
  In agony bowed down :

While you, O gentle sufferer, feel,
  Though bending 'neath the rod,
A holy joy, the sign and seal
  Of a sustaining God !

Within your grated prison cell
  A gracious guest abides,
And by the same low-spoken spell
  Which stilled the raging tides

Of fierce Tiberias, he exerts
  A spirit-soothing calm,
And heals the sting of earthly hurts
  With heavenly peace and balm.

Around you in unending play
  The bounding billows roar,
And white with crests of seething spray
  Break thundering on the shore.

These ocean-surges well express
  The love, the hopes, the care,
Which to you in your loneliness
  Your faithful people bear.

Chains and a prison cannot wrest
  Your empire from its throne;
You find in every Southern breast
  A kingdom and a home!

The stately land you strove to save,
  In sable robes arrayed,
Majestic mourns beside the grave
  Where all her hopes are laid.

But though she weeps her cherished dead
  With sorrow deep and true,
No tears of bitterness are shed
  Like those that fall for you!

You hold her heart-strings in your hand,
  And every blow and slur
That strikes you as you helpless stand
  Falls doubly hard on her!

Heaven help us all! The New Year dawns
  Again with gladsome birth;
God grant, ere many smiling morns
  Have glorified the earth,

That one may break amid the stars,
    Which, by His blest decree,
Beaming across your prison bars,
    Shall shine upon you free!
                    FANNY DOWNING.

"GONE FORWARD."

[General Robert E. Lee died October 12, 1870. His last words were: " Let the tent be struck !"]

YES, " Let the tent be struck": Victorious morning
    Through every crevice flashes in a day
Magnificent beyond all earth's adorning:
    The night is over; wherefore should he stay ?
    And wherefore should our voices choke to say,
        " The General has gone forward !"

Life's foughten field not once beheld surrender,
    But with superb endurance, present, past,
Our pure Commander, lofty, simple, tender,
    Through good, through ill, held his high purpose
        fast,
    Wearing his armor spotless,—till at last
        Death gave the final " Forward !"

All hearts grew sudden palsied : Yet what said he,
    Thus summoned ?—" Let the tent be struck !"—
        For when
Did call of duty fail to find him ready
    Nobly to do his work in sight of men,
    For God's and for his country's sake—and then
        To watch, wait, or go forward ?

We will not weep,—we dare not ! — Such a story
    As his large life writes on the century's years
Should crowd our bosoms with a flush of glory,
    That manhood's type, supremest that appears
    To-day, he shows the ages.   Nay, no tears
        Because he has gone forward !

Gone forward ?—Whither ?—Where the marshalled
        legions,
  Christ's well-worn soldiers, from their conflicts
        cease,—
Where Faith's true Red-Cross Knights repose in
        regions
  Thick studded with the calm white tents of
        peace,—
  Thither, right joyful to accept release,
    The General has gone forward !

                  MARGARET J. PRESTON.

VANQUISHED.

[*General U. S. Grant, died July* 23, 1885.]

I.

NOT by the ball or brand
Sped by a mortal hand,
Not by the lightning-stroke
When fiery tempests broke,—
Not mid the ranks of war
Fell the great Conqueror.

II.

Unmoved, undismayed,
In the crash and carnage of the cannonade,—
Eye that dimmed not, hand that failed not,
Brain that swerved not, heart that quailed not,
Steel nerve, iron form,—
The dauntless spirit that o'erruled the storm.

III.

While the Hero peaceful slept
A foeman to his chamber crept,
Lightly to the slumberer came,
Touched his brow and breathed his name :

O'er the stricken form there passed
Suddenly an icy blast.

IV.

The Hero woke : rose undismayed :
Saluted Death—and sheathed his blade.

V.

The Conqueror of a hundred fields
To a mightier Conqueror yields ;
No mortal foeman's blow
Laid the great Soldier low ;
Victor in his latest breath—
Vanquished but by Death.

FRANCIS F. BROWNE.

SECOND REVIEW OF THE GRAND ARMY.

I READ last night of the Grand Review
    In Washington's chiefest avenue—
Two Hundred Thousand men in blue,
    I think they said was the number,—
Till I seemed to hear their trampling feet,
The bugle blast and the drum's quick beat,
The clatter of hoofs in the stony street,
The cheers of people who came to greet,
And the thousand details that to repeat
    Would only my verse encumber,—
Till I fell in a revery, sad and sweet,
    And then to a fitful slumber.

When, lo! in a vision I seemed to stand
In the lonely Capitol.   On each hand
Far stretched the portico ; dim and grand
Its columns ranged, like a martial band
Of sheeted spectres whom some command
    Had called to a last reviewing.

And the streets of the city were white and bare,
No footfall echoed across the square;
But out of the misty midnight air
I heard in the distance a trumpet blare,
And the wandering night-winds seemed to bear
    The sound of a far tattooing.

Then I held my breath with fear and dread;
For into the square, with a brazen tread,
There rode a figure whose stately head
    O'erlooked the review that morning,
That never bowed from its firm-set seat
When the living column passed its feet,
Yet now rode steadily up the street
    To the phantom bugle's warning:

Till it reached the Capitol square, and wheeled,
And there in the moonlight stood revealed
A well-known form that in state and field
    Had led our patriot sires;
Whose face was turned to the sleeping camp,
Afar through the river's fog and damp,
That showed no flicker, nor waning lamp,
    Nor wasted bivouac fires.

And I saw a phantom army come,
With never a sound of fife or drum,
But keeping time to a throbbing hum
    Of wailing and lamentation:
The martyred heroes of Malvern Hill,
Of Gettysburg and Chancellorsville,
The men whose wasted figures fill
    The patriot graves of the nation.

And there came the nameless dead,—the men
Who perished in fever-swamp and fen,
The slowly-starved of the prison-pen;
    And, marching beside the others,
Came the dusky martyrs of Pillow's fight,
With limbs enfranchised and bearing bright:

I thought—perhaps 'twas the pale moonlight—
  They looked as white as their brothers !

And so all night marched the Nation's dead,
With never a banner above them spread,
Nor a badge, nor a motto brandishèd ;
No mark—save the bare uncovered head
  Of the silent bronze Reviewer ;
With never an arch save the vaulted sky ;
With never a flower save those that lie
On the distant graves—for love could buy
  No gift that was purer or truer.

So all night long swept the strange array ;
So all night long, till the morning gray,
I watch'd for one who had passed away,
  With a reverent awe and wonder,—
Till a blue cap waved in the lengthening line,
And I knew that one who was kin of mine
Had come ; and I spake—and lo ! that sign
  Awakened me from my slumber.

                                        BRET HARTE.

COMRADES KNOWN IN MARCHES MANY.

COMRADES known in marches many,
Comrades tried in dangers many,
Comrades bound by memories many,
    Brothers ever let us be.
Wounds or sickness may divide us,
Marching orders may divide us,
But whatever fate betide us,
    Brothers of the heart are we.

Comrades known by faith the clearest,
Tried when death was near and nearest,
Bound we are by ties the dearest,
    Brothers evermore to be.

And, if spared, and growing older,
Shoulder still in line with shoulder,
And with hearts no thrill the colder,
    Brothers ever we shall be.

By communion of the banner,—
Crimson, white, and starry banner,—
By the baptism of the banner,
    Children of one Church are we.
Creed nor faction can divide us,
Race nor language can divide us ;
Still, whatever fate betide us,
    Children of the Flag are we.
            CHARLES G. HALPINE.

IN MEMORY.

OLD Greece hath her Thermopylæ,
    Brave Switzerland her Tell,
The Scot his Wallace heart, and we
    Heroic souls as well.
The graves of glorious Marathon
    Are green above the dead ;
And we have royal fields whereon
    The trampled grass is red.

Oh, not alone the hoary Past
    Spilled precious princely blood ;
Oh, not alone its sons were cast
    In knightly form and mood ;
Perennial smells of sacrifice
    Make sweet our sickened air ;
And troth, as leal as Sidney's, lies
    Around us everywhere.

Swords tried as that Excalibur
    Which graced King Arthur's thigh,

What time our battle instincts stir,
  Flash bare beneath the sky.
We feel the rowels of Honor prick
  As keenly as did he
Who sowed his savage epoch thick
  With perfect chivalry.

Cœur-de-Leons on every field,
  Sweet saints in every home,
Through whose dear helping stands revealed
  The joy of martyrdom;
Compassed by whose assuring loves,
  Our comrades dared and died
As blithely as a bridegroom moves
  To meet his waiting bride.

Though tears be salt, and wormwood still
  Is bitter to the taste,
God's heart is tender, and He will
  Let no life fail or waste.
O mothers of our Gracchi! when
  You gave your jewels up,
A continent of hopeless men
  Grew rich in boundless hope.

Renown stands mute beside the graves
  With which the land is scarred;
Unheralded, our splendid braves
  Went forth unto the Lord:
No poet hoards their humble names
  In his immortal scrolls,
But not the less the darkness flames
  With their clear-shining souls.

Beneath the outward havoc, they
  The inward mercy saw;
High intuitions of Duty lay
  Upon them, strong as law;
Athwart the bloody horizon
  They marked God's blazing sword,

And heard His dreadful thunders run
   When but the cannon roared.

Shield-bearers of the Sovran Truth!
   We count your costly deeds
Devoutly as a maiden doth
   Her consecrated beads.
You thrill us with the calms which flow
   In Eucharistic wine;
And by your straight tall lives we know
   That Life is still divine.

                RICHARD REALF.

A DIRGE.

Low lies in dust the honored head,
   Cold is the hand that held the sword;
Slowly we bear them to the dead,
   And lay them down without a word.

What is there to be said or done?
   They are departed, we remain;
Their race is run, their crowns are won,
   They will not come to us again.

Cut off by fate before their prime
   Could harvest half the golden years,
All they could leave they left us—time,
   All we could give we gave them—tears.

Would they were here, or we were there,
   Or both together, heart to heart.
O death in life, we cannot bear
   To be so near—and so apart!

         RICHARD HENRY STODDARD.

LINES FROM "COMMEMORATION ODE."

[Recited at the Harvard Commemoration, July 21, 1865.]

WE sit here in the Promised Land
That flows with Freedom's honey and milk ;
But 'twas they won it, sword in hand,
Making the nettle danger soft for us as silk.
    We welcome back our bravest and our best ;—
    Ah me ! not all ! some come not with the rest,
Who went forth brave and bright as any here !
I strive to mix some gladness with my strain,
        But the sad strings complain,
        And will not please the ear :
I sweep them for a pæan, but they wane
        Again and yet again
Into a dirge, and die away in pain.
In these brave ranks I only see the gaps,
Thinking of dear ones whom the dumb turf wraps,
Dark to the triumph which they died to gain :
    Fitlier may others greet the living,
    For me the past is unforgiving ;
        I with uncovered head
        Salute the sacred dead,
Who went, and who return not.—Say not so !
'Tis not the grapes of Canaan that repay,
But the high faith that failed not by the way ;
Virtue treads paths that end not in the grave ;
No bar of endless night exiles the brave ;
        And to the saner mind
We rather seem the dead that stayed behind.
Blow, trumpets, all your exultations blow !
For never shall their aureoled presence lack :
I see them muster in a gleaming row,
With ever-youthful brows that nobler show ;
We find in our dull road their shining track ;
        In every nobler mood
We feel the orient of their spirit glow,
Part of our life's unalterable good,
Of all our saintlier aspiration ;

They come transfigured back,
Secure from change in their high-hearted ways,
Beautiful evermore, and with the rays
Of morn on their white Shields of Expectation !

*   *   *   *   *

Not in anger, not in pride,
Pure from passion's mixture rude
Ever to base earth allied,
But with far-heard gratitude,
Still with heart and voice renewed,
To heroes living and dear martyrs dead,
The strain should close that consecrates our brave.
Lift the heart and lift the head !
Lofty be its mood and grave,
Not without a martial ring,
Not without a prouder tread
And a peal of exultation :
Little right has he to sing
Through whose heart in such an hour
Beats no march of conscious power,
Sweeps no tumult of elation !
'Tis no Man we celebrate,
By his country's victories great,
A hero half and half the whim of Fate,
But the pith and marrow of a Nation
Drawing force from all her men,
Highest, humblest, weakest, all,
For her time of need, and then
Pulsing it again through them,
Till the basest can no longer cower,
Feeling his soul spring up divinely tall,
Touched but in passing by her mantle-hem.
Come back, then, noble pride, for 'tis her dower !
How could poet ever tower,
If his passions, hopes, and fears,
If his triumphs and his tears,
Kept not measure with his people ?
Boom, cannon, boom to all the winds and waves !

Clash out, glad bells, from every rocking steeple!
Banners, advance with triumph, bend your staves!
    And from every mountain-peak
    Let beacon-fire to answering beacon speak,
    Katahdin tell Monadnock, Whiteface he,
And so leap on in light from sea to sea,
    Till the glad news be sent
    Across a kindling continent,
Making earth feel more firm and air breathe braver:
" Be proud! for she is saved, and all have helped to
    save her!
  She that lifts up the manhood of the poor,
  She of the open soul and open door,
  With room about her hearth for all mankind!
  The fire is dreadful in her eyes no more;
  From her bold front the helm she doth unbind,
  Sends all her handmaid armies back to spin,
  And bids her navies, that so lately hurled
  Their crashing battle, hold their thunders in,
  Swimming like birds of calm along the unharm-
    ful shore.
  No challenge sends she to the elder world,
  That looked askance and hated; a light scorn
  Plays o'er her mouth, as round her mighty knees
  She calls her children back, and waits the morn
Of nobler day, enthroned between her subject seas."

Bow down, dear Land, for thou hast found release!
  Thy God, in these distempered days,
  Hath taught thee the sure wisdom of His ways,
And through thine enemies hath wrought thy peace!
    Bow down in prayer and praise!
No poorest in thy borders but may now
Lift to the juster skies a man's enfranchised brow.
O Beautiful! my Country! ours once more!
Smoothing thy gold of war-dishevelled hair
O'er such sweet brows as never other wore,
    And letting thy set lips,
    Freed from wrath's pale eclipse,

The rosy edges of their smile lay bare,
What words divine of lover or of poet
Could tell our love and make thee know it,
Among the Nations bright beyond compare?
　　What were our lives without thee?
　　What all our lives to save thee?
　　We reck not what we gave thee;
　　We will not dare to doubt thee,
But ask whatever else, and we will dare!

　　　　　　　　　JAMES RUSSELL LOWELL.

———

HEROES OF THE SOUTH.

*[From an Ode on the Valor and Sufferings of Con-
federate Soldiers.]*

　FOUR deadly years we fought,
Ringed by a girdle of unfaltering fire
That coiled and hissed in lessening circles nigher.
　　Blood dyed the Southern wave;
From ocean border to calm inland river,
There was no pause, no peace, no respite ever.
　　Blood of our bravest brave
Drenched in a scarlet rain the western lea,
Swelled the hoarse waters of the Tennessee,
Incarnadined the gulfs, the lakes, the rills,
　　And from a hundred hills
Steamed in a mist of slaughter to the skies,
Shutting all hope of heaven from mortal eyes.
The Beaufort blooms were wither'd on the stem;
　　The fair Gulf City in a single night
　　Lost her imperial diadem;
And wheresoe'er men's troubled vision roamed
They viewed MIGHT towering o'er the humbled crest
　　of RIGHT !

But for a time, but for a time, O God!
The innate forces of our knightly blood
Rallied, and by the mount, the fen, the flood,
    Upraised the tottering standards of our race.
O grand Virginia! though thy glittering glaive
Lies sullied, shattered in a ruthless grave,
    How it flashed once!
    They dug their trenches deep
(The implacable foe), they ranged their lines of
        wrath ;
But watchful ever on the imminent path
    Thy steel-clad genius stood ;
North, South, East, West,—they strove to pierce thy
        shield :
    Thou wouldst not yield!
Until—unconquered, yea, unconquered still—
Nature's weakened forces answered not thy will,
And gored with wound on wound,
Thy fainting limbs and forehead sought the ground ;
And with thee, the young nation fell, a pall
Solemn and rayless, covering one and all!

God's ways are marvellous ; here we stand to-day
Discrown'd, and shorn in wildest disarray,
The mock of earth! yet never shone the sun
On sterner deeds, or nobler victories won.
Not in the field alone ; ah, come with me
To the dim bivouac by the winter's sea ;
Mark the fair sons of courtly mothers crouch
    O'er flickering fires ; but gallant still, and gay
As on some bright parade.   Or mark the couch
    In reeking hospitals, whereon is laid
The latest scion of a line perchance
Whose veins were royal.   Close your blurred
        romance,
Blurred by the dropping of a maudlin tear,
And watch the manhood here ;
    That firm but delicate countenance,
Distorted sometimes by an awful pang,

Borne in meek patience.   When the trumpets rang
" *To horse !*" but yester-morn, that ardent boy
Sprung to his charger, thrilled with hope and joy
To the very finger-tips; and now he lies,
The shadows deepening in those falcon eyes,
  But calm and undismayed
As if the Death that chills him, brow and breast,
Were some fond bride who whispered, " Let us
  rest !"

Enough ! 'tis over ! the last gleam of hope
Hath melted from our mournful horoscope—
  Of all, of all bereft ;
  Only to us are left
Our buried heroes and their matchless deeds.
These cannot pass ; they hold the vital seeds
Which in some far, untracked, unvisioned hour
May burst to vivid bud and glorious flower.
  Meanwhile, upon the nation's broken heart
Her martyrs sleep.   Oh, dearer far to her
Than if each son, a wreathéd conqueror,
  Rode in triumphant state
  The loftiest crest of fate ;
Oh, dearer far, because outcast and low,
She yearns above them in her awful woe.

    PAUL HAMILTON HAYNE.

———

HYMN FOR MEMORIAL-DAY.

[Magnolia Cemetery, Charleston, S. C.]

SLEEP sweetly in your humble graves—
  Sleep, martyrs of a fallen cause !
Though yet no marble column craves
  The pilgrim here to pause,

In seeds of laurel in the earth
  The blossom of your fame is blown,

And somewhere, waiting for its birth,
    The shaft is in the stone!

Meanwhile, behalf the tardy years
    Which keep in trust your storied tombs,
Behold! your sisters bring their tears
    And these memorial blooms.

Small tributes! but your shades will smile
    More proudly on these wreaths to-day
Than when some cannon-moulded pile
    Shall overlook this bay.

Stoop, angels, hither from the skies!
    There is no holier spot of ground
Than where defeated valor lies
    By mourning beauty crowned.

                              HENRY TIMROD.

ODE FOR DECORATION-DAY.

BRING flowers to strew again
With fragrant purple rain
Of lilacs, and of roses white and red,
The dwellings of our dead, our glorious dead!
Let the bells ring a solemn funeral chime,
And wild war-music bring anew the time
    When they who sleep beneath
    Were full of vigorous breath,
And in their lusty manhood sallied forth,
    Holding in strong right hand
    The fortunes of the land,
The pride and power and safety of the North!
It seems but yesterday
The long and proud array—
But yesterday when even the solid rock
Shook as with earthquake shock,—
As North and South, like two huge icebergs, ground

Against each other with convulsive bound,
And the whole world stood still
   To view the mighty war,
   And hear the thundrous roar,
While sheeted lightnings wrapped each plain and hill.

Alas! how few came back
From battle and from wrack !
Alas ! how many lie
Beneath a Southern sky,
Who never heard the fearful fight was done,
And all they fought for won.
Sweeter, I think, their sleep,
More peaceful and more deep,
Could they but know their wounds were not in vain,
Could they but hear the grand triumphal strain,
And see their homes unmarred by hostile tread.
Ah ! let us trust it is so with our dead—
That they the thrilling joy of triumph feel,
And in that joy disdain the foeman's steel.

We mourn for all, but each doth think of one
   More precious to the heart than aught beside—
Some father, brother, husband, or some son
   Who came not back, or coming, sank and died :
   In him the whole sad list is glorified !
" He fell 'fore Richmond, in the seven long days
   When battle raged from morn till blood-dewed eve,
And lies there," one pale widowed mourner says,
   And knows not most to triumph or to grieve.
" My boy fell at Fair Oaks," another sighs;
" And mine at Gettysburg !" his neighbor cries,
   And that great name each sad-eyed listener
      thrills.
I think of one who vanished when the press
Of battle surged along the Wilderness,
   And mourned the North upon her thousand hills.

O gallant brothers of the generous South,
   Foes for a day and brothers for all time !

I charge you by the memories of our youth,
    By Yorktown's field and Montezuma's clime,
Hold our dead sacred—let them quietly rest
In your unnumbered vales, where God thought best !
Your vines and flowers learned long since to forgive,
And o'er their graves a 'broidered mantle weave ;
Be you as kind as they are, and the word
Shall reach the Northland with each summer bird,
And thoughts as sweet as summer shall awake
Responsive to your kindness, and shall make
Our peace the peace of brothers once again,
And banish utterly the days of pain.

And ye, O Northmen ! be ye not outdone
    In generous thought and deed.
We all do need forgiveness, every one ;
    And they that give shall find it in their need.
Spare of your flowers to deck the stranger's grave,
    Who died for a lost cause :
A soul more daring, resolute, and brave
    Ne'er won a world's applause !
(A brave man's hatred pauses at the tomb.)
For him some Southern home was robed in gloom,
Some wife or mother looked with longing eyes
Through the sad days and nights with tears and
        sighs,—
Hope slowly hardening into gaunt Despair.
Then let your foeman's grave remembrance share ;
Pity a higher charm to Valor lends,
And in the realms of Sorrow all are friends.

Yes, bring fresh flowers and strew the soldier's
        grave,
    Whether he proudly lies
    Beneath our Northern skies,
Or where the Southern palms their branches wave !
Let the bells toll and wild war-music swell,
    And for one day the thought of all the past—
    Of all those memories vast—

Come back and haunt us with its mighty spell !
Bring flowers, then, once again,
And strew with fragrant rain
Of lilacs, and of roses white and red,
The dwellings of our dead.

HENRY PETERSON.

ODE FOR DECORATION-DAY.

THEY sleep so calm and stately,
  Each in his graveyard bed,
It scarcely seems that lately
  They trod the fields blood-red,
    With fearless tread.

They marched and never halted,
  They scaled the parapet,
The triple lines assaulted,
  And paid without regret
    The final debt.

The debt of slow accruing
  A guilty nation made,
The debt of evil-doing,
  Of justice long delayed,—
    'Twas this they paid.

On fields where Strife held riot,
  And Slaughter fed his hounds,
Where came no sense of quiet,
  Nor any gentle sounds,
    They made their rounds.

They wrought without repining,
  Till, weary watches o'er,
They passed the bounds confining
  Our green, familiar shore,
    Forevermore.

And now they sleep so stately,
  Each in his graveyard bed,
So calmly and sedately
  They rest, that once I said :
    " These men are dead.

" They know not what sweet duty
  We come each year to pay,
Nor heed the blooms of beauty,
  The garland gifts of May,
    Strewn here to-day.

" The night-time and the day-time,
  The rise and set of sun,
The winter and the May-time,
  To them whose work is done,
    Are all as one."

Then o'er mine eyes there floated
  A vision of the Land
Where their brave souls, promoted
  To Heaven's own armies, stand
    At God's right hand.

From out the mighty distance
  I seemed to see them gaze
Back on their old existence,
  Back on the battle-blaze
    Of war's dread days.

" The flowers shall fade and perish,"
  In larger faith spake I,
" But these dear names we cherish
  Are written in the sky,
    And cannot die."

            THEODORE P. COOK.

THE BLUE AND THE GRAY.

[*This poem is founded upon an incident that occurred at Columbus, Miss., on Memorial-Day, 1867, when flowers were strewn upon the graves of Confederate and Federal soldiers alike.*]

By the flow of the inland river,
　Whence the fleets of iron have fled,
Where the blades of the grave-grass quiver,
　Asleep are the ranks of the dead ;
　　Under the sod and the dew,
　　　Waiting the judgment day ;
　　Under the one, the Blue ;
　　　Under the other, the Gray.

These, in the robings of glory,
　Those, in the gloom of defeat ;
All with the battle-blood gory,
　In the dusk of eternity meet ;
　　Under the sod and the dew,
　　　Waiting the judgment day ;
　　Under the laurel, the Blue ;
　　　Under the willow, the Gray.

From the silence of sorrowful hours
　The desolate mourners go,
Lovingly laden with flowers
　Alike for the friend and the foe ;
　　Under the sod and the dew,
　　　Waiting the judgment day ;
　　Under the roses, the Blue ;
　　　Under the lilies, the Gray

So, with an equal splendor,
　The morning sun-rays fall,
With a touch impartially tender,
　On the blossoms blooming for all ;
　　Under the sod and the dew,
　　　Waiting the judgment day ;

Broidered with gold, the Blue;
　　Mellowed with gold, the Gray.

So, when the summer calleth,
　　On forest and field of grain,
With an equal murmur falleth
　　The cooling drip of the rain;
　　　　Under the sod and the dew,
　　　　　　Waiting the judgment day;
　　　　Wet with the rain, the Blue;
　　　　　　Wet with the rain, the Gray.

Sadly, but not with upbraiding
　　The generous deed was done;
In the storm of the years that are fading,
　　No braver battle was won;
　　　　Under the sod and the dew,
　　　　　　Waiting the judgment day;
　　　　Under the blossoms, the Blue;
　　　　　　Under the garlands, the Gray.

No more shall the war-cry sever,
　　Or the winding rivers be red;
They banish our anger forever,
　　When they laurel the graves of our dead.
　　　　Under the sod and the dew,
　　　　　　Waiting the judgment day;
　　　　Love and tears for the Blue;
　　　　　　Tears and love for the Gray.

FRANCIS MILES FINCH.

THE TOURNAMENT.

I.

LISTS all white and blue in the skies;
　　And the people hurried amain
To the Tournament under the ladies' eyes
　　Where jousted Heart and Brain.

II.

Blow, herald, blow!   There entered Heart,
   A youth in crimson and gold.
Blow, herald, blow!   Brain stood apart,
   Steel-armored, glittering, cold.

III.

Heart's palfrey caracoled gayly round,
   Heart tra-li-raed merrily ;
But Brain sat still, with never a sound—
   Full cynical-calm was he.

IV.

Heart's helmet-crest bore favors three
   From his lady's white hand caught ;
Brain's casque was bare as Fact—not he
   Or favor gave or sought.

V.

Blow, herald, blow!   Heart shot a glance
   To catch his lady's eye ;
But Brain looked straight a-front, his lance
   To aim more faithfully.

VI.

They charged, they struck ; both fell, both bled ;
   Brain rose again, ungloved ;
Heart fainting smiled, and softly said,
   " My love to my Beloved !"

———

Heart and Brain! no more be twain ;
Throb and think, one flesh again !
Lo! they weep, they turn, they run ;
Lo! they kiss: Love, thou art one!
                              SIDNEY LANIER.

INDEX OF AUTHORS.

www.ingramcontent.com/pod-product-compliance
Lightning Source LLC
Chambersburg PA
CBHW072337090426
42741CB00012B/2825